While yet a boy I sought for ghosts, and sped
Through many a listening chamber, cave and ruin,
And starlight wood, with fearful steps pursuing
Hopes of high talk with the departed dead.
Percy Shelley

TALKING WITH THE DEAD

Collected by Troy Taylor and Rob & Anne Wlodarski
Casebooks from American Ghost Hunters
Limited Edition Copy _____ 9 _____ of 100

WHITECHAPEL PRESS
OTHER BOOKS IN THE HAUNTED FIELD GUIDE SERIES

Ghost Hunter's Guidebook by Troy Taylor
Strange Frequencies by Craig Telesha
Ghosts on Film by Troy Taylor
Field Guide to Haunted Graveyards by Troy Taylor
Confessions of a Ghost Hunter by Troy Taylor
So, There I Was.. By Troy Taylor & Len Adams
Lighter Side of Darkness by Luke Naliborski
Paranormal Investigators Logbook by Kelly Davis
Strange Frequencies by Craig Telesha

THE HAUNTED FIELD GUIDE SERIES

TALKING WITH THE DEAD

CASEBOOKS OF AMERICAN GHOST HUNTERS

EDITED BY TROY TAYLOR AND ROB AND ANN WLODARSKI

- A Dark Haven Entertainment Book from Whitechapel Press -

Special Thanks to:
Jill Hand - Editor
Rob & Anne Wlodarski - Original Idea & Inspiration
All of the Contributors to the Book
Members of the American Ghost Society
Mike & Sandra Schwab -- Long-suffering Cover Designers
Crusty & Houseshoe
& Haven Taylor

ORIGINAL COVER ARTWORK DESIGNED BY

©Copyright 2009 by Michael Schwab & Troy Taylor
Visit M & S Graphics at http://www.manyhorses.com/msgraphics.htm
Front Cover Photograph by Sandra Schwab

THIS BOOK IS PUBLISHED BY

Whitechapel Press
A Division of Dark Haven Entertainment, Inc.
15 Forest Knolls Estates - Decatur, Illinois - 62521
(217) 422-1002 / 1-888-GHOSTLY
Visit us on the internet at http://www.americanhauntings.org

First Printing -- September 2009
ISBN: 1-892523-67-1

Printed in the United States of America

TALKING WITH THE DEAD
CASEBOOKS OF AMERICAN GHOST HUNTERS
COLLECTED BY TROY TAYLOR AND
ROB AND ANNE WLODARSKI

INTRODUCTION BY TROY TAYLOR

I have always had an interest in ghosts and the supernatural. It's been with me for as long as I can remember. I have a boring confession to make about this lifelong fascination: there was no single event that caused me to devote most of my adult career to the pursuit of the unexplained. It was really simply a mixture of things, from my taste in reading to my fascination with horror films.

Books had a great impact on my life. I wanted to be a writer for as long as I can remember, from the time that I began scribbling stories in battered notebooks. I was one of those kids who could always be found with his nose buried in a book. I didn't really care what I was reading, as long as it could transport me somewhere else and, preferably, give me a good scare or two along the way.

I was also the kid at school who was obsessed with monsters, ghosts, horror movies and anything else that was sure to creep out my friends or incur the wrath of my teachers. I can't count how many times my monster magazines were confiscated by some well-meaning (but very misguided) educator or the number of disapproving glances that I received while poring over an already dog-eared copy of a new horror novel.

My reading habits gained me a reputation for being a bit eccentric in school and everyone knew that if they had a good scary story I would be interested. While many of my teachers frowned on my literary tastes and morbid interests, not all of them were concerned. In fact, some of them even brought me newspaper clippings about strange stories and haunted houses, which is how I first heard about the so-called "Columbus Poltergeist" case of 1984.

At that time, the Resch family in Ohio began experiencing violent poltergeist activity that seemed to be centered around their teenage daughter, Tina. The case made national news before eventually dying out. Some of the experts involved believed that the strange events in the house had nothing to do with ghosts, but rather was caused by an unconscious energy that came from Tina. The Tina Resch case continues to be debated to this day and at the time, it was pretty exciting stuff.

Little did I know that just over a decade later, I would have my own poltergeist case to deal with.

It wasn't the only poltergeist incident that I have investigated over the years, but it was definitely the first. It was also the first case in which I found myself wishing that I had done things differently.

It was in 1997 that I got involved in the case of a young woman whom I have since referred to as "Christine M." Besides being the first, it was also the most active human agent poltergeist incident with which I was involved. In the case of "Christine M.", I believe that the outbreak in her home was genuine, not only because of eyewitness accounts of unexplained goings-on but because I saw some of them myself. To this day, I cannot explain what I saw and heard in that house, other than to say it was paranormal in nature.

This case could almost be described as "textbook" compared to many of the others that I had read about. Remember, at the time, my only knowledge of poltergeists was from what I had been able to glean from the writings of researchers like Dr. William Roll, Loyd Auerbach and D. Scott Rogo. My information was all second-hand but I went into the investigation with my eyes wide open. I discovered then what I would find repeated in the future: that people usually suspect their house is haunted before they come to believe that they might be the cause of the eerie happenings.

This is what occurred in Christine's case. She contacted me because she believed her house was haunted. She told me of a wide variety of weird phenomena that was taking place like knocking sounds, lights turning on and off by themselves, doors slamming without anyone touching them, cabinets opening and closing, windows breaking and other destructive happenings. Because Christine was under eighteen at the time, I contacted her mother and she assured me that the events described were actually taking place. She also agreed that an investigation might be in order.

During this initial interview, I asked her about the history of the location and if she had any thoughts on why the phenomena were taking place. I also asked how long it had been going on. Her answer surprised me. She explained that the so-called haunting had started just two years before, when Christine had gotten pregnant at age fifteen. The girl was very upset at the time and became so depressed, and anxious, that her mother had taken her to see a therapist. She stopped going, however, and the weird activity began a short time later. While Christine believed that the house was haunted, her mother (who had no experience or interest in the paranormal) believed that her daughter was somehow causing the things to happen. She had no idea how this could be so, but she believed that it was possible.

With the home owner's permission, I began a series of five in-depth investigations of the house. These investigations were the first that I had ever conducted of this sort of activity and I feel that I learned a lot from them, including what not to do! In some of my later writings, I used quite a few examples of the things that happened during these investigations as the basis for conducting good research.

My interviews with Christine and her mother collected numerous accounts of the activity that was taking place. The events began one night when Christine was lying on the living room floor watching television. The room was the largest on the first floor and when I visited the house, it was furnished with a couch, some chairs, a table and a large piano. There were three doors leading into the room. These led to a spare room, a screened-in porch and to the kitchen. On that first night, as Christine and her mother were watching television, the piano began to play loudly by itself.

Not long after that, things began to escalate. Doors began to open and close, windows broke inside empty rooms and the sounds of knocking and footsteps began to be heard, usually on the upper floor of the house when no one was up there. Lights flicked on and off, radios turned on and off and the volume of the television would often raise and lower without assistance. The footsteps and noises from upstairs became so bad that Christine insisted that her mother put a padlock on the door leading to the second floor. She remained convinced, even after my initial visit and after her mother's insistence otherwise, that the house was haunted by ghosts.

Nothing that occurred could convince her otherwise. The strangest event that reportedly took place (and I did not witness this for myself) was when Christine's sister sustained a savage bite mark on the back side of her upper arm. There were no pets in the house and no way that the girl could have managed to bite herself in that area of her body. I don't think that it was any coincidence that the bite mark appeared just shortly after Christine and her sister had an argument. It should be noted that the argument was not a violent one. Christine did not bite her sister during the conflict but the mysterious bite mark somehow appeared.

As you can imagine, I was having some reservations about the house being infested by spirits at this point, especially since the girls' mother again told me that she was convinced that the activity centered around Christine. However, the young woman insisted that the house was haunted and would only agree to cooperate with the investigations if we would proceed as if ghosts were actually infesting the house. I reluctantly agreed and the five investigations began.

Most of the time, things were fairly quiet, including the two uneventful investigations that were conducted when Christine was not at home. When she was not present, there was absolutely no sign of any activity at all. However, on two occasions, I was present when violent phenomena occurred and I was also present when one of the other investigators snapped a photograph of a bright ball of light in the downstairs hallway. According to his account, the light was actually moving down the hallway, literally following Christine's little boy, who was two years old at the time. I was in the kitchen with Christine when this occurred but I did see the resulting photograph, which shows a glowing light (apparently in motion), just a foot or two behind the boy as he is running into the living room.

One evening, Christine, her mother, three other investigators and I clearly heard what seemed to be someone banging loudly on the walls of the second floor of the house. There was no one else present at the time but the sounds really seemed to be made by a person upstairs, walking down the hallway and hitting the walls with his fists. Christine's mother told me that these were exactly the sorts of sounds that they had become used to over the past months. Unsure of what to do, I ran up the stairs to see if anyone else was there. I was certain that we were alone in the house but I had to make sure. The downstairs door, as mentioned, had been padlocked, so Mrs. M. had to open it for me and I hurried up the staircase with another one of the investigators behind me. The pounding noises had stopped by the time we reached the upper floor, but if anyone had been there, we would have found him. Instead, we discovered the hallway and the rooms to be dark, quiet and empty.

During an investigation on another night, I saw two cabinet doors actually shut under their own power. The incident occurred while I was in the living room with Christine, her mother and one other investigator. As we were sitting and talking, we began to hear a repeated rapping sound coming from the kitchen. It began to increase in volume until it started to sound like someone rapidly hammering on a wooden surface. The first sound was joined by a second and then a third. Each of the sounds was identical and my first thought was that it sounded just like someone slamming a cabinet door closed. Since it was coming from the kitchen, this was not a far-fetched idea, expect for the fact that I knew that no one was in that room!

Just as I had done when we heard mysterious sounds upstairs, I ran for the kitchen as quickly as possible. The two rooms were separated by an open archway. Hurrying from the carpeted living room and onto the linoleum floor of the kitchen, I slipped just as I was going under the archway. I stumbled but didn't fall and was able to look up quickly enough to see two of the cabinet doors waving back and forth and cracking against the wooden frame. The movement ceased almost immediately as I came into the room but it was certainly the first time that I had ever seen "paranormal movement" during an investigation.

Over the next several weeks, the activity in the house continued until it did begin to decrease after two months. Thanks to the relentless interviews that I had with Christine, and the fact that we conducted the two completely uneventful investigations with the girl removed from the house, I felt that we could determine that the cause of the haunting was indeed Christine.

Eventually, her mother and I were able to get her to agree with these findings and she returned to the therapist. Not surprisingly, the phenomena ceased completely soon after and to this date, nothing out of the ordinary has occurred at her home. Christine has been happily married for many years now, has more children and has never been bothered again by paranormal activity.

This investigation was just one of many that I have been involved with over the years, but it was one of the best learning experiences that I could have had. I learned that if I had been more patient and careful, and perhaps employed more investigators and more cameras, I could likely have captured some of the activity in the house as evidence. I also learned a lot about interviewing witnesses, as well. And that not everything that we think is a ghost actually is. We can learn a lot about the paranormal, about ghost research, and about ourselves in the course of an investigation.

And this is something that all of the contributors to this book have discovered over the years, as well.

My friend Rob Wlodarski approached me about putting this book together more than a year ago, hoping to compile at least thirteen accounts of paranormal investigations from around the country. Each of us contacted people we knew who had been active in ghost research for a number of years and asked them each to add one chapter from their casebooks to this volume. I think you will be as pleased as we were with what they submitted. The stories come from all over the country, from coast to coast, and delve into some famous and many little-known locations. Rob and I hand-picked each of the investigators who contributed to the book and I don't think you will be disappointed by what they chose to send us.

You have a chilling read ahead of you and I would suggest keeping a light on and occasionally glancing back over your shoulder. You never know what might be sneaking up on you in the dark!

Happy Hauntings,
Troy Taylor
Summer 2009

1. THE HOUSE OF SPIRITS

BY ROB AND ANNE WLODARSKI

**1019 NORTH ROXBURY DRIVE
BEVERLY HILLS, CALIFORNIA**

HISTORICALLY KNOWN AS THE MONTE BLUE; RUSS COLUMBO; GEORGE AND IRA GERSHWIN; GINNY SIMMS; AND ROSEMARY CLOONEY HOUSE

Few places in the United States had a Hollywood legacy as grand and storied as 1019 N. Roxbury Drive. The legendary musical tradition associated with this house is mystical and magical and the memories associated with it could fill hundreds of photo albums. It was a unique incarnation encompassing movie lore and musical wonderment. The house was constructed for actor Monte Blue around 1928. The architect was Don Uhl and the builder was C.R. Senteny. The lot included a garage, guesthouse, pool, tennis court and extensive landscaping. The white Mediterranean-style house contained eight bedrooms, six bathrooms, a basement, breakfast room, sun room, den, dining room, family room, living room, and covered patio.

A veritable Who's Who in Hollywood history lived in or visited this house from 1929 until 2003 when the last owner, singer Rosemary Clooney, succumbed to cancer. Clooney occupied this house for five decades, longer than all of the prior owners combined. Despite efforts to

The house on North Roxbury Drive

save the historic structure, one of the last of the old-time Hollywood mansions, it was razed in the summer of 2005 to make way for a new home. Gone are the music-filled soirées, the dancing, backyard pool parties, the cadence of tennis balls, the composers who made musical history here, and the energy that lasted until the city of Beverly Hills preferred progress to preservation, and money to memories. This was a house of music, a place of legendary Hollywood parties and a magical spot, where during the course of our investigations, an olive tree that was declared dead by arborists came back to life. We witnessed shadowy figures pass through walls and heard voices from the past echo through the darkened hallways and abandoned rooms. The house is now gone, but during the three years that the International Paranormal Research Organization (IPRO) investigated this historic and haunted location, we were able to talk to the dead.

HISTORY

Our history begins sometime in 1928 when gifted actor Monte Blue either built the house, or had it built for him. Blue was born Gerard Montgomery Bluefeather on January 11, 1890 in Indianapolis, Indiana. One of five children, his father died in a car crash when Blue was eight. His mother could not raise five children alone so Monte, along with another brother, was admitted to an orphanage. In his twenties, the part-Cherokee Blue held jobs ranging from stevedore to cowboy. While working as a fireman he broke both arms and legs in an accident and had to spend eighteen months in a hospital. He became a movie-studio handyman around 1910.

Monte Blue

As an extra and stunt man, Blue graduated to featured parts in D.W. Griffith's *Birth of a Nation* in 1915. Because of his work with Griffith and Cecil B. DeMille, Blue became a dependable box-office attraction during the 1920s. He ended up playing everything from a lawyer to a baseball player.

In 1928, Blue was cast as the drink-sodden Dr. Matthew Lloyd in *White Shadows In the South Seas*, one of his greatest roles. After making a successful transition to talkies, Blue decided to retire from filmmaking and toured the world, returning to the United States in 1931. Blue lost his fortune through bad investments, and had dropped out of the public eye as far as motion pictures went. He rebuilt his career, playing bit parts in "A" pictures and supporting roles in "B"s. He was extremely busy in Westerns and also appeared in several serials. Movie mogul Jack Warner, out of gratitude for Blue's moneymaking vehicles of the 1920s, made sure that he was steadily employed at Warner Brothers, and that his name would appear prominently in the studio's advertising copy. Blue continued accepting character roles until he retired from acting in 1954. Blue ended up acting in about 250 movies during his lifetime and was also a screenwriter. Blue was married three times. He and his first wife, Erma Gladys divorced in 1923. Blue and his second wife, the former Tova Jansen, were married on November 11, 1924, and they and their children, Barbara Ann and Richard most likely moved into the N. Roxbury Drive house around 1929 and remained in residence until 1932. At the end of his life Blue worked as an advance man for the Hamid-Morton Circus. He died of a heart attack in Milwaukee, Wisconsin, on February 18, 1963.

The second occupant of 1019 N. Roxbury was gifted singer Russ Columbo, known as "The Romeo of Song" and "The Singing Valentino." In the early 1930s, many considered Columbo to be the finest singer of love songs in the United States and the one who had the greatest appeal to women. Columbo phrased rather like his "rival," Bing Crosby, in a voice more silkily textured. Russ Columbo represented the most serious challenge to Crosby and at only 26 years of age – he was five years younger than Bing – it is reasonable to assume that his best years were still to come. It says something for his talent and popularity that it would be almost six years before another serious challenger – in the person of Frank Sinatra – forced his way into the reckoning.

Russ Columbo

Columbo was born Ruggerio Eugenio di Rudolpho Colombo, on January 14, 1908, in Camden, New Jersey. The son of Italian immigrants, Columbo learned to play accordion and violin. In 1927 he joined Gus Arnheim's band at Hollywood's Coconut Grove as one half of a two-violin string section with future film star Fred MacMurray. A later addition to the band was Crosby, who proved to be Columbo's main competition, along with Rudy Vallee. Columbo formed his own band in 1931 and replaced the "o" in his last name with the more phonetic "u." This gave rise to the legend that he was descended from Christopher Columbus. He was an immediate success both in person and on records. His dark good looks and romantic baritone voice prompted Hollywood to star him in several movies including *Broadway through a Keyhole* (1933) and *Moulin Rouge* (1934). By 1934 he also had his own NBC radio series, and his total earnings for the year were estimated at $500,000.

Russ Columbo spent most of Friday, August 31, 1934, recording the songs from Universal Studio's *Wake Up and Dream* for the Brunswick label. That evening, he attended the preview of *Wake Up and Dream* at the Pantages Theater on Hollywood Boulevard with his close friend, Carole Lombard. After appearing in almost a dozen films, Columbo had finally received top billing. His best friend of ten years, portrait photographer Lansing Brown, Jr., was also in the audience, but he was not seated near Lombard and Columbo.

A Universal press release written for the preview ended with this quote from Columbo: "At 26, I find that I have just about everything I want from life and am pretty happy the way things have turned out for me."

On Saturday, September 1, Columbo drove to Santa Barbara for the film's out of town preview. Lombard and Columbo planned a late supper Sunday evening with Carole's mother, Elizabeth Peters, and brother, Stuart. Feeling a premonition of disaster, Lombard tried calling Columbo upon her arrival at Lake Arrowhead, where she had gone to relax, but found the telephone exchanges closed for the evening. They would never speak again. Lansing Brown returned Columbo's telephone call Sunday morning, and Russ asked to come over to Brown's home.

It was rumored that the two friends had a falling out earlier in the month and Columbo was determined to talk to his friend and patch things up. In an interview before the tragedy, Columbo describe "Lansa" as his best friend – "my confident, my advisor for ten years. No matter what I asked of him he would never fail me. And I too—I would never fail him."

Russ arrived at his friend's bungalow located at 584 Lillian Way about 12:30 p.m. and found

Russ Columbo in from of the North Roxbury House

Brown's parents there, as well. The two friends talked in the library while the elder Browns retired to the kitchen, located in the back of the house. According to statements given at the inquest, Brown was toying with one of a pair of antique dueling pistols and holding an unlighted match in his left hand. The "trick" was that the hammer would ignite the match, although Brown would later testify that he did not know why he had the match and the gun in the first place, other than a sort of odd "habit." Unfortunately, the old relic contained both gunpowder and a vintage mini ball. Somehow, the match and the hammer triggered the gun powder, and the bullet was discharged. Detectives later determined that the bullet must have ricocheted off the mahogany desk between the two men, striking Columbo in the left eye and lodging at the back of his brain. He slumped in the chair and immediately lost consciousness. It was 1:45 p.m. Although Brown's father later testified that there was no evidence of any quarrel, and no one had been drinking liquor that afternoon, rumor claimed that servants heard loud voices shortly before the shot. The senior Brown, assuming that Columbo had died instantly, called the police.

When the coroner's ambulance arrived to pick up the body, it was discovered that Russ was unconscious, but still alive. He was taken first to Hollywood Receiving Hospital, and then transferred to the Hospital of the Good Samaritan. Doctors attempted surgery to save his life, but it was too late. Carole Lombard rushed down by automobile from Lake Arrowhead after being telephoned by surgeon George W. Patterson, but it was Columbo's close friend, actress Sally Blane (sister of actresses Polly Ann Young and Loretta Young), who was at his bedside when he died at 7:30 that evening.

His body would lie in the Delmar Smith Mortuary for three days while Jack Pierce, Universal Studio's legendary makeup artist responsible for Boris Karloff's unforgettable makeup in *Frankenstein* and *The Mummy*, repaired the damage done by Brown's pistol.

In a coroner's inquest held on Sept. 5, a tearful Lansing Brown took the stand and testified, "We were friends...he was my best friend...I didn't know there was powder and a slug in it...there was noise...Russ was slumped in the chair...I put ice on his head...he couldn't speak to me."

The jury found the death to be an accident. Brown, by all accounts, was left a broken man.

A requiem Mass was held before 3,000 mourners at Hollywood's Blessed Sacrament Church at 10 a.m. on Thursday, September 6, 1934. Hundreds of fans gathered outside the church on Sunset Boulevard to pay respects and to glimpse the pallbearers: Bing Crosby, Walter Lang, Stuart Peters, Gilbert Roland, Sheldon Callaway, and Zeppo Marx. Carole Lombard and her mother sat with the Colombo family. Lombard provided a blanket of gardenias – the singer's favorite flower - that covered the bronze casket. Lansing Brown was spotted alone at the back of the church; he remained on his knees throughout the service, crying and trembling.

After the mourners left, the casket was returned to the mortuary while the Columbo family debated whether to tell the tragic news to Russ's mother, Julia, 68. She had been hospitalized with a heart attack and her condition was serious. Doctors feared the news would kill her, so she wasn't told of her youngest son's death. Columbo's story, already strange, became even stranger as a get-well card was sent to his mother, signed with his name.

Not long after Russ' death, Carol Lombard stated in an interview, "(Julia Columbo) was told that Russ and I flew to New York suddenly, to avoid publicity, and we had been married. When I went east, his family arranged wires signed 'Russ and Carole.' Presumably, from New York we sailed to England on our honeymoon. Cables from London are currently being sent signed with our names."

The Columbo family decided to tell Julia that Russ' European tour had been extended, and they continued to send her cards, gifts and a monthly check (actually his insurance dividend) in his name. This bizarre charade would continue for 10 years until the time of Julia's death. Carole Lombard's 1939 marriage to Clark Gable was withheld from her, as was Lombard's 1942 death in a plane crash. News stories with headlines such as "Russ Columbo's Mother Still Doesn't Know" were carefully cut out of her daily paper.

On October 18, a full seven weeks after his death, Russ Columbo was finally interred at Forest Lawn, in the Sanctuary of the Vespers of the Great Mausoleum, near his older brother, Fiore, who had been killed in an automobile accident in 1929.

Lansing Brown vacated the Lillian Way bungalow and for the next year he lived with his parents at 916 North Genessee Avenue. Brown died in February 1962. Never married, Brown's last home was a Victorian mansion at 637 S. Lucerne in Hancock Park, later used in William Castle's 1964 horror film, *The Night Walker,* with Barbara Stanwyck and Robert Taylor. His ashes reside in an unmarked crypt at Forest Lawn near Anna, Julia and Nicholas Colombo. The contents of Lansing Brown's will have never been made available to the general public.

Columbo had vacated the N. Roxbury Drive house prior to his death. The next celebrity occupants of the house were George and Ira Gershwin and Ira's wife, Leanore. They, too, didn't live there long. The Gershwins moved into the house in August 1936. George died suddenly on July 11, 1937 from a brain tumor. Ira and his wife stayed in the house for a short time before moving out.

George Gershwin was born Jacob Gershowitz in Brooklyn, on September 26, 1898. He was the son of immigrant parents. His compositions are still used today by teachers everywhere as examples of the American entrance to the serious musical world of Stravinsky, Debussy, Bartok, etc. Gershwin's first experiences came as a piano was rolled into the house for Ira. But it was George who took the most interest in the instrument and immediately began to play by ear. His parents invested in some piano lessons for him and George began to play professionally in his late teens.

Essentially self-taught, he was first a song plugger in Tin Pan Alley and an accompanist. In his teens he began to compose popular songs and produced a succession of musicals from 1919 to 1933 (*Lady, be Good!,* 1924; *Oh, Kay!* 1926; *Strike Up the Band,* 1927; *Funny Face,* 1927; *Girl Crazy,* 1930); the lyrics were generally by his brother Ira (1896-1983). In 1924 he became famous when he wrote "Rhapsody in Blue" as a concerto for piano and Paul Whiteman's jazz band. Its success led him to devote increasing energy to serious

George & Ira Gershwin

composition.

His more ambitious works include the "Piano Concerto in F" (1925) and the tone poem "An American in Paris" (1928). But he continued composing for the musical theatre, and some of his most successful musicals (*Strike Up the Band, Girl Crazy, Of Thee I Sing*) date from this period. In 1934-5 he wrote his American folk opera, *Porgy and Bess*, which draws on African-American idioms and characters. When it was first performed on Broadway, it was only a limited success. It is now recognized as one of the seminal works of American opera. Gershwin went to Hollywood in 1936 and wrote songs for films. He was a sensitive songwriter of great melodic gifts and did much to create syntheses between jazz and classical traditions in his concert music and between black folk music and opera in *Porgy and Bess*. Over the course of the next four years, Gershwin wrote 45 songs; among them were "Somebody Loves Me" and "Stairway to Paradise," as well as a 25-minute opera, "Blue Monday." Composed in five days, the piece contained many musical clichés, but it also offered hints of developments to come. In the early thirties, Gershwin experimented with some new ideas in Broadway musicals. *Strike Up the Band, Let 'Em Eat Cake,* and *Of Thee I Sing*, were innovative works dealing with social issues of the time. *Of Thee I Sing* was a major hit and the first comedy ever to win the Pulitzer Prize.

While the Gershwins' time at North Roxbury Drive was a brief 11 months, they are linked closely with the Beverly Hills home. After moving in, they wrote songs for the Astaire-Rogers movies. There are stories that Fred Astaire, who rarely left his studio, came to the house to work with Ginger Rogers and the Gershwins on several numbers. The house became a gathering place for friends such as Lillian Hellman, Oscar Levant and Harold Arlen.

The lush backyard on a given day might find Moss Hart, Harpo Marx and Paulette Goddard poolside, composer Arnold Schoenberg playing tennis, and comedian Fanny Brice planting night-blooming Jasmine. There were dinners and poker games and plenty of work completed at the house. The Gershwins began with the Astaire-Rogers *Shall We Dance,* followed by the Astaire picture, *A Damsel in Distress*, and finally, Sam Goldwyn's *The Goldwyn Follies.* During his brief time at the Roxbury house George Gershwin created songs like "They All Laughed," "Let's Call the Whole Thing Off," "They Can't Take That Away From Me," "Love Walked In" and "Our Love is Here to Stay," which

Ginny Simms

he never lived to complete. Thirty-eight-year-old George Gershwin died of a brain tumor on July 11, 1937. After his brother's untimely death, Ira swore that he would never set foot in the house again. Instead, he and Leanore bought the house next door, where Ira lived out his life.

The next owner was Ginny Simms, a band singer and actress. Simms lived at 1019 N. Roxbury for about 15 years during the 1940s and 1950s. She was born in San Antonio, Texas, on May 25, 1915. She was a gifted pianist but it was her singing voice that launched her career. She formed a singing trio while at Fresno State Teachers College and was performing at a club in San Francisco where bandleader Kay Kyser heard her and offered her a job as his featured singer. Simms also kept busy recording swing and pop albums. Some of her well-known recordings included "Deep Purple," "Indian Summer," "I'd Like to Set You to Music," "I Can't Get Started," "I Love Paris," and "Stormy Weather."

Simms had originally wanted to teach. While an undergrad, she organized a singing trio as a means of earning tuition money. After a few engagements, she was encouraged by friends and fans to try her luck as a solo vocalist. At the age of twenty, Simms signed as female songstress with the Tommy Gerun band, and then joined the Kay Kyser orchestra in 1938. She was featured on Kyser's popular College of Musical Knowledge weekly radio show, and then accompanied Kyser and the band to Hollywood, where they made their film debut in 1939's *"That's Right, You're Wrong."* Reportedly, Simms and Kyser fell in love, but she broke off the relationship when the shy bandleader dragged his heels concerning marriage. Simms left the Kyser troupe in 1941, when she was signed to her own radio program.

Her career lost momentum when she turned down a marriage proposal by newly divorced MGM head Louis B. Mayer. The scorned Mayer immediately dropped Simms' contract at the studio. She went on to star or co-star in such lightweight film fare as *Here We Go Again* (1942, with Edgar Bergen and Charlie McCarthy and Fibber McGee & Molly), *Hit the Ice* (1943, with Abbott & Costello) and *Broadway Rhythm* (1944), and was also featured in the 1946 Cole Porter biopic *Night and Day*. She appeared in eleven movies from 1939 to 1951, before retiring. Ginny left Hollywood for good in 1951 and her recording career ended shortly thereafter. She retired and ran a travel agency while developing an interest in interior decorating. (Her first husband, Hyatt von Dehn, was the man who started the Hyatt Hotel chain, for which she did much of the interior decorating). She also was involved in real estate with third husband Donald Eastvold. The mother of two sons from her first marriage, Ginny died of a heart attack on April 4, 1994 at the age of 78. She was married three times: to von Dehn from 1945 to 1951, to Bob Calhoun from 1951 to 1952, and Don Eastvold from 1962 to 1994. She is buried at the Desert Memorial Park Cemetery in Cathedral City, California.

The final owners of the house were José Ferrer and Rosemary Clooney. Ferrer, Rosemary's husband, bought the North Roxbury home in 1952 and she was only 25 when she moved in. She died there in June 2002.

Rosemary Clooney was born May 23, 1928, in Maysville, Kentucky. She was the aunt of actor George Clooney. Her unpretentious, rich, and smooth voice earned her recognition as one of America's premier pop and jazz singers. Frank Sinatra stated, "Rosemary Clooney has that great talent which exudes warmth and feeling in every song she sings. She's a symbol of good modern American music."

Her childhood was a difficult one; Clooney and younger siblings Betty and Nick were shuttled among their alcoholic father, Andrew, their mother, Frances; and relatives, who would take turns raising the children. When Clooney was 13, her mother moved to California, taking Nick with her but leaving the girls behind. Her father tried to care for Rosemary and Betty, but he left one night to celebrate the end of World War II, taking the household money with him; and never returned. She and Betty were left to fend for themselves. They collected soda bottles and bought meals at school with the refund money. The phone had been disconnected, the utilities were about to be turned off, and the rent was overdue when Rosemary and Betty won an open singing audition at a Cincinnati radio station. The girls were hired for a regular late-night spot at $20 a week each.

Rosemary Clooney

Jose Ferrer, Rosemary Clooney and their beloved family pets at the North Roxbury House

The Clooney Sisters began their singing career in 1945 in Cincinnati. This work brought them to the attention of Tony Pastor, a big band leader with a national reputation who happened to be passing through Ohio. In 1945, The Clooney Sisters joined Pastor's orchestra.

They toured with Pastor as featured singers until 1948, at which point Betty decided to return to her radio career in Cincinnati. Rosemary continued as a solo vocalist with Tony Pastor for another year. Then, in 1949, at age 21, she left the band, struck out on her own and went to New York City. Clooney's arrival in New York was perfectly timed with the rage for orchestra-backed singers; she was immediately signed with Columbia Records. While at Columbia, Clooney and Mitch Miller hooked up, and Miller convinced Clooney to record an oddball song "Come On-a My House," written by Ross Bagdasarian with lyrics by William Saroyan. The skeptical Clooney finally recorded the song, which was an immediate success, and became a gold record, making Clooney a star and a household name.

In the early 1950s Clooney co-hosted a radio show with Bing Crosby. Clooney also appeared in *White Christmas,* the top grossing film of 1954. Accompanied by the music of Irving Berlin, Clooney was praised for her performance of "Love, You Didn't Do Right by Me." She began a romance with dancer Dante Di Paolo, her co-star in the films *Here Come the Girls,* and *Red Garters.* Rosie first met Miguel José Ferrar when she was singing with Tony Pastor's band. Ferrer was promoting *Cyrano de Bergerac.* They kept running into one another, and the two fell in love and were married. During the summer of 1953, Ferrer, 16 years her senior, married Rosie and they moved into 1019 N. Roxbury. The couple entertained with lavish poolside parties attended by Hollywood's best and brightest stars.

Ferrer loved sports and would get up early for tennis, singing, and fencing lessons, and friends would constantly drop by. According to Clooney in her 1999 book, *"Girl Singer: An Autobiography,"* co-written by Jean Barthel, "Joe's idea of a fine evening is sitting at home with our four dogs underfoot [Cuddles, the Great Dane; George, the basset hound; and the two little Pomeranians], and some good intimate friends on hand. A big evening for me used to be games and noise and festivity."

In a March 1997 interview, Clooney incorrectly maintained that Columbo accidentally shot himself in the den of the N. Roxbury Drive house while cleaning a gun. She told the interviewer that his spirit still haunts the house, "...right here, where we are sitting is where Russ Columbo killed himself. The bullet...ricocheted off three walls. When the kids were young they wouldn't come down here at night unless I was standing at the head of the stairs. And even then, they'd walk in the room, switch on all the lights and say, 'excuse me, Mr. Columbo, I'm just coming in for a minute to get something and then dash out as quickly as they could."

Clooney became the star of her own television series in 1956. The *Rosemary Clooney Show* ran through 1957 and was syndicated to more than 100 television stations. However, by that time,

Clooney had begun to feel the strain of stardom and her relentlessly hectic schedule.

The pressure of raising five children while pursuing careers as a television, movie, radio, and recording star, coupled with the deteriorating state of her marriage, soon took its toll. Clooney developed an addiction to tranquilizers and sleeping pills. She and Ferrer divorced in 1961, reconciled for a few years, then divorced again in 1967. For Clooney, the world came crashing down in 1968. She was standing only yards away when her close friend Robert Kennedy, then campaigning for the Democratic presidential nomination, was assassinated in Los Angeles at the Ambassador Hotel. The tragedy, compounded with her drug addiction, triggered a public mental collapse.

In 1976 Clooney's old friend Bing Crosby asked her to join him on his 50th anniversary tour. It would be Crosby's final tour and Clooney's comeback event. The highlight of the show came when Clooney joined Crosby in a duet of "On a Slow Boat to China." The next year, Clooney signed a recording contract with Concord Jazz, taking the next step on her comeback trail. Along with her renewed recording efforts, Clooney created a living memorial to her sister Betty, who died in 1976 from a brain aneurysm: the Betty Clooney Center in Long Beach, California, a facility for brain-injured young adults.

Rosemary collaborated with Ira Gershwin, singing ten Gershwin standards on an album recorded in 1979. Ira penned a note on the album that said, "Dear Rosie, I am delighted to be connected with your latest recording. Your singing and interpretations have never been better - With appreciation and love, Ira Gershwin." Clooney, in her autobiography, talked about living next to Ira Gershwin. She wrote that strange things often went on at his house and that it was haunted. After years on her own, she married her longtime companion Dante DiPaolo, a graceful Hollywood dancer. They married in November of 1997. Her last performance was December 15, 2001 at the Count Basie Theatre in Red Bank, New Jersey. She was still singing well. In January of 2002, Rosemary underwent lung cancer surgery. She remained hospitalized at the Mayo Clinic until early May, at which time she returned to her Roxbury home to share Mother's Day and her birthday with her family, that included her five children, ten grandchildren, brother and sister-in-law Nick and Nina Clooney, sister Gail Stone Darley and their and Betty's children. She succumbed to cancer on June 29, 2002.

INVESTIGATION #1: DECEMBER 28, 2003

Our group was privileged to first enter this house of music and creativity on December 28, 2003. For the next three years we were welcomed by the living and the dead to partake of the history and hauntings of this house of souls. Sadly, the house is gone now, and during our parting investigation involving four individuals, four crystals from the original chandelier fell at our feet; one at a time. It was as if the house was letting us know that it appreciated our visits and attempts to preserve this landmark that truly embodied the greatness of Beverly Hills. In the end, the city of Beverly Hills cared more about money than memories. The loss of this house represents the loss of a part of the spirit that gives soul and substance to this community.

IPRO normally takes a multi-stage approach to investigations. We usually visit a reportedly haunted location more than once. We try, as a service to the dead, to let them get to know us as we get to know them. Therefore, we proceed in stages, with the first stage being a preliminary walk-through. On Sunday, December 28, 2003, Anne and I met Judy Cameron in the driveway at 1019 Roxbury Drive, at around 2:00 p.m. Judy got our name from a mutual friend and after obtaining permission from the owner, the three of us went into the house. Judy related to us the fact that the current owner was having a few problems with keeping workers from leaving. They were apparently being provoked by unseen energies. We began by taking a few exterior shots, then we unloaded our equipment on the front porch and found the key to open the front door. We noted that Ira Gershwin's old house was next door and to the north and that Lucille Ball's former house was directly across the street. Other former nearby neighbors included: Jack Benny, Diane Keaton, Jimmy Stewart, Eddie Cantor, Agnes Moorehead, Jeanine Crain, Polly Bergen, and Marlene Dietrich.

Judy opened the wrought-iron screen door and then opened the front door. We all felt a strong "whoosh," as the front door opened. It was freezing inside and Anne said that it felt like we just entered a tomb. We tried to disconnect the burglar alarm using the code we were provided, but were unsuccessful. The alarm went off and for the next four minutes, we had to endure the shrill sound until Judy was able to reach someone on my cell phone to get the new code. Not a soul, police or neighbors, came to see what the fuss was all about. We shut the door behind us and unloaded all our equipment in the foyer. The place was devoid of furniture and unkempt. Nothing was cleaned, and it was as if someone came in hastily and removed everything inside and then left without so much as vacuuming. An eerie and pervasive sense of solitude and sadness overcame us. We felt alone and extremely apprehensive for the first few minutes. I immediately took out my IR thermometer and took readings inside and out. The average exterior temperature based on ten readings was about 70 degrees F. I proceeded upstairs and took 20 readings in various rooms where the average temperature was about 48 degrees F (and as a side note, many of the windows were wide open, which should have allowed the warmer outside air to filter in). About 15 readings from the entry level rooms were roughly 45 degrees F. The downstairs cellar was about 43 degrees F (based on about five readings). None of us could figure out why, with the windows open, not one room in the house was over 48 degrees F. If ghosts or spirits as some suggest, emanate cold, then this house was filled to the brim with strong energy.

We always say a prayer once we enter, to ask permission to access the place, seek communication with any spirits and let them know why we have come. After the opening prayer, we used dowsing rods to ask the following questions:

R.W. –"I sense that Rosemary, Miss Clooney is here to greet us, is that correct?"
Rods – (Quickly) to Yes!
R.W. –"Thank you. Are there other spirits who inhabit this space here as well?"
Rods – Yes
R.W. –"Is Monte, I mean, Mr. Blue here?"
Rods – Yes
R.W. –"Is Mr. Gershwin also here in the house?"
Rods – Yes
R.W. –"What about Mr. Columbo and Miss Simms?"
Rods – Yes
R.W. –"Thank you, and here we go."

Judy then gave us a tour of the house, beginning back in the foyer. Steps led down into a spacious living room. This was where Russ Columbo and George and Ira Gershwin composed their music. According to a few historic photographs of the house, a piano stood in the northwest corner dating to the time of Russ Columbo through Rosemary Clooney's occupation. While the piano was no longer there, you could still see the imprints from its legs deeply imbedded in the carpeting.

Strange photographs plagued the investigation, including weird lights in the upstairs bathroom, an odd anomaly near Rob Wlodarski while using the dowsing rods, and others.

There was a sense of being watched and we heard the faint sound of a piano being played. This occurred for a fraction of second, but we all heard something. This room was alive with energy. This seemed to be the heart of the house. Gershwin wrote "Shall we Dance" at the piano in this room.

While still in the foyer, we admired the marble floor and wrought iron banister that led from the foyer to the second floor. A crystal chandelier hanging from the ceiling on the second floor illuminated the entire area. So far, I was able to obtain EMF spikes in the corner where the piano once stood and in the foyer.

Judy picked up the presence of an African-American female, while I sensed a Caucasian female, perhaps a maid or cleaning woman. The kitchen led to a utility room and then a hallway that went to the back of the house where the staff quarters were. There was a small bedroom followed by a larger bedroom, bath and walk-in closet. Judy told us that George Clooney used to stay in the smaller middle room in the back.

We exited a small door off the hallway near the kitchen area, and reached the concrete, awning covered, back patio. Once outdoors, the chill from the house immediately vanished. The temperature had gone from the 40s inside the house to around 71 degrees F outside. We were all immediately drawn to a large olive tree. (According to Judy, it was Rosemary's favorite).

Beyond the tree was a pool, bathhouse, pool house and tennis court. A flagstone walkway led from the right side of the patio, circled the olive tree, then led to the pool and bathhouse. Walking through the backyard, I was over whelmed by the energy of the place. We walked the path that Rosemary must have taken hundreds of times. By the pool, I looked back at the house and saw someone peering out of a second-floor window at us. It was a woman with blonde hair, probably about 30 years old. Her hair was worn short in the front, with a bun in the back. I noticed a boy, around 11 years old beside her. He had dark hair and the woman had her arm around him. This was on the northwest wing of the house, above the kitchen.

Rob sensed a man related to movie Westerns and he felt that several dogs that had been buried in the backyard. As we were standing near the pool, I could feel people all around me. I saw the pool filled and lounge chairs scattered around the pool. There were people drinking, swimming and, mingling.

Near the bathhouse, Judy wanted to ask a few questions, so I got out my dowsing rods;
J.C. –"Was this bathhouse original to the house?"
Rods – No
R.W. –"This was added later, is that correct?"
Rods – Yes
R.W. –"Was this here when Mr. Columbo occupied the house?"
Rods – No
R.W. –"Was this after Mr. Columbo?"
Rods – Yes

R.W. asked for a spirit count in the backyard for animals and the rods spun quickly, four times. There was also an indication of animals in the house and backyard belonging to several different owners. R.W. sensed that at least one dog was Rosemary's pride and joy, and that her children loved the dog. R.W. also sensed another pet dog that belonged to either Monte Blue or Russ Columbo. As we continued to walk through the place, there was a very strong sense of Rosemary still ruling the roost in this house. She seems to be the greeter and caretaker. The upstairs studio area, which turned out to the place where I saw the woman and boy watching us through a west-facing window is the only place outside of the master bedroom that I felt José Ferrer's presence. I didn't sense that he was here that much; this was a stopover for him.

After completing a thorough walk-through of the entire house, and property, we said our closing prayer, turned on the alarm, locked the front door and left. We planned to return, with the owner's approval, as soon as possible. We all sensed that the strongest energy in the house belonged to Rosie, followed by George Gershwin, Russ Columbo and a former housekeeper who was very loyal to Rosemary Clooney. The saddest rooms in the house seemed to be the master bedroom and former Gershwin Room. The happiest rooms were the living room and music room. The rooms with the most unsettling energy were the basement and den. We all sensed that the living room was the heart of the house. We had all the temperature readings from the various rooms which never changed while we visited, exhibiting constant ambient readings of between 43 and 49 degrees F, although it was over 70 degrees F outside and most of the windows were open in the house. There were numerous spikes in the Gauss and EMF meters, and a Natural EMF meter went off by itself in the corner of the living room while the three of us were standing in the foyer.

INVESTIGATION #2: JANUARY 11, 2004
Time of Investigation: 10:30 p.m.-5:00 a.m.
Equipment: "L" Rods (5 sets); Natural Tri-field Meter (1); Gauss Meter (2); Tape recorders (2); IR Thermometers (2); Camera (1 mini dv)
Participants: Robert J. Wlodarski; Matthew Wlodarski; Dan Larson; Anne Wlodarski; Matthew Cope; Ginnie McGovern; Victoria Gross; Deann Burch; Christi Flowers; Kristin Collier; Robin Collier; Alma Carey; Palah Sandling; Peggy Stahler; Judy Cameron; Len, Selma and Lisa Fisch (owners); Nancy Gershwin; Jan Perry, and Drew and Laurel. There were a few more people who came in after the investigation began.

Photographs taken during the séance portions of the investigation.

This was our first full-blown investigation courtesy of the owners, and was arranged by our friend, Judy Cameron. We employed equipment and utilized several psychics, during this investigation. As the psychics entered, they were each given a clip board and a rough diagram of the house and were encouraged to walk through at their own pace. None of the psychics were given any information about the house or its occupants prior to visiting. All they received was the address. Two of the psychics used tape recorders to record their thoughts during the walk-through. A tape recorder was placed in the basement and left on in an attempt to pick up EVP (Electronic Voice Phenomenon.) A psychic summary session began at 1:45 p.m. in the den/recreation room. Each psychic shared his or her sensory feelings and impressions. A summary of major impressions follows:

* In the living room was a loving female presence in her mid-to-late thirties or early forties. She is tall, with a medium-to-thin build, and a fair complexion with shoulder length, golden brown hair. The woman is waiting for a young lover or husband who may have gone off to the war. A little girl is in the closet, playing hide and seek. In the dining room is a male energy with black hair. He has a medium to heavy build and is in his mid-fifties to mid-sixties. He was facing the window nearest the driveway, longing for someone.

* In the studio I sensed several children playing.

* In the pool area I sensed a child drowning.

* I felt a love triangle gone awry and a dispute over a baby. I also felt a "revolving door" sensation in the late '40s or early '50s. I don't think it was necessarily sold numerous times, but the owners had quite an open door policy and never knew who would be staying at or partying at their home on any given night or weekend.

* In the living room I sensed a woman standing at the window to the left of the fireplace. She was facing out as though waiting for someone to come home. There is sadness in her stance although I

ı grace about her, a dignity. I feel sad for her; there is an essence of
s wearing a below-the-knee length dress that is cinched in or belted at

window at the back of the room I have lower back pain and a light-
the result of a miscarriage or childbirth. I feel a great sense of energy in
coming into the room from out in the garden;

rts with FR, Frank? Fred? I just keep hearing "Frrrrr."

e a couple who are angry with each other. There is a sound of shattered
the floor. The fight takes place in front of others. She is very angry and
woman I witnessed from the window in the living room.

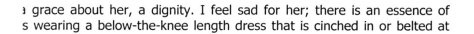

ʋm I see a fight between two men. One man is hit in the right jaw by a not-too-
man with dark hair.

ı sense heart or chest pain related to a man in his early fifties or late forties.

* In the pantry I sense lots of chatter and gossip involving three young women in their late teens or early twenties saying, "Don't tell" and then whispering to each other.

* In the basement I sense a lot of alcohol being consumed. This place is like a night club filled with gambling, drinking, smoking and sex.

* In the second bedroom to the left of the stairs I sense a strong masculine energy wearing brown clothes and a brown top hat who is writing feverishly at his desk. He has brown thinning hair, wears a sweater, is younger than 40, with the name of Frank or Albert.

* In the vanity area off the master bedroom I sense a woman named Carole or Celeste. She is a blonde, elegant woman putting on lipstick in the mirror.

* When I walked up to the house, I sensed a woman looking down at me from a second floor window. She did not seem very friendly, and was watching over the house. She did not like outsiders, and was rather stern.

* On the tennis court I felt lots of celebrities playing tennis and hanging out; it was a great place to be.

* In the upstairs master bedroom there was a lot of female energy, and I sensed that a woman named Jenny or Lenore was not happy here.

* In the upstairs studio I sensed a male working on projects all night long. He did not take good care of himself and didn't remember to eat and rest as much as he should have. I sensed that he

wrote music and also played a piano there.

* In the foyer I felt that a woman was having a lot of trouble breathing.

* In the dining room I made contact with a woman who said that she really loved the room. I sensed that she spent a lot of time in that room. This woman, whoever s... this house for a long time and she was ill at the end of her life. I just felt really con... dining room. She kind of used that as her window to the world. She looked out those wi... I'm almost thinking that they may have used it as a bedroom for her when she was ill. walking through the house with her, my feet were hardly moving. It was just a lot of trouble and walk. While in the den, I got a strong pressure in my lungs and had difficulty breathing.

* Once in the studio room all I wanted to do was dance and I'm not a dancer. I just kept danc... and dancing in that room. There was a man in there and all he kept showing me was blue, blue, blu... He was showing me pieces of cardboard paper that were covered in blue. He was trying to show me the color blue. For some reason I didn't get the impression that the room was ever blue but rather the color was a metaphor for a personality that once inhabited the house. There was a man in his late thirties or early forties who loved this room. This room is like music to me and I felt that a piano had been in here at one time. I sensed a piano, cello, base instrument and a trumpet being played. I sensed the name Count Basie, dancing, writing, theater and music associated with this room.

* In the light blue room upstairs, I felt very ill. I went back in there later and got the impression of a younger woman in her twenties, blonde, and I wanted to take a one-two punch to my stomach. It wasn't as if someone was hitting her, it was like stomach pain.

* In the master bedroom I sensed a couple who had been in there who loved each other very, very much; it was a wonderful romantic love in this room. Then I had the woman come back to me with the breathing problems. She continually made me feel sad. I think she was a really wonderful woman who was humming to me and singing to me in the dining room. She was definitely a singer with Hollywood connections, and may also have been an actress. She had a hard time toward the end when she got ill. She really didn't want people to see her there. There was one point where I was having trouble breathing inside, and I went outside to get some fresh air. She came out with me and said that she did that a lot too. She always kept bushes in the front of the house to give her privacy. Because when she would walk out to get some air, she didn't want anybody to see her the way she was. That means to me that she must have had a devastating illness, because she would have changed a lot toward the end.

* On the other side of the master bedroom, the energy switched to the man from the music room, and he gave me the worst headache. Several people in the group also experienced the headaches. At one point I heard the words cerebral hemorrhage. I don't know whether he had that, or whether he died from that. The man was dressed like Hugh Heffner. He had on a long, silk bathrobe and he was very fashionable like Howard Hughes. He had dark hair and he was around 40 and came from the 1920s or 1930s.

kenness. My head was spinning and it was wild down there. It ... felt like excessive drinking. I felt like someone had died in the ... man killed during a party. He was a heavier, old gentleman in ... eart attack at the party in the basement. I got a dead body ... is very oppressive. I think it was a feeling from more than

...derland with a lot of energy focused around the olive ... lots of fun. It's a great backyard and a magical place.

...ux; a woman from the 20s era; a male servant; and, ...nething like that. I also sensed that someone had fallen or ...hind the house after a party.

...n I got a really strange buzzing sound or feeling. Then, I got a really severe ...uld come and go as I walked around the house. I sensed an older man in who was ...us. He was talking as if he was glad that we were having a party. He seemed really happy ...e were all here.

* In the pool area, I kept feeling a head injury.

* I picked up on a young woman wearing 1920s clothing with a flowing Art Deco dress and spaghetti straps. She was very adventurous and traveled a lot. I sensed that she had a pet monkey that was kept in the backyard in a cage. I keep sensing a male servant who spoke more than one language, like French and Indonesian, or French Polynesian. He's somehow connected to the young woman. I got him strongly in the kitchen wearing a black tie. I got the name Natalie or Natalia for the woman, and the name Huxley or Leslie, or Wesley for the man.

* The bedroom directly above the den, that overlooks the back porch, had a strong scent of perfume. It was very powdery, sickly sweet, and I picked up a female, around 56 (or perhaps from 1956). As I walked towards that bathroom, I got a pain in my shoulder that went straight through to my chest, and my arm was paralyzed, so I don't know if it was a stroke or heart attack. I went into the bathroom, and once I got inside, the feeling became worse.

* When I got out the bathroom and went to the other side, I picked up a male who had pain under his left rib. What I got was that this man had died from this internal injury or illness.

* In the basement, I sensed a lot of drinking and that people needed a secret knock to enter. I felt women coming in and giggling like they were getting away with something.

* In the large downstairs living room I picked up on the 1920s-1940s and then the 1970s. In the late 1920s, I had a little girl who loved to sit by that window, and that's where she would talk to her friends. She was a little blonde girl and I remember a blue ribbon in her hair. She had her hair pulled back. I got a name of something like Bethany. She loved to play by that window.

Several very clear "orb" photographs were taken during the investigation, usually when other activity was taking place

* At the pool I heard child saying something like, "Pool bad."

* While standing near the tennis court, I heard two men actually playing tennis and calling out the score.

* In the tennis court I heard people playing tennis. I also picked up the names, Tyrone Power and June Havoc.

* I sensed a chauffeur in the back of the house or servant's quarters.

* Downstairs in the room with patterned wallpaper, I got the main female presence or energy in the house. I got this woman everywhere. I sensed nostalgia and longing, as if waiting for someone. She seemed alone in the house.

* In the upstairs bathroom, near the master bedroom, there was an etched mirror. What I saw was the older woman facing into the mirror and disappointed with her looks. She had once been very beautiful but now she was saying, well, I guess that's it. She had just given something up, like a marriage, or a good relationship.

Following the psychic summary session, a séance took place. These EVP snippets follow from a review of the tape.

GM –"I also forgot to say when I was upstairs in the music room, my favorite room, a dog came out. At first I thought it was like a poodle. It was champagne colored dog, and now I've got another animal here, under the table that keeps brushing my leg. Almost like a cat would brush my leg." [A distinct bark can be heard on the tape at this moment].

GM —"Somebody told me it was champagne colored and I said, "Oh how Beverly Hills to tell me that the dog is champagne colored!" [One sharp click can be heard on the tape]

CF —"Whoever it is, is a male and they are showing me a brooch. It's an oval-shaped brooch with a peach background, and green cameo of a female in front with a gold frame around it. That's here on the property." [On the tape there's a word that sounds like "couch" between people talking]

CF – "It wasn't intentionally hidden." [A discernable knock can be heard on tape]

GM – "Victoria, what do you have?" [A voice on tape says something like, "Case, okay."]

VG – "It's a big, heavy warning. If you fill that pool, be very careful with small children, because the potential for accidents is very strong." [Faint EVP of a child's voice... can't make out what it's saying, followed by louder EVP of a child's voice whispering something unintelligible... something like, "Hop in."]

INVESTIGATION #3: MARCH 21, 2004

Time of Investigation: 11:30 p.m.-7:00 a.m.
Equipment: "L" Rods 1 set; Tri-field Meter: 1; Gauss Meter: 1; Tape recorders: 2; EVP Equipment: 1 analog tape player; IF Thermometers: 1; Camera: Digital: 1-35mm;
Personnel: Rob Wlodarski; Alma Carey, Carlos Penaranda; Ginnie McGovern; Robin Collier, Peggy Stahler, Peter James and Judy Cameron.

During this session, 28 photos with anomalies were taken in the house. This investigation allowed psychics Carlos Penaranda and Peter James to explore the house. It was also designed to use dowsing rods to communicate with energies in the Blue Room, where J.C. saw the figure of a man the last time we were in the house.
The dowsing rod communication session and some highlights in the Blue Room follow.

Q."Is there someone in this room with us right now?"
Dowsing Rods: Yes.
Q."The last time we were here on January 11, I saw a man standing in this room. Was it George Gershwin?"
Dowsing Rods: Yes.
Q."Is George the one who brought me (J.C.) to this house?"
Dowsing Rods: Yes.
Q."Is there something I need to do for you and this house?"
R.W. —"My sense is that you have already done it."
Q."Do you frequent this house and the one where Ira lived?"
Dowsing Rods: Yes.
Q."Are the people in Ira's house aware of spirits or have paranormal activity?"
Dowsing Rods: Yes.

Q. "Does Leonore Gershwin's spirit visit this house?"

Dowsing Rods: No.

Q. "Is Leonore Gershwin's spirit next door?"

Dowsing Rods: Yes!

Q. "Are you [George] aware of what's happening to this house?"

Dowsing Rods: Yes. As Judy is asking another question, the word "Yes" in a male voice, can be heard over her voice

Q. "Are you aware of Rosemary Clooney?"

Dowsing Rods: Yes!

Q. "Is Ira in communication with George?"

Dowsing Rods: Yes.

Q. "Was Rosemary aware of your presence in the house when she was living in it?"

The Blue Room, where the dowsing rod session took place during the investigation.

Dowsing Rods: No. The dowsing rods begin pointing in back of me, toward Ira and Leonore's house.

Q. "Are you pointing to where you are?" A "Ha ha ha ha ha" can be distinctly heard.

Q. "You lived here with Leonore and Ira, correct?"

Dowsing Rods: Yes.

Q. "Was this their room?"

Dowsing Rods: No.

Q. "Did you use it for a specific purpose?"

Dowsing Rods: Yes.

Q. "Although this was not your bedroom, did you spend a lot of time in this room?"

Dowsing Rods: Yes. An unidentifiable sound can be heard on the tape, like a tap step?

Q. "Were you aware of Ira facing at this particular room from his house?"

Dowsing Rods: Yes.

Q. "Did Ira talk to you?"

Dowsing Rods: Yes.

Q. "So you would purposefully come into this room so you could be closer to Ira, is that correct?"

Dowsing Rods: Yes.

Q. "Was Leonore more of a skeptic then Ira?"

Dowsing Rods: No.

Q. "Was Ira more of a skeptic?" A woman's voice says something like "He was very aware of him."

Dowsing Rods: Yes. - On tape you can hear a male voice distinctly saying the words "Skeptic." A woman's voice then says "Would you communicate with us?"

Q. "You communicated a lot through your music, is that correct?"

Dowsing Rods: Yes.

Q."From your perspective, are there a lot of parties still going on in this house?"
Dowsing Rods: Yes.
Q."I get the feeling that sometimes you don't stay here because it is too noisy." A voice says "Yep," or "You bet!"
Dowsing Rods: Yes.
R.W. –"I'm getting a sense that he knows we are talking about him." (A click) "I know he's here… I'm getting chills."

R.W. walked over toward the window where we feel that George's spirit stares out hoping to connect with Ira. We are both chilled to the bone at this moment. I take a few photographs of the room and J.C.. Later, after developing the film, I find three photographs of the room with orbs and other anomalies. J.C. says that we have to come at night, because that's when she saw George Gershwin in the room. There is another cadenced voice on tape but I can't make it out.

My camera jams and I can't get the film out and then the camera flies out of my hands and onto the floor. We stop the question and answer period at this point. A curious event took place while A.C. and R.W. were in the Blue Room later on, around 2:30. As A.C. and R.W. began discussing what had happened earlier, Alma began to get a strong whiff of sweet perfume from the adjacent small room between the bedroom and bathroom. R.W. walked into the room and also experienced a whiff of perfume, followed a smell of dirty diapers. It was a very strange sensation. A.C. continued to smell perfume and R.W. began sensing that someone unseen was now in the room with us. R.W. took out the IR thermometer and began taking readings. At that moment, A.C. began sensing a young girl, around seven or eight years old in the room. As R.W. began trying to locate the spirit with the IU thermometer, the reading went from 57 degrees to 60, 63, 66, 68, 71, and then 73 degrees within seconds. A.C. said a playful child was walking around us, checking us out. As AC sensed the child moving, R.W. followed to where A.C. was pointing. Everywhere A.C. pointed the readings were 70 to 73 degrees, while other parts of the room; registered around 57 degrees. A Gauss Meter was also used and fluctuations were noted in the areas where AC felt the little girl and the IR temperature readings were high. This was good corroborative evidence for us. As C.P. entered the room, he immediately sensed the little girl. At that moment, the readings around Alma ceased, and the energy shifted to C.P. The child's energy seemed to circle around C.P., and this was confirmed by high IR temperature fluctuations and Gauss Meter spikes. Everyone in the room was getting the chills when A.C. said that she now sensed a ghostly teenage boy come in the room. As R.W. took IR readings of both Alma and Carlos, the equipment picked up noticeable fluctuations. There were areas around C.P. and A.C. registered 70 to 74 degrees, while other parts of the room continued to produce readings of 56 to 58 degrees. This continued for about seven or eight minutes before we all felt that the two energies had left the room. At that point, there was no registration in the room higher than 58 degrees. It was amazing to sense the presence of an energy form, but also track its movement. Once both energies left the room, we also left.

Peter James provided the following insights during this investigation:

* While in the den, Peter picked up on some sweet smelling perfume. It was a floral scent. Just then, others at the table began smelling the fragrance. The group of onlookers began hearing what sounded like several people talking in the vacant den.

* Peter yelled out, "Hello! Who is here? Communicate with me!" Peter heard a voice that he said belonged to Russ Columbo.. People then began hearing footsteps coming from upstairs. Peter called out once again, "Hello, who is here? Identify yourself. Make your presence known now." Several of the onlookers began hearing faint voices or whispers coming from upstairs. [There is a loud thump followed by a sharp screeching sound on tape].

Psychic Peter James

* As Peter reached the master bedroom, he felt the presence of Rosemary Clooney and Russ Columbo. He had a very strong sense of a dominant female energy throughout the house. Peter said that the master bedroom was the heart of the house, and there was extensive energy in the room... almost like a portal to another dimension. This area is a very strong spot where the spirits gather and enter. It is an energy vortex!

* When Peter was talking about the death of Russ Columbo there was an audible whisper on the tape. Peter said, "I am going to ask him (Russ Columbo) if he was murdered. I am leaning more toward murder. I would say that there are three ghosts in this house, at least three. Some come and go."

* Peter began sensing (silent film star) Pola Negri. He said, "Out of respect for Russ Columbo and with respect to the choices that people make in their lives (at this point you can hear an audible laughter on tape), I believe that the tryst that he had with Lansing Brown... well, I feel that they were more than just friends... that they were lovers. I believe that Carole Lombard and someone else named Sally were a cover for Russ Columbo. I believe this Brown person had a lover's quarrel." (a click on tape) "That's what I feel, and I'm not judging his lifestyle."

* On the stairs, Peter felt that an accident took place there and paramedics had been called to the house on a number of occasions. There may have even been an attempted suicide in the house. Rosemary Clooney was well aware of the spirit of Russ Columbo and before going to bed some nights, she would actually call out, "Goodnight, Russ."

* He also sensed that a person or persons had a drug problem and that this left an imprint in the house.

* James felt that a man with the name Lance or Lancer, something like that, attempted to strangle Russ Columbo in this house. There was an altercation between the men in the house, at least once.

* James picked up a baby dying in the house. He also sensed that a woman of color named Blanche became Rosemary's closest confidant toward the end of her life. They would be in telephone contact all the time.

* According to James, there were some not-so-happy times in this house. There are a couple of unusual sounds on the tape as James called out for Rosemary to let herself be heard or let us know that she is here. One sound seemed like creaking or breathing. This was not caused by the camera, people talking or the sound of people walking because everyone was still. Once again, Peter picked up on the close relationship between Rosemary and a woman named Blanche.

* James reiterated that there are a several strong energies that stay here, but that many others come and visit. The house is filled with very good, positive vibrations. The place is very active with most of the energy of a playful nature. James sensed that many deals were made in the house and contracts signed. The house contains abundant energy reflecting celebrities, parties, negotiations and business dealings.

* James had a sense that Rosemary Clooney believed in metaphysics. She was a very spiritual person and very open to these types of things. She was a believer who had a personal psychic or attended readings.

* According to Peter, many of the spirits return to this house because of the wonderful memories they had here. This was the home for many of those in Hollywood to come to when they needed to get away or relax. There were also very painful times in this house for Rosemary. She went through quite a bit of trauma, disappointment and loss here. It contains the good and bad times; happy and sad memories.

* While upstairs in the music room James sensed dancing and music. He also suggested that meetings took place with moguls in the industry and deals were made there.

* According to James, the basement has its own essence and character. It was a kind of hideout, away from the rest of the house. He felt that gambling, bootlegging, and clandestine activities took place here. He felt like someone had been seriously injured down here or that a man's legs had been purposefully broken. There was strong gangster activity in this part of the house with people coming and going through the back door and not through the house. The place was thick with Prohibition energy.

INVESTIGATION #4: MAY 1, 2004

Time of Investigation: 5:00 p.m. to midnight

Equipment: "L" Rods 1 set; Tri-field Meter: 3; Gauss Meter: 3; Tape recorders: 4; EVP Equipment: 2 sets

IF Thermometers: 4; Cameras: Digital: 3- 35mm; 2; Digital 8MM; 28 photos with anomalies were taken in the house

Investigators: Rob Wlodarski and Alma Carey of IPRO; Chad Patterson, Virginia Marco, José Marco, Dede Miller, Darcy Hogan, Karen Johl, Mike Ash, Tracy Austin, Nancy Richling, Jason Lithgow of the California Society for Ghost Research (CSGR). Guests: Lonnie Sill, Alex Sill, Nicci Sill, JoJo Wright, Megan Steinbeck, Steve Clark, Clete Keith, Jan Perry and two children, Selma Fisch, Max Pierce, and Johnny Gorman.

R.W. arrived at 2:30 p.m. and entered the house alone. R.W. unloaded all his equipment and felt a strong rush of energy upon entering the house and set up the equipment in the den. After taking six photos in the den and foyer, R.W. felt as if he was being watched and followed as he went from room to room to get a feel for the house. R.W. heard a dog bark from the kitchen area, a child crying upstairs and a gunshot come from the basement area. Checking each of these locations out, R.W. found no one else in the house. A.C. arrived at 3:00 and R.W. and AC heard footsteps coming from upstairs; the sounds of furniture being moved; people talking and whispering. A woman in a blue robe walked into the den and then dematerialized. A man walked into the pool house wearing a black bathing suit and then waved. The guest house was locked when R.W. arrived. When R.W. and A.C. went out to the guest house to check out the strange-looking man in the bathing suit, the doors to the guest house were wide open. We were both chilled to the bone after entering and stayed only a few minutes before locking the doors and leaving. By 5:00 p.m., 25 people were in the house. From 8:30 p.m. to 2:30 a.m. we conducted a thorough investigation of all the rooms. Four groups of five people began switching rooms and monitored all the room in the house for the next six hours.

The group got numerous orbs by the pool and floating orbs in the tennis court. There were EMF fluctuations in the guest house. A door opened in front of a group monitoring the guest house and several group members reported hearing tennis balls being hit back and forth on the deserted tennis court. Team members heard music and people partying in the living room. A misty shape and apparition were sighted in the Blue Room and master bedroom; and a dog was heard scratching the rug in the family room. The group captured orbs on film, saw balls of light shoot across the ceiling or down the hallways; witnessed mists, heard voices and unexplained noises, noted frequent spikes in equipment and captured EVP. Scents of perfume, flowers, cologne and pipe or cigar tobacco were noted in various parts of the house.

INVESTIGATION #5: JANUARY 9, 2005

Time of Investigation: 12:15 p.m. to 4:15 p.m.

Guests: Rob Wlodarski; Ginnie McGovern; Don; Judy Cameron; Ruth; and, Johnny Gorman

Equipment: "L" Rods 1 set; Tri-field Meter: 1; Gauss Meter: 1; Tape recorders: 2; IF Thermometers: 1; Camera: Digital: 0 - 35mm; 2; 74 photos were taken. About 20 had anomalies

This was a very rainy day and by the time we had to leave, a massive storm was in full swing. Over ten inches of rain would fall in Beverly Hills by the time this three-day rain cycle had ended. Water was coming into the house from several locations including the upstairs roof, which was leaking in the master bedroom and music room. The ambient temperature was roughly 58 to 61 degrees from noon to 4:30 p.m. The humidity was about 80 percent. Our focal point was the sunken living room where a table had been set up near where the piano had been in place since the time of Russ Columbo and the Gershwins. During the walk through, R.W. lit candles and played Gershwin, Clooney and Columbo tunes on the CD player. The house seemed to come alive when the music began playing. Prior to recording the EVP, we heard a baby cry three times and the group witnessed several shadowy figures on the second floor; two members smelled woman's perfume; and, three group members heard footsteps coming from the unoccupied upstairs area. As a final preliminary note, the olive tree in the backyard, which was declared dead by an arborist last year, is sprouting back to life. Judy had been watering it during the summer and the recent rains seem to have rejuvenated it.

We essentially used this time to talk about the former occupants, listen to Columbo, Gershwin, Simms and Clooney tapes, and reminisce about what they all contributed to Hollywood, the world of music and how they impacted our lives. As the rain continued to pour, we began noticing that we could see our breath as we talked. The humidity apparently created this odd phenomenon, which certainly enhanced the paranormal ambiance of the house. During the entire four-hour event, we continually heard unexplained voices and noises coming from various rooms inside the house. By the end of our time in the house, only four of us remained (R.W., G.M., J.C. and J.G.). As we stood in a circle under the chandelier in the entryway, four crystals from the chandelier above us proceeded to fall at our feet; one by one, we heard a clink and saw a crystal from the chandelier near each of our feet. It was almost as if the house or the four main spirits of the house (Rosemary, Monte, Russ and George) were giving us a going away gift. Needless to say, we were all stunned and very appreciative of the experience.

INVESTIGATION #6: MARCH 12, 2005

Time of Investigation: 4:15pm-1:00am
Investigators: Rob Wlodarski, Lonnie Sill, Alex Sill, Nicci Sill, and Natasha Sill of IPRO; Judy Cameron; Maritza Skandunas, and Karen Ridens (San Diego Ghost Hunters), Johnny Gorman, and Dave Deelo and Donavan McDougle
Equipment: "L" Rods 1 set; Tri-field Meter: 3; Gauss Meter: 3; Tape recorders: 5; IF Thermometers: 3; Camera: Digital: 5 - 35mm; 2; roughly 300 photos were taken by all investigators

This ended up as our last investigation because the house was being sold. The group arrived between 4:30 p.m. and 5:30 p.m. We began setting up the equipment and doing a walk through. AS and R.W. went to the Blue Room to try our luck at EVP while J.C. was being interviewed by D.D. and D.M. M.S. and her group were making their way through the house for the first time. A.S. and R.W., with the tape recorder running began the EVP session with the following summarizing the results:

There are several noticeable clicks as A.S. and R.W. are talking.

R.W. —"It is now 6:05 p.m., we are in the Blue Room. Alex's camera batteries went dead on him." [Loud click – Tape #4]. "They were fully charged when we began."

R.W. –"We've set up a candle and a natural Tri-field meter, EMF meter on the "sum." (Loud pop.)

The sum setting detects a combination of magnetic and electric fields. The EMF meter is a scientific instrument for measuring electromagnetic fields. It has also been suggested that spirits may disrupt the EMF within a location or emit their own EMF, although there is no scientific proof for this belief as yet.

R.W. –"We are going to try and contact George Gershwin or anyone else who would like to come through. Leave a voice answer, use long sentences, whatever you can do with your energy, we'd appreciate it." [a bell-like sound can be hear in the background – Tape #17]

R.W. –"The last time we were here you were standing near the window trying to communicate with Ira. Are you still doing that?" [A noise in the background – Tape #18] The dowsing rods indicate a "Yes."

R.W. –"The last time we were here, we got the word skeptic when we were asking whether Ira was a skeptic. I will ask you again. Was Ira a skeptic?" The dowsing rods indicate a "yes" and there is a faint click on the tape followed by a discernable voice saying, "I believe so."

R.W. –"Would you point to where you are?" [A bell-like sound in the background of Tape #23] The dowsing rods point to the north wall of the Blue Room.

R.W. –"If you allow us to take a picture of you that would be super." [A loud thump – Tape #24] "George, Did you like your stay in this house?" The dowsing rods indicate a "Yes" followed by an "Okay" on tape #32.

R.W. –"Maybe Alex could shut the door and we could be isolated." [As AS shuts the door to the room, there is a loud popping sound on tape #50]

 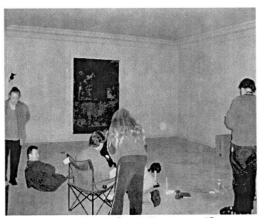

Photographs of the team taken during the March 12 investigation of the North Roxbury House

R.W.- "Is Rosemary downstairs now?" [What sounds like a faint woman's or child's voice is heard in the background – tape #53]

R.W. –"So the skeptic remark was just in answer to my question that Ira was a skeptic in life, correct?" [A loud click on tape #67 followed by an "ah" that can be heard following R.W.'s "Okay."]

R.W. –"Do you know that there are new owners?" [A woman's voice says something like "Oh..." tape #72]

R.W. –"You probably know the outcome." [A loud crashing noise or "boom" sound in the background – tape #74]

As there is general talking, a popping sound can be heard on tape #80

R.W. – "George could say something on tape, now that Judy's here." [Thumping sounds can be heard on tape #84]

R.W. –"Are you still playing tennis?" J.C. – "Did you win, George?" [A low moan can be heard on tape #86]

J.C. –"Is this his (George Gershwin's) bedroom?" ["Yeah... that's right, that's right" on tape #90]

R.W. –"Is there a young boy here in spiri?"t ["Yes" on tape #85]

The Natural EMF meter on the floor begins to register on its own. [A loud sound in the background of tape #104]

R.W. –Okay, that was your sign?" [A popping sound on tape and the EMF meter moves]

R.W. –"Yeah. okay... work with the Tri-field meter... George, are you here?" [Whispering in the background on tape #111... could be J.C. or AS??? – a child's voice in the background on tape #112]

R.W. –"Monte, are you here?" [Several clicking sounds on tape #132]

J.C. –'In the book about Ira, I just read that Ira saw you in the other room. Do you remember that?' [The dowsing rods immediately show a "yes" response and the EMF meter goes wild]

R.W. –"It's a song?" [Laughter and a deep voice says "Yes," on tape #166]

R.W. –"Could you turn this up and make it louder?" [The word "Oh" is on tape #168] "Or stop altogether?".

R.W. –"Could you stop for a second, George? Hello?"... [A very loud snap on tape# 171]

R.W. –"Do you think you could knock? Go ahead; it's your show tonight." [Whistle at tape #221]

R.W. –"Ira, did you like to drink while you were writing your lyrics?" [Two grunting-like sounds on tape #235]

R.W. –"I've got a feeling George had a great sense of humor. George, did you like a good joke?" [Whistling in the background on tape #273. At tape#288 there is a clicking sound followed by "Yes."]

J.C. –"Are you tired of being here?" [a clunking noise on tape #313]

R.W. –"If you wanted to go to New York [Loud "pop" on tape #328] you could go there instantly, right?" [Fluttering sound on tape #332]

R.W. –"Are you cold where you are?" [a snapping sound on tape #336] "Or do you just suck our energy and change it?" [A snapping sound on tape #337] "By contacting us are you able to manipulate our environment and make things colder? And that's how we know you are here?"

A.S. –"I don't think you die; you just go to another dimension… another life…" [A thump on tape #390]

A.S. –"There is no death." [Another thump on tape #39

R.W. – "Does Oscar Levant play tennis with you?" [Female whisper on tape #497 says "Oscar!"]

R.W. –"Would you mind if we came out and watched you play tennis later?" [A loud click on tape #527]

We concluded our last investigation inside and our two-year ongoing research project had come to an end. We gathered our equipment and bags, and then turned the alarm back on and shut the door for good on 1019 N. Roxbury Drive. There is little doubt from those who spent time in the house (both skeptics and believers) that it was haunted by passive and active energy. You could feel the palpable energy upon entering and even the most skeptical guest could not help but feel something unusual inside. We heard a baby crying and disembodied footsteps. We felt cold spots, smelled perfume and tobacco, witnessed shadowy figures, and captured quite a bit of EVP including George Gershwin saying "skeptic," and numerous instances of tapping, clicking, clapping and other sounds were captured on tape.

Further proof of the paranormal energy in the house comes from the unusual spikes in meters, the rapid fluctuations in IR thermometer readings, the numerous photographs taken of orbs, and unusual mists, funnels and blobs of light witnessed by many of the investigators and guests. We have little doubt that some of what we experienced was because not only did we want something to happen, or even psych ourselves into a haunted house experiential mode, but, there were too many things that happened that could not be explained as paranoia, wishful thinking, or other natural causes. There were too many independent observers, investigators, psychics and sensitives who came up with similar evidence and impressions for what we experienced to be dismissed as some kind of mass hallucination.

We would soon find out that the property had been purchased by a developer and soon the city of Beverly Hills approved the demolition of one of America's most historic celebrity homes. The residence stood for 77 years, and the list of owners and guests was like a Who's Who of entertainment personalities. Rosemary Clooney would be the last celebrity occupant and with her death, the house met an untimely end. We hope that by chronicling what we encountered inside, that we have somehow honored the dead and provided some memories for the living. Perhaps in some inter-dimensional sense, only the shell of the house is gone and its true spirit is and will always be alive.

2. THAT STEAK JOYNT

BY DALE KACZMAREK

FORMERLY AT 1610 N WELLS STREET
CHICAGO, ILLINOIS

Unfortunately, That Steak Joynt is no longer open and what a shame, as it was, without a doubt, Chicago's most haunted restaurant! In the 1870s, the building at 1610 North Wells St. was Henry Piper's Bakery, a growing concern that employed over five hundred workers, housed a school for their children and shipped baked goods to 39 states. This was also a time when Chicago was busy exporting its share of the 60,000 pounds of sturgeon caviar produced annually in the Great Lakes.

The original site was razed by the Great Fire of 1871 then raised in height by twelve feet. A magnificent Victorian showpiece was constructed on the new, "modernized" street but after 60 years of successful operation, Henry Piper closed his bakery and too, Chicago stopped shipping Lake Sturgeon caviar. The building never closed its doors, however, subsequently housing a variety of businesses including a launderette and a hardware store. In 1962, the location underwent a transformation and reopened as That Steak Joynt, an exquisitely restored tribute to Chicago's past. The late Billy Siegel was the owner and the late Raudell Perez the driving force behind its success story.

The building's interior was spectacular. The most eye-catching of the original pieces created for the Piper Bakery over a century ago was the bakery display case, which served as a back-bar. Henry Piper brought artisans from Europe specifically to hand-carve the casework from black walnut. The extraordinary shelving was installed along with the leaded glass window. In the center section sits a Carrara marble bust of a smiling peasant gripping a wine flask, a relic from the defunct Matson Steamship Line. Some say if you stare at the sculpture too long, its features will come to life. Sometimes the expression on the face will change from a smile, to a frown, to a grin. A stockbroker once claimed it fed him tips while others say they use its so-called powers for curative purposes. Suspended over the bar was a three hundred pound German silver candle and gas fixture that once hung over a billiard table in Peel Castle on the Isle of Man, built in the eleventh century by the Vikings.

The gilt-accented sculptured baroque ceiling of the lounge was also the original from the Piper Bakery, as was the grandfather clock, which once stood by the entrance to the main dining room. The

The former That Steak Joynt on Wells Street in Chicago

pink leather banquettes, the window shutters and panels behind them and the stained glass window valances behind and above were from a Lake Geneva Wrigley Mansion as were the matching pieces and the etched glass doors in the alcove across the room. To the rear was another original Piper Bakery display case, hand-carved from the now-rare black walnut, used at one time as a sideboard.

The foyer housed some great treasures. The mahogany stair railing was removed in sections from Chicago's old L'Aiglon Restaurant. Atop the newel post was a bronze statue that served as a light fixture - a signed piece by French sculptor Gustave Moreau; Renoir's prized pupil. The crystal chandelier suspended from the twenty-foot ceiling, formerly a gas fixture, came from the McCormick estate. On the wall opposite the staircase was a six hundred pound second empire Viennese mirror from the French-style manor of James W. Thorne in Lake Forest.

At the top of the stairs was a marble female figure from the Armour mansion's rose garden. Representing summer, it was one of a group of statues portraying the four seasons. The statue's teak and gold leaf pedestal was a support from the Thorne family dining table, one of Chicago's finest examples of boule inlay. Nearby were two Russian ceremonial candlesticks, five feet tall, weighing seventy pounds each; handmade of onyx and bronze.

The entryway to the Edwardian Room had French pocket doors that could be pushed into the wall to create more space. The hand-etched Lalique glass panes were said to be the upper sections of the originals, which were made for a mansion in Lombard, Illinois. Inside, the velvet-tufted room was decorated with the hand-painted oils of Stanley Kozakiewicz - faithful reproductions of French masterpieces in Chicago's Art Institute. Overhead, another souvenir from the 19th century L'Aiglon restaurant: the stained glass skylight.

The hand-carved wine racks in the Wine Room were made in China from East Indian teak and once held 287 bottles of wine. Still in place is the original Piper Bakery wall safe manufactured by Herring-Hall. Decorating the safe are paintings of a clipper ship with decorative lettering and artistic scrolls.

Along the staircase leading to the upper dining room and washrooms once hung the portraits of William and Catharine Devine, milk merchants of the early history of Chicago. William Devine was a city treasurer who was born in Ireland, on September 18, 1844. After his father died in 1856, William, although just a lad, assumed responsibility of his family's farm and applied himself to the job at hand. It was on that farm that Devine first carried on a regular milk and dairy business in which his family eventually became the largest operator in the west of Ireland, if not the entire country. In 1864, he came to America where his brother, M.A. Devine, was already doing a flourishing milk business. In May 1866, he started in the milk business for himself with $1,000 capital, $400 of which was borrowed. His yearly sales were in excess of $130,000. Devine married Catharine McManus of Camden, New Jersey, on October 1, 1869 and together they had eight children.

The pictures of William and Catharine Devine were purchased from Al Morlock formerly of Victorian House Antiques, 806 W. Belmont Avenue in Chicago. They came from the contents of the Devine residence formerly at 4 E. Huron Street. Soon after acquiring the portraits Morlock said that the woman's portrait made him feel jumpy and uneasy. In fact, he claimed that one afternoon the picture came off the wall striking and breaking his toe. He wanted to destroy the picture but instead, he sold it to Warren Black, who was the interior designer for That Steak Joynt.

Black also admitted that he felt something unnatural about the portrait and many restaurant patrons claimed to have felt a cold spot in the area directly between the two paintings. This cold spot has been reported at various times throughout the year, no matter what the season or temperature may be. Some say they have actually seen the lady smile when the painting is reflected in the Viennese mirror mounted at the bottom of the steps. But when viewed straight on, the smile disappears. Others claim to have had the unnerving experience of her eyes following them as they climbed the stairs. Manager Raudell Perez often commented about this feeling of uneasiness on the staircase and he combated it by smoking a cigarette whenever he passed the portraits. He said it was a way to ward off the spirits of those people portrayed in the paintings.

During the 1980s, in particular, séances were regularly held in the upstairs dining room by a prominent Chicago medium named Robert Dubeil. With a group of around 15 or so adventurous souls, Dubell claimed to have made contact with three spirits. One was an architect who designed the building, the second was a female patron from when it was a bakery and it is unclear as to the identity of the third. Attending the séance was a reporter from the *Chicago Sun-Times*, Celeste Busk, who became violently ill during the séance.

There had been reports in the past verified by Billy Siegel that a murder had taken place in the alleyway next to the restaurant while it was still Piper's Bakery. Perhaps this is one of the many ghosts still inhabiting the building?

Perez related on many occasions that he had a difficult time holding on to night help, especially janitors and clean-up crews, because of reports of strange singing sounds and apparitions that would appear to be floating throughout the restaurant after hours. On one occasion, a night worker became so frightened by what he had seen that he left the restaurant unlocked and fled, not bothering to pick up his paycheck!

Perez and other waiters have seen shadowy forms on numerous occasions. One time, he said he was sitting by the bar and happened to look towards the staircase leading up to the second floor. He saw what appeared to be two people going upstairs. The restaurant was closed and he wondered who could still be in the building. He went upstairs and searched around but found no one. There was no way to way a pair of intruders could have left the restaurant without Perez spotting them.

In May of 1991 one of the other employees, a man named Avalino, was locking the front doors at closing when he felt someone grab his shoulder from behind and pull him backwards. When he spun around to see who it was, there was not a living soul nearby.

Another bartender, John, also felt something pull him back while he was attempting to climb the stairs to the second floor. Again, nobody was around but he was sure it felt like a human hand.

There have been reports of strange sensations in the women's washroom as though someone entered the room but there was no one visible. Women using the facility would often complain of hearing the distinct sound of high heels on the tile floor but no one was ever visible. Other times the door to the stalls would inexplicably jam shut. Since the restaurant had a piano bar on weekends, the music and singing could be quite loud. Any unfortunate souls locked in the washroom often were imprisoned for some time before the next patron came to the door and opened it as though there wasn't a problem at all.

The most frightening occurrence happened to a waitress bussing tables one night in the upstairs lounge. Suddenly she felt something grab her wrist and begin pulling her towards the staircase. She could see nothing, but the force was quite strong and continued to half-drag her towards the carpeted

Ghost Research Society investigation team at That Steak Joynt in the early 1990s

stairway. She began screaming at the top of her lungs for help. Perez and another waiter ran upstairs to see what the commotion was. They found the waitress sprawled on the floor with one of her high heels broken and painful red marks on her wrist as though someone had applied a firm grasp. Immediately thinking that it was an intruder, Perez grabbed a steak knife from a nearby table and searched the upstairs all the way back to the emergency exit, which was closed and sealed. No intruder was found and the waitress was quite adamant that it wasn't a real person at all that had grabbed her wrist but an invisible entity of some kind. She did not return to work the next day and later quit her job.

On two separate occasions, in April of 1991 and in April of 1994, members of the Ghost Research Society stayed overnight at That Steak Joynt from closing time to dawn. The first time they were joined by Celeste Busk of the *Chicago Sun-Times* and the second occasion by Janet Davies of WLS-TV Chicago. Davies later commented that she had been to a lot of haunted places in the past, but that this place gave her the creeps.

The restaurant was divided into several outposts that were manned by GRS members with cameras, tape recorders and other electronic devices. Many encounters were recorded during the initial investigation in 1991 including psychic observations of a strange energy near the bust of the peasant holding the wine flask, which was later verified by strange bluish white fingers of lights captured with a 35mm camera. A red light was seen near the north corner of the west wall by several witnesses, magnetic disturbances were noted along the entire west wall, and candle-like glows of an orange color were reported by two outpost members. A crescent-shaped area of white light was photographed near the women's washroom. Most unusual were the two cameras that captured a monk-like figure superimposed in the middle of a dining room table. The upper torso and lower extremities can clearly be seen, however the middle of the body is missing as though the tablecloth blocked that portion of the figure.

During our second investigation in April 1994 a downstairs door leading to the kitchen suddenly began to swing open by itself. A GRS member captured the movement with a camcorder. Airflow tests were immediately conducted and what was found proved amazing. The door apparently opened against the airflow! This gave us the impression that there were other forces at work here beyond that of nature or physics.

Other unexplained events included a burning odor, a strange figure of unknown origin which was seen seated at a downstairs dining room table, flickering lights, chills and cold spots, footsteps and creaking sounds, floral scents, a howling sound followed by pounding noises and the sound of something being dragged across the floor. Compasses deflected from true north several times. Investigators reported the smell of freshly-cut flowers, hissing sounds, a very faint woman's voice, sulfur smells, sounds of clanging pots and pans coming from the kitchen and the sound of a synthesized, mechanical growling noise that was picked up on the audio portion of a video tape recorder that was monitoring the stairway. One camcorder was constantly monitoring the staircase where the portraits of the Devines hung. Toward the end of one tape there was a high-pitched squeal followed closely by deep guttural sounds which were repeated in a few seconds Absolutely no one was anywhere near the camera or the area when the sounds were recorded. What produced them is still a mystery.

Greg Gracz and his wife, former members of the GRS, were in the downstairs dining room during one of the two overnight investigations of the place. They were using a night vision camera when suddenly the swinging door between the dining room and the kitchen swung open by itself. Quickly

calling out, I ran to the area and soon discovered that it was impossible for this to happen. Tests of airflow in the corridor by lighting a match and watching for the direction the smoke traveled clearly showed that the door had opened against the normal flow of air.

During the initial setup of one investigation a number of GRS members clearly saw a person sitting quietly in the downstairs dining room near the rear. Thinking it was one of the investigative team, they called to the figure to join them in the briefing. When the figure failed to respond, they walked in the direction of the form, only to see it slowly disappear in front of their eyes.

A former GRS member who was also a sensitive was being videotaped walking around the bar area when she distinctly picked up a wave of unusual energy emanating from the left of the bust of the peasant. Pictures were taken with a 35mm camera just before and after the walk through by the psychic. Later, when the pictures were examined, evidence of fingers of whitish light were seen from the left-hand side of the bust, just as the psychic had felt. No one was allowed to smoke during our investigation so the mist was definitely not cigarette smoke illuminated by a flash.

All in all, investigators not only saw many inexplicable visions, but their other senses were also affected by the environment including odors, sounds, cold spots and the feeling of physical presences in many parts of the room.

Shortly after the death of Perez, the building was sold and stood empty for many years. Eventually, after a major reconstruction effort of the Piper Alley area, the place reopened as an Adobo Grill. This Mexican restaurant reports no unusual occurrences today, as far as we can tell. Attempts have been made to contact the new owners but calls have gone unanswered to date. Usually ghosts stay in a locale even though that location has changed hands. Only time will tell if the spirits are still in residence at 1610 N. Wells St.

I feel quite confident that the many ghosts of the once-famous That Steak Joynt are still around today and may find it a bit confusing. Once a Victorian-style restaurant, the location has a more casual atmosphere and attracts a different type of clientele today than it once had. Due to the long history of the building, I truly believe that the ghosts still make themselves known to employees and patrons and hopefully we'll be able to once again step through the doors and greet them again.

3. A MESSAGE FROM TRICKSTER

BY ROSEMARY ELLEN GUILEY

Anyone who becomes involved in the paranormal soon comes face to face with Trickster. In mythologies, Trickster is the god who portrays and embodies the forces of chaos and destruction. He is a clever, sneaky character who swings easily from being a good guy to a mean and nasty guy, and he loves to have a belly laugh at your expense.

In the paranormal, Trickster is more a force or characteristic than an entity, and strikes with such things as the failure of fresh batteries and equipment (usually at a crucial moment), bizarre phenomena, and events that suddenly go twisted and awry – all without explanation.

I've had a good share of Trickster phenomena over the years, but one investigation stands out in that respect: an evening at the former Western State Penitentiary in Moundsville, West Virginia. I received a clear message from Trickster in real-time communication.

The Gothic-style prison, opened in 1876 and now a historical site, was the scene of some of the most bloody and violent events in U.S. prison history. It is a favorite with paranormal investigators.

On this particular evening in June 2009, I was working with two investigators from the Center for Paranormal Study and Investigation, based in the Pittsburgh, Pennsylvania, area. The founder, Tom Harter, and I have been friends for several years, and I have done investigations with CPSI from time to time.

At Moundsville, I teamed up with CPSI members Scott Philips and Maureen Davis. We moved around the prison, setting up our equipment at several known hot spots. In addition to cameras, recorders and EMF meters, I was running a Minibox, a version of Frank's Box.

Frank's Box, named after its inventor, Frank Sumption, of Littleton, Colorado, is a device that rapidly scans radio frequencies (either AM or FM). This scanning creates a noise matrix that purportedly enables spirits (the dead or entities from other dimensions) to communicate in real-time. Instead of putting out a recorder, asking questions, and listening for answers in playback, in the traditional

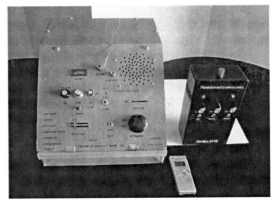

A Frank's Box device & a Mini-Box

technique for EVP, the operator of a Frank's Box hopes to get real-time, two-way talking. The spirit voices seem to ride on top of the radio scan. On a properly set scan, you do not hear sustained portions of radio broadcast, and you especially do not hear sustained portions of music. Scans are quite broken, a racing stream of random words and maybe a note or two of music as the scan momentarily hits a station and then moves on to another one. The sound is like what you would hear if you moved your radio tuner rapidly up and down the band without end.

Experiments for two-way communication have been done for decades, and have involved a variety of devices besides radio scanners. Frank's Box is the latest to hit the paranormal scene. The Minibox, created by Ron Ricketts of Carrollton, Texas, works along the same lines. That's it in a nutshell. I have an article on Frank's Boxes on my website, and the information for that is at the end of this article.

I have three Frank's Boxes and a Minibox, and have gotten responses over them that I cannot explain naturally. This field is highly controversial and unpredictable, and I consider it to be one of the most exciting areas in paranormal investigation.

On this night at Moundsville, I had been running the Mini in every spot we set up. The prison was quite active paranormally, and we had gotten interesting results in several places. It was one of those investigation nights that clipped along on high energy.

Toward the end of our evening, we made our way to the Sugar Shack, one of the prison's famous paranormal hot spots. The Sugar Shack, as you might well guess, had once been the scene of some questionable forms of recreation. It is a large basement room where prisoners went for indoor recreation when the weather was too severe to send them outside into the yard. Supervision was lax there, and inmates engaged in violence and certain "recreational" activities.

We set everything up, and I sat down beside the Mini, with my recorder running and a camcorder focused on me and the box. We had high expectations, having heard a great deal about the Sugar Shack. We were quickly disappointed. The atmosphere in the room seemed "flat," and nothing came over the box in response to questions.

After a few minutes, the Mini suddenly cut out and went silent. I hadn't touched it. I examined it and found that somehow the volume knob had been turned all the way down. I readjusted it, and the box resumed its audible scan.

After a few more minutes, the Mini cut out again. I examined it and found that this time, the speaker jack was pulled partway out – not completely, but enough to cut the audio. I pushed the jack back in and the scan sound resumed. Exasperated, I commented to Scott and Mo about what had happened twice – as though someone was playing with our equipment.

I said out loud, addressing whatever entity or entities might be present, "Is that you?"

Nothing responded over the Mini, which scanned away in a jumble of radio noise.

Maureen said, "You don't want to talk to us, do you?"

I repeated, "Is that you? Are you messing with our equipment?"

Without a beat, an answer came over the Mini – an impossibly long and sustained portion of the theme music from *The Twilight Zone.*

We burst out laughing.

The message? Trickster is alive and well, and working diligently in the paranormal to give you a hit-and-run upset when you least expect it!

4. A PSYCHIC INVESTIGATION AT THE GLEN TAVERN INN

BY RICHARD SENATE

134 NORTH MILL STREET
SANTA PAULA, CALIFORNIA

The moment Psychic Debbie Senate opened the door of the room she felt the icy cold seeping out. She quickly closed the door. She wanted the rest of the team to feel the wave of supernatural cold. This was part of a psychic investigation conducted on October 28, 2008 of the historic Glen Tavern of Santa Paula by the Ventura College Community Services class on ghosts and haunted houses. The team was on the second floor and when they caught up with Debbie, she again opened the door. The cold greeted them as they stepped into the tastefully decorated room. The cold seemed to sink into the skin, driving to the bone. It was the first time that the ghost hunting team struck pay dirt in their investigation of the 1911 Inn. The Santa Paula landmark has long been rumored to have ghosts wandering its halls and the owners graciously permitted the class to come and try their hand at ghost hunting. The students were not disappointed with the results.

THE HISTORY

The Glen Tavern Inn owes its existence to the oil boom that spurred growth in Santa Paula in the latter decades of the nineteenth century. By 1910 the town fathers recognized the need for a classy hostelry as the community was then the headquarters for the Union Oil Company of California. Twenty-five wealthy townspeople hired well-known architects Burns and Hunt to design a three-story hotel in the then-popular Tudor-Craftsman style. The hotel was completed in 1911 and opened with a gala party and dinner for the movers and shakers in the county. The top story was never really finished but demand wasn't that great and "the attic" was used for storage. As time progressed it would be put to other uses.

The inn was purposely constructed next to the train depot so as to be convenient to businessmen traveling by rail. It wasn't long before the Glen Tavern became the social center of the valley, providing a place for gatherings and events. This was the era before the popular arrival of the automobile and travel was restricted to the railroads. It was only a few years after its construction that the hotel with its first class accommodations attracted the eye of early Hollywood. A number of silent films, mostly Westerns, were filmed in the area (movies are still filmed here). The movie people added

The historic Glen Tavern Inn

their mark to the colorful history of the Inn. Stories were told of visits by such famed people as magician Harry Houdini and stars Carol Lombard, John Wayne, and the famed canine performer Rin Tin Tin, who stayed in room 307 during the filming of *The Night Cry* in 1926.

In the dark days of Prohibition the third floor became a sort of speakeasy and brothel that attracted both the oil workers and the movie people. It was best known for its poker games and rumors say that one of the members of a movie company was found cheating at cards and, in the best tradition of the West, was shot dead and buried somewhere on the property. The tale was never confirmed but, a bloody hat was found hidden in the walls years later. There were stories of murdered prostitutes as well. Some tell of the mistress to a prominent political leader, who, when she became too curious about his shady dealings, was silenced permanently and buried on the grounds. The tales are yet to be proven but are part of the colorful legends and lore of the establishment.

As the years passed the oil money moved on to richer fields and the movies found other locales for their Westerns, leaving the old hotel next to the railroad station to settle into a quieter life. There were still balls and lavish dinners but they were more for locals and executives of the rich agricultural companies like Sunkist than the movie studios. People travelled by car now as highways laced the nation together. Now the auto court and motel replaced the stately grandeur of country hotels. The grand Glen Tavern Inn slowly declined with the fortunes of the town, a monument to the past with a host of new owners and uses until it was at long last restored.

Over its long decades of existence the old place has attracted a number of ghost stories giving credibility to its motto: "where the past comes to life." Since the 1980s, stories swirled around the hotel of ghosts and odd happenings. Perhaps the most reported phantom being that of a man called "Calvin." He, according to the story, was the fellow caught cheating at cards on the third floor and shot. There is also a tale of a French woman who sold perfumes who died here and continues her residency as a sweet-smelling ghost. Then there is the account of a prostitute shot because she knew too much. Some have named her Rose, because of the scent associated with her, but others say she was a story made up by some of the ghost hunters who now make the pilgrimage to the inn.

The hotel was listed in several works as one of the most haunted places in California. Here paranormal conventions were held and groups have discovered odd events and strange readings with their ghost-finding equipment. One section where the bizarre seems to be documented is on the third floor, now arranged with rooms. The place was bought in 2005 by the Jennett Investment Group, and underwent a two-year renovation

The lobby of the Glen Tavern Inn

before reopening as a full service hotel, restaurant and bar. It is frequently rented for private parties and events and has largely reclaimed its faded status as a center for social life. Most observers hold that the renovation successfully preserved the inn's historical attributes alongside the addition of more modern amenities. A fire in April of 2006 delayed some of the renovations but the damage was limited and left opportunities for several upgrades. After the fire, some of the staff reported an increase in paranormal events, indicating that the supernatural traditions continue.

The Glen Tavern Inn was awarded a special certificate in 2008 by the U.S. Senate and House as well as the California State Assembly for its successful renovations

A HAUNTED HISTORY

Former owner Dolores Diehl said of the inn, "All I know is that my staff saw lots of things happening that could not be explained." She herself had a mysterious event happen while staying in the building. "When I first moved in here, I lived in the apartment over the pub area. At around 2 o'clock in the morning I would hear sounds below me as if carts were moving. They were loud enough to make the floors vibrate. When I looked down there it was always deserted."

Psychic Debbie Senate also heard the rumblings and felt carts used to go up and down here. A local student did some research and discovered records that there was a mine shaft right under Diehl's apartment. The mine was for extracting chemicals for the manufacture of explosives and they used heavy iron carts to carry the material. Over the years many have felt things on each of the three floors. Those staying there have heard loud banging on the doors. Actor Joe Estevez was awakened

from a sound sleep by a furious pounding on his first floor room late one night. The staircase, like many in haunted locations, is the focal point of several continuing psychic events. Over the last 30 years a number of people have encountered ghosts in the rooms and in the lobby. The reported phantoms include:

THE GHOST CHILDREN

Controversial Ghost Hunter Dan Hobbit managed to record EVP of children's voices on the second floor hallway. He believed these were from the victims of a fire that once occurred at the hotel. This tragedy, so he believed, took the lives of several children. Research into the history of the hotel turned up no trace of a fire or any event that claimed the lives of a group of children. The story of the burned children was unconfirmed but that doesn't mean that the encounters with children are false as many have experienced children's ghosts here. Years ago my wife, Debbie Senate, was working at the inn late one night and heard children laughing and running down the stairs. As they drew near she saw nothing but the sounds went past her as did a wave of cold air. The ghost children were one of the targets of the investigation and the group did secure information that confirmed the story of the phantom children.

THE HAUNTING WESTERNER

The name of the man in the Western hat and coat is believed to have been Calvin but others call him Wilber, Jonathan, JT and CJ. He is linked to the days when silent films were made at the inn in the 1920s. His apparition has been encountered at the inn since the early 1980s. The legend of the figure, which resembles Western showman Buffalo Bill Cody, is closely linked to the movie history of Santa Paula. Western two-reel films were shot in the local hills, and the film company and its actors were housed at the inn. This was the era of Prohibition and the third floor became a place where strong drink, a friendly game of poker or a willing woman could be found if one had the right price. The man known as Calvin was an older fellow who had once worked for Buffalo Bill's Wild West Show and sported a goatee and long hair like his former boss. He worked as the wrangler with the motion picture company, taking care of the horses. Sometimes, he served as an extra when needed. The fellow was lucky at cards and each Friday an all-night poker party would clean out the crew leaving the Westerner rich. He placed his winnings in a Gladstone bag. Then, one night, five aces turned up in the deck. The Westerner was accused of cheating. Guns were drawn and a single shot hit the Westerner in the forehead. The members of the movie company got his key and let themselves into his second floor room. They searched for the money he had won from them only to find it gone! It seems he had hidden the cash somewhere in the inn. The murder was never reported and the killers were said to have taken the body down the dumbwaiter and buried it somewhere on the grounds. The ghost has been seen in Room 306, where it is thought he was killed. He has been encountered on the second floor, on the staircase, as well as the lobby. He has even been reported in the women's bathroom. One of the earliest sightings took place in Room 307 when Ojai psychic Cheryl King walked into the room and saw a cowboy actor on the TV screen even though the set wasn't on at the time.

The door to infamous Room 307

"I saw a man who looked like Buffalo Bill Cody, with long hair, a beard and a white shirt and a string tie," King said.

The psychic tried automatic writing in the same room and produced three words in 19th century-style scratchy writing. The words were, "Murder. Gold. Attic." In a séance King reported that the ghost told her he was "guarding the attic where he hinted there were important maps and papers. In the large closet, where the dumbwaiter was once located, there is a persistent cold spot. The ghostly man sometimes manifests as the sweet smell of a cheroot cigar. This smell has been detected on the stairs and in the lobby.

No gold was found during the renovation of the inn, which now has 41 guest rooms, many with antique beds and some with Jacuzzis.

Psychic Grace Conveney encountered the Westerner in the hallway. To her, he seemed to be laughing.

Former head waitress Johnnie Britton was on the staircase years ago when she may have received a communication from the phantom cowboy.

"I was on the stairs when a voice said, 'tell them to leave me alone.' I couldn't see anybody. It scared me really bad."

THE WESTERNER: ATTEMPTS AT STIMULATION

Years ago an attempt was made to try stimulation of the Westerner's ghost in Room 307 by having team members play poker there. It was hoped this might enhance psychic results and there were some spikes in the readings as well as a curious EVP recorded. A voice clearly says three words, well in keeping with past results at this site. The words were, "You will die" but the meaning was hard to interpret. Were that the people in the room under a threat or was the voice just stating the fact that all human being will someday die. Who can say?

A psychic visiting the place in 2001 got the distinct impression that Calvin was dumped in a dry well. Another psychic felt that his real name wasn't Calvin but Henry. A bloody hat was discovered hidden in a wall long ago but it has vanished over the years. By all accounts the Westerner is a friendly spirit who may have been stimulated when movie companies filmed years ago in Santa Paula. As an actor, maybe he wants to step in front of the cameras one more time. Or he may well be seeking justice for his murder or a proper burial for his remains. Who knows?

THE FRENCH PERFUME SALESWOMAN

Perhaps the second most-seen phantom is the sad French perfume saleslady. Her name is believed to have been Elaine or Marie. Her story is a simple one. She was traveling from town to town with suitcases of perfume samples, taking orders from stores. While staying in Santa Paula, then wealthy with oil money, she suffered a sudden aneurism and dropped dead in her room. She is believed to have stayed in Room 210. The phantom is manifest by a sudden drop in temperature, a sweet smell of perfume, and the sound of heartbroken sobbing. Like the Westerner, she wanders the hotel, even down to the lobby where she has been seen near the front door. She sometimes manifests as a moving cold spot. It is thought she dates back to the late 1920s or early 1930s, due to the style of her dress.

An illustration of the French Perfume Saleswoman

THE GHOSTLY LADY

Some believe this is a mistaken sighting of the French woman. She is seen as a classic Lady in White. Her story is perhaps a more recent addition to the phantom family of the Glen Tavern. It is said she was a prostitute or the mistress of a very prominent political leader. He was married at the time but kept his mistress "Rose" as his confidant, bringing her with him on his many railroad trips. It was in the Glen Tavern that the two had a falling out. She had overheard something important, something she should not have heard. Fearing that she might go to the newspapers, the decision was made to have her eliminated. Some versions of the story say a man went into her room and choked her to death and some say she was drugged and suffocated with a pillow. The crime was hushed up but her vengeful spirit still lingers on the first floor. The story of Rose, is thought by some to be a creation of a ghost hunter. Others believe there really is a ghost lady, while others think the woman in white is actually the French saleswoman. Time will tell is Rose is real or a fantasy.

THE PHANTOM COOK

Many paranormal events have surfaced in the old restaurant of the inn. It was damaged by fire several years ago and was recently remodeled but some feel that the ghosts still linger there. In the past a ghostly chef wearing a white hat and coat was seen. Several times an ice scoop flew across the room and chairs were moved by unseen hands. Former head waitress Johnnie Britton described an encounter with the cook one time when she was standing in the dining room. "After I had a month off, I felt a tap on my shoulder and (a male voice) said, "Welcome back." I turned around to thank whoever it was. There was no one there...that really frightened me."

Years ago a sensitive picked up the name Adam in the dining room. Adam could that be the name of the cook or is he related somehow to the old mine that once operated at the site of the kitchen and pub?

GEEKS VS FREAKS:
AN EXPERIMENT IN PSYCHIC INVESTIGATION

One of the great debates in psychic investigation is between that of psychic impressions and the reliance upon technology to record paranormal events. The popularity of such TV programs as *Ghost Hunters* has given an advantage to those who seek a strictly scientific approach to ghost hunting. Having come from the Hans Holzer age of psychic research, and one who has successfully used metaphysical means to attain answers to questions in a haunted site, I am reluctant to cast them aside for the dubious results of e-meters and the like. I believe that both techniques can be used for a better understanding of the paranormal. In an attempt to reconcile these two traditions I gathered two groups. One was made up of psychics, sensitive readers, and their followers, armed with dowsing rods, pendulums, Ouija boards, cameras, crystals, and tape recorders. The other was strictly scientific with Tri-field meters, e-meters of every type, special cameras, electronic thermometers, recoding devises and more. The target of this groundbreaking investigation was the Glen Tavern Inn.

In the lobby, as the two groups eyed one another from opposite sides of the room, I met with the leaders of each faction. It was the scientific group who asked why I had brought "those freaks" along, pointing to the psychics. Later one of the psychics asked why I had invited the "geeks" along on the investigation. These comments gave me the names for the two factions: the "geeks" with electronic equipment, and the "freaks" being the psychics and those with a metaphysical point of view. Could the two groups work together? Could they both pick up data at the haunted hotel? Small groups made up of members of each faction began to search the inn and through they started out somewhat hostile to those in the opposite camp, they slowly began to work together. Psychics would sense something and the scientific types would use their tools to confirm that they were really picking up something. Amazingly, in many cases the psychics and the scientists gave overlapping confirmation of supernatural events. At the end of the investigation, the two groups were getting along like old friends. The experiment seemed to indicate that the two groups could be mutually important in a psychic investigation and confirmed that together, the freaks and the geeks can collect and analyze a great deal of information. A blended approach is a positive way to conduct an investigation. The Glen Tavern provided a great testing ground for a unique experiment, one that will need further data to confirm.

The Ventura College ghosts and haunted houses class is offered in two parts. Lectures tell the story of ghost hunting from ancient times to today with a focus on how to do an investigation. The second part of the class involved an investigation of a haunted site. This class the target was the restored Glen Tavern Inn where they were experiencing a spike in supernatural activity.

GHOST WATCH INVESTIGATION

Glen Tavern Inn
Case Number SP-891 =0 A
Field Notes
Date: October 26, 2008
Place: Glen Tavern Inn
  134 North Mill Street
  Santa Paula, CA 93060
  Phone 805-525-6658

The Team
Leaders: Richard and Debbie Senate, Assistant: Megan Senate
Video: John Anthony Miller, Jennifer Cubitt, Melinda Hauser, Barbara McKinnon, Leta Meyer Tuiaana, J.R. Tuiaana, Patty Hass, Nick Mungal, Sheigh O'Brien, Patricia Garcia, Yolanda Juarez, Dena DeSimone, Peter DeSimone and Katie Crawford

NOTES
The team met in front of the fireplace in the lobby of the Tudor-style hotel. This would serve as the meeting place headquarters for the investigation. There were some outside disturbances from the public coming and going. A private room would have been preferable for this purpose. The team members were interviewed then placed in small groups to conduct their investigations. A set period of time was allocated to each group. Debbie and I floated between the groups to collect data and answer questions. Our role was to keep things moving and stimulate the investigations. Debbie was given the task of being the keeper of the keys, opening rooms and making sure the teams had access but didn't disturb the rooms in any way. She also helped by providing her psychic insights. I was kept busy keeping a record of the events and suggesting ways to help in the experiments, such as when a number of readings on the equipment were gathered at a location, I would have the metaphysical members see what they detected in the same site.

The goal was to gather new information at a site that had been well worked over by many teams over the last three decades. In order to do this I keep my information from past groups to myself until the de-briefing at the conclusion of the investigation. Some members did have prior knowledge of the inn and several had conducted their own experiments here as well. I was most impressed with the team members who were new to the site. They were the ones who came away with the most data. The goal was to see if this team could point out places where past events have occurred.

When Debbie opened the door to Room 210, she felt the distinct cold linked to haunted places and knew that whatever haunted the chamber was active at that moment. She closed the door and waited for the team to arrive. She wanted them to confirm what she knew. The room was long rumored to be haunted by a woman who died there decades ago and her spirit has manifested off and on over the years. Whatever was there was active at this moment. Like volcanology, the study of

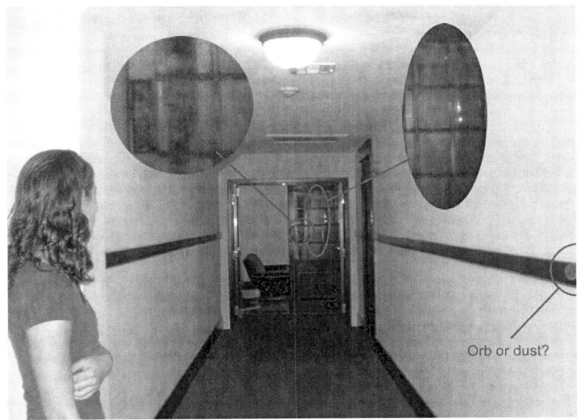

Orb or dust?

A photograph taken on the night of the investigation showed potential paranormal phenomena and a possible apparition caught on film near the door at the end of the hallway.

volcanoes, ghost hunting is dependent upon events as they happen and luck is always a part of any investigation.

The minute the team stepped over the threshold of Room 210 they began to rub their arms as if they felt a chill. They smelled the sweet odor of perfume. Legends say this was the room where Elaine, (Or Marie) the French perfume saleswoman, collapsed as the result of an aneurism long ago. She had just checked in after arriving by train with her samples when she was stricken. Team member Patricia Garcia smelled the sweet perfume smell as soon as she walked into the room. It was like a mixture of flowers. She also felt the distinct cold that seemed to sweep her up in a sort of supernatural envelope. It was most manifest on the backs of her arms. Another team member, Barbara McKinnon, also felt the odd cold in the room and sensed activity over the bed. Team Member Yolanda Garcia used a pair of dowsing rods over the bed and had the rods cross over the pillow. As she was using the rods, her arms began to tingle and become cold. She also saw something in the room, a figure standing in the doorway to the bathroom. It was the misty image of a man. She said the male figure vanished when she looked directly at it.

Perhaps the team member who was most affected was Melinda Hauser. She tried holding dowsing rods over the bed and, once again, they moved violently. Like many ghost hunters who stumble into a hot spot, Melinda became disoriented and almost passed out. She staggered back and slid to one side. Perhaps she was feeling the leftover sensations of the French woman at the moment of her death. The students with ghost hunting tools got reactions from the bed area. It is a modern bed, perhaps in the same location as the one where the Frenchwoman collapsed so long ago. Some believe that when people die suddenly, some form of amnesia takes place and the spirit doesn't realize that it is dead. That is why some linger on as ghosts.

The team continued on and found more evidence of ghosts in Room 308, the infamous Houdini Room. This time it wasn't the ghost of the famed magician but the mischievous spirits of young children. There are no known reasons why ghost children would haunt the inn but they have been reported there for years. J.R. Tuiaana went into the bathroom of Room 308, where be felt the cold of a ghostly presence. It's a feeling he has felt before. He snapped a photograph with his digital camera and got the image of a blue orb, a mysterious glowing ball. It didn't seem like any sort of reflection. He then used a tape recorder in the bathroom in an attempt to get EVP, electronic voice phenomena. He asked questions then paused, leaving room for answers. He heard nothing but when he played back the tape, at the point where he asked; "Do you want to play?" there was a harsh whisper-like child's voice saying, "Yeah."

Leta Meyer Tuiaana smelled the flowery scent of perfume at the end of the second floor hallway. It had a distinct rose quality this time. Was it the spirit of the French woman, wandering from Room 210, or was this the ghost called Rosie from the first floor? Another team member also smelled the scent and reported that it suddenly vanished.

Jennifer Cubitt detected something in Room 224. She felt it was children and when she began to record in the room, hoping to capture EVP, the tape recorder flew out of her hand as if it was jerked. She did pick up one word, "May," but it was undetermined if this was the name of a child or woman or had something to do with the month of the same name.

The target of the investigation, the cowboy ghost called Calvin, didn't manifest himself but many e-meter recordings were discovered that seemed to confirm the places where events had happened in the past. The Westerner who captivated so many over the years did not make his presence known at this time but enough evidence was collected to confirm to the team that the Glen Tavern Inn was still very haunted. The historic hostelry once again lived up to its reputation as a place where the past is never really gone and the essence of her former visitors lingers still.

The Glen Tavern Inn remains the most opulent establishment of its kind in Santa Paula. The three-story mock Tudor-style inn has captivated ghost hunters and investigators for many decades and it had attracted some of the biggest names in the study of the paranormal from Dr. Kenny Kingston, to psychic Chris Fleming and investigator Rob Wlodarski. The ghosts gave the Ventura College team a thrill, showed them how to use their new tools and confirmed that something paranormal is going on at the 1911 inn.

5. HAUNTED NEMACOLIN CASTLE

BY RENE' KRUSE

BRASHEAR AND FRONT STREETS
BROWNSVILLE, PENNSYLVANIA

Situated high on a bluff overlooking the Monongahela River sits the Nemacolin Castle. The castle, a stately red brick mansion with a three-story crenellated tower gracing the front of the building and an architectural folly tower facing the back garden, has its roots buried deep in the history of southwest Pennsylvania and the westward progression of settlers heading toward the new frontier in the later eighteenth century.

Nemacolin Castle is located in Brownsville, Pennsylvania, but actually predates the town. The historical significance of the land beneath the castle may be as important as the castle itself. Legend has it that the land was originally an ancient Indian burial ground. Because of the elevation of the bluff

Nemacolin Castle in Brownsville, Pennsylvania

The back of Nemacolin Castle showing the rear entrance

and proximity to the Monongahela River, this same land was used by the English during the French and Indian War for the construction of Old Fort Burd in 1759. This was also the destination of Delaware Indian Chief Nemacolin and Thomas Cresap, a Maryland frontiersman, who cleared a path across the mountains between the Potomac and Monogahela rivers, creating the Nemacolin Trail, later to approximate the path of the National Road. Because of this, Brownsville was known as the Gateway to the West.

As settlers followed the Nemacolin Trail while migrating westward, Jacob Bowman, a settler himself, realized the need for trade goods and a stopping off point before the settlers moved on across the Monongahela River. In 1780, Bowman purchased the land and named it in honor of Chief Nemacolin. By 1786 he and his partner, Colonel Robert Elliott, had established a trading post on the site of the former Fort Burd. This trading post is still contained within the mansion and exists as the oldest part of the building with its large stone fireplace and exposed hand-hewn timbers.

Jacob Bowman, being an enterprising and hard-working man further realized that the huge cost of transporting goods across the mountains illustrated the need for products to be made locally. Following this logic, he built a nail factory and a paper mill, and produced machine parts. He also became a postmaster and a justice of the peace and established the first national bank in the area.

As his wealth grew, so did his family. Married and having fathered nine children, there was great need for a larger home. This led to the construction of the central section of the house, built around the original trading post, which was completed in the early 1800s. Jacob was also a practicing abolitionist and the castle became a stop on the Underground Railroad, helping runaway slaves escape to find freedom in the North.

Following Jacob's death, the house was passed to his son Nelson and his wife Elizabeth. The Victorian wing of the house was constructed by Nelson and was completed by 1850. This wing added a grand staircase, a large carriage entrance, an ornate drawing room, and a well-appointed library on the ground level and three grand bedrooms on the upper level. This last phase of construction brought the house to a total of 22 rooms, all beautifully furnished.

In time, the house passed on to Nelson's son Charles and his wife Lelia, who raised their two sons in the house. Lelia, the last of the Bowmans to reside in the house, lived there until her death in 1959. For the entire history of the castle as a home, four generations of Bowmans had lived there with no other exceptions other than servants and caretakers.

Within a few years of Lelia Bowman's passing, Nemacolin Castle was donated to Fayette County and is lovingly preserved by the Brownsville Historical Society. Nemacolin Castle is also listed on the National Register of Historic Places.

The Historical Society has supported the maintenance of the building by conducting historical tours since the 1970s. Since then, thousands of people have visited the castle, many of whom have walked away having had much more than just an historical experience. Many have had glimpses into the past that they would never have expected and have thrilling tales to tell as a result.

THE HAUNTINGS

Since the Brownsville Historical Society has taken over the general operations of the castle, many people working there as well as visiting the site have had a variety of unexplained experiences and stories started to spread about the possibility that the castle might be haunted. As these stories continued to accumulate over the years, people began to realize that many of them were being repeated by a fairly large number of people and that many of the events and stories seemed to be very similar, as though they were happening over and over to a variety of people. Unfortunately, there was no one left who had ever lived in the house as a Bowman who might be able to shed some light on what was happening. For decades, there were only the stories...

During the course of a single year, many people put countless hours working in the castle. Tours are conducted in the house from March until January, including Christmas tours where different individuals, families, and groups lovingly decorate nearly every room. During this time there are people conducting tours, cleaning, decorating, doing maintenance and a myriad of other jobs, most of which are done by volunteers. Following are some of their experiences.

Nancy Franks has been the tour and guide coordinator for several years and now assists when additional people are needed for large events. She has probably spent more hours alone in the castle than any other person in the past decade. It is her routine, on tour days, to arrive before anyone else to open up and get the building ready for tours then wait for the first visitors to arrive. Because of this, she very often finds herself sitting alone, waiting.

A common occurrence for Nancy is to hear heavy footfalls pacing around on the second floor where there happens to be a long straight hallway connecting all three sections of the building. She frequently hears pacing along this hallway and on occasion, doors opening and closing. Footsteps on the grand staircase are also common. The unique aspect is that when this happens, there is no way that anyone else could have entered the building without Franks' knowledge. Sometimes she hears voices coming from upstairs, although not they are not speaking clearly enough for her to hear what is being said. She has also related that there have been times when she has distinctly heard someone walk up behind her and stop. She then turns to realize that there is no one there. That is usually when Nancy decides it is a good time to sit outside and enjoy the day!

One of the ghosts who roam the castle is a young girl who stays mostly in the middle section of

The seemingly endless second story hallway where footsteps are frequently heard pacing up and down with occasionally slamming doors

the house. She has been seen by literally dozens of people and is a favorite. She is described as being somewhere between six and nine years old with dark hair hanging in ringlets around her shoulders. She appears to be wearing a full-length nightgown. Who this little girl is, no one is sure but many believe that she has worked hard to make her presence known.

A few years ago, two volunteers were doing some spring cleaning in preparation for re-opening the Castle after being closed for the winter months. After working for some time in the nursery, they went down to the kitchen to get more cleaning supplies. When they returned a few minutes later, they found that some antique tinker toys had been taken from the display shelves and laid out on the bed forming the letters "M*A*R*Y." Ironically – or maybe not – many visitors who are able to catch a glimpse of the little girl tell the guides that they somehow know that her name is Mary, without having heard the story of the tinker toys. She seems to be rather mischievous and is frequently seen peeking around corners, moving toys in the nursery, and causing the springs to bounce on an antique toy riding horse. She has also been seen peeking out from beneath the tablecloth in the sitting room below.

Mary's most striking appearance happened late one night in mid-winter. The security alarm was triggered and the police were called as well as Bob Mammarella, president of the historical society. The police officer arrived first and waited outside the rear entrance for Bob to arrive and unlock the building. When Bob arrived, the officer laughed and said that he already knew why the alarm went off. He believed, a young guide must have fallen asleep and had been left behind, locked in the building. He said she had been looking down at him, smiling and waving from the upstairs hall window that overlooks the rear entrance. Bob explained that this wasn't possible because the house had been locked up and unused for weeks. Bob and the officer determined that the security zone that had triggered the alarm was in the same area that the little girl had been seen. After a thorough check of the entire building it was found to be empty. The officer left immediately and has never again set foot on the Castle grounds.

Although Lelia, the last Bowman to live in the castle, has been dead for several decades, there are a few people remaining who had worked for her. Occasionally, one of them will visit the castle for old times' sake. On one such occasion, a very elderly lady who had lived with and cared for Lelia in her later years asked the volunteers working that day if anyone had ever seen the "little girl ghost" in the nursery. She explained that when she lived there in the 1950s, she had seen the little girl several times. She also said that she discussed what she had seen with Lelia, who just smiled and said that the little girl had been there for a very long time – as long as anyone could remember.

Several people have seen three other apparitions over the years. A small boy who has been named Peter has been seen sitting on the steps in the tower bedroom and also under the tablecloth in the sitting room. A stern-looking woman has been seen walking the long second story hallway and bedrooms. The third is a slight, elderly man who might be Jacob Bowman himself. Occasionally, people will report seeing a soldier in varying places in the castle. Cold spots abound and snippets of long ago conversations coming from empty rooms are common.

The most unusual apparition is that of a small dog, most often reported in the Victorian wing of the house. Numerous visitors have described feeling it weaving around their legs or even feeling a tug on the bottom of their pant legs. Young children have been known to ask if they can play with the little dog by the library. No one seems to know where this little one came from but he certainly seems to enjoy interacting with visitors.

THE INVESTIGATIONS

As far as prime locations for a paranormal investigation go, the Nemacolin Castle has it all. This site is a textbook checklist of possible reasons for a haunting. It is a stately old mansion on the site of an ancient Indian burial ground, an eighteenth century fort having had thousands of pioneers passing through, as well as an unknown number of runaway slaves and nearly two centuries of occupation by the same family, several of whom were "laid out" in the Victorian wing prior to their funeral. Best of all, the hauntings date back at least a hundred years and have been witnessed by a large number of people. The only thing missing is a graveyard.

I and the other members of the Pennsylvania Paranormal Research Group (PaPRG) have been the primary investigators of the Nemacolin Castle since 2001 and we have been privilege to investigate there many times. We have been fortunate to have three members who are also on the board of directors for the castle and others who volunteer many hours working there, so we have had additional opportunities to observe when not investigating and to interact with visitors relating their experiences. In addition, a few other paranormal groups have been allowed to conduct investigations, with the assistance of PaPRG members.

Since the house has 22 rooms and there have been such a variety of experiences, a great deal of time and equipment has been put into each of the formal and informal investigations. Generally, two systems are used in this huge house because some of the events such as pacing in the upstairs hallway and doors opening and closing have occurred in unoccupied spaces and other events have been witnessed or experienced directly. We frequently set up video cameras up in some areas and just let them run. Due to the castle's size, this site is uniquely appropriate for our DVR and IR camera system for remote viewing in the unoccupied spaces. We also set up video and audio equipment in areas where we tend to interact.

Temperature fluctuations are monitored with the use of IR thermal scanners and digital thermal probes. Monitoring temperatures becomes problematic in winter months. The house is over 200 years old and has all the air leaks and drafts common to a building of that age. A cold windy night outside

The nursery with the large bay window where Mary is most frequently seen

means a cold drafty night inside – except around the radiators! Summer works out better as there is no air conditioning, making it easier to identify genuine cold spots.

A favorite spot to investigate is, of course, the nursery. With so many sightings of Mary there and toys moving around, any number of things can happen there. The room itself is rectangular with a beautiful bay window at one end and the closet and hall doors at the other. One side contains a fireplace and the other has a doorway connecting to the master bedroom.

There is a small bed and many antique toys, including the previously mentioned bouncing-type riding horse. This horse is often described as rocking but it is in fact fitted with a flat spring so the child would instead bounce up and down rather than rock. This particular horse seems to be a favorite toy of Mary's as it has been known to bounce on its own. We have suspected that this might be due to people walking through the room, stepping on very old floorboards, the movement of which causes the horse to bounce. One visiting ghost group told us that during their investigation two of their members saw the horse bouncing on its own. Always a bit skeptical when natural explanations are possible, I determined that I was going to try to get Mary to come out and play. After requesting that no one come into the room during my experiment, I sat on the floor, in the dark, camera in hand, along the opposite wall from the bay window and the notorious riding horse, waiting for something to happen. As a back up, I also had set up a night vision video camera, trained on the horse and the shelves holding the antique toys.

After a disappointing, uneventful hour I decided to try to actively coax Mary out by repeatedly asking her to come out and play – to ride the horse. After about 15 minutes of this, as I was ready to give it up for that night, the horse began to bounce. At first I just froze and watched in utter astonishment as the horse bounced away. After about five good bounces, finally able to move again, I was able to take one digital photo, and then there was still the video! Two more bounces and the horse stopped dead. It didn't slow to a stop; it just came to a dead stop. The digital photo could not show the horse bouncing, of course but it did show an interesting light anomaly. The video however was another story. Upon reviewing the event, I found that for about two minutes, right when the horse was bouncing, the camera recorded only snow. No video backup!

Sometimes things like that just happen, whether or not it was a fluke, a malfunction or paranormal interference. One more reminder that the single most important piece of equipment any of us possess sits atop our shoulders. No photograph or piece of video can provide the information and understanding that a thoughtful and attentive observer can. The event I just described is a prime example. If I had not been sitting in the right place at the right time, there would have been no new experience and nothing new learned.

Another favorite investigation site in the castle is the master bedroom. In addition to being a very "active" room, it is also very conducive for a group of people to be working together. This lovely room is on two levels. The part of the room with the bed, dresser and fireplace is directly off the hallway. The dressing room is at the back of the bedroom and is elevated by two steps. There are two long, narrow, walk-in closets on either side of the dressing room. The two wide steps

This photo of the antique child's riding horse was taken as the horse was bouncing on its own

dividing the bedroom and sitting room work very well as a resting spot for weary investigators, especially since no one is allowed to sit on most of the antique furniture in house. Most of the EVP recordings done in the castle have come out of the master bedroom. I have often wondered if that is because of those long steps that are so inviting to sit on.

The master bedroom is also a room where cold spots are frequently encountered. A common practice in there is for investigators to gather a group and sit on the floor in a circle to do observations and EVP. There have been several times when a cold spot forms at someone's back or side then moves from person to person around the circle. This sounds very much like the power of suggestion at work, however with the use of a hand-held thermal probe we have been able to determine that this roving cold spot is real and measurable, with temperature variations in excess of 40 degrees F.

On one specific occasion, while doing an EVP circle in the master bedroom, we were interrupted by loud footsteps coming down the hallway, stopping just outside the door, taking a few steps away and then returning to the bedroom door and stopping again. We waited to see who had come to join us so that we could continue the EVP session, however we soon realized that no one was there. The only other people in the building that night were two people who had gone outside for a smoke break. Eight people all distinctly heard the footsteps but the digital recorder in operation at the same time didn't pick up any sounds other than the people in the room talking about hearing the steps and calling out to see who was there.

At any given time, day or night, the sounds of indistinct conversations can be heard, with no indication of who is talking or where they are conversing. Late one night, as we were packing up equipment in the Victorian wing following an investigation, we began hearing what seemed to be a gathering of several people, carrying on several conversations at once. It sounded like both men and

Photo taken outside the Victorian wing of the Nemacolin

women. We joked that it seemed that the ghosts were having a cocktail party in the old trading post in the opposite end of the house. We decided that we needed to check to make sure that someone hadn't sneaked in. Half of us went upstairs to check the second floor while the other half walked the main floor. We met in the opposite wing, having found nothing. As we reached our destination, we could still hear the talking but now it sounded as if it was coming from the area we had just left.

During any investigation, we do our best to check and photograph the exterior of the site. The castle is no exception. In 2005, I was out walking the grounds and photographing the exterior of the building. As I was standing outside the Victorian wing preparing to take a picture, I suddenly felt goose bumps spring up all over my body and it seemed as if someone whispered in my left ear. I don't know what was whispered but I was so startled that I snapped the picture. The resulting photo showed a large cloud of mist that wasn't visible earlier.

The most striking experiences in ghost hunting are quite often those that are totally unexpected – or those that occur in such a way that we don't quite realize that we have experienced something supernatural until it is all over. We have a saying about times like that: "If I had known it was a ghost, I would have paid more attention!" Well, fellow investigator Bob and I had just such an experience at the conclusion of an investigation.

We have a practice of dividing up and walking the entire house to make sure that we have all our equipment packed up and that everything is turned off and closed up and to make sure that no one has gotten into the house while we were there. On this night, Bob and I were checking the second floor. As we reached the top of the grand staircase, we turned left to walk down the long hallway. Just as we turned, we both saw a very solid-looking woman walking away from us about 10 feet down the hallway. She was wearing a black blouse with long sleeves and high neck and a floor length black skirt. Her dark hair was pulled back in a severe bun. Bob and I stared at each other and then followed her down the hall as she turned into the master bedroom. As we reached the master bedroom doorway, we could see the hem of her skirt disappearing through the adjoining doorway into the nursery. We quickened our pace but as we arrived at the nursery, we found the room empty.

In the Nemacolin Castle, the only thing you can really count on is that almost anything can be seen, heard or felt at just about any time, and all of this while being surrounded by over two hundred years of history.

Special thanks to the members of the Pennsylvania Paranormal Research Group, including Dave Ross, Edgar Harris, Bob and Nellie Mammarella and Linda Davis, and to all of the generous volunteers who keep the Nemacolin Castle in operation.

6. THE SPIRIT OF RALPH MESA SPEAKS

PARANORMAL INVESTIGATIONS AT THE MACHADO STEWART HOUSE

BY MARITZA SKANDUNAS, KAREN RIDENS AND SHARON GAUDETTE HIESERICH

We invite you to take a step back in time with us as we explore San Diego's Old Town, considered the birthplace of California. San Diego became the first Spanish settlement in California in 1769. Old Town is reminiscent of that era rich in the flavor of the early days of San Diego, with several old homes including the Whaley House, Derby-Pendleton, which sits behind the Whaley House, Casa De Estudillo, Robinson-Rose House, Machado-Stewart House and the Campo Santo Cemetery, to name a few of our favorite "haunts."

Heritage Park Victorian Village also rests in the Old Town area. This is an almost eight-acre county park which is dedicated to preserving San Diego's Victorian architecture. These wondrous homes give visitors a glimpse into the past, the splendor and the glory of the boom years of early San Diego. After World War II, with downtown San Diego expanding, many of these buildings were threatened with demolition on their original sites. Thankfully, through the generosity of private and public funding, seven of these "painted ladies" were acquired, relocated and restored in the Heritage Park. The county now leases out the lovely structures to commercial and private entities that are responsible for the interior renovation and operation which is in keeping with the

The Machado Stewart House

park's Victorian theme. Here, you can find wedding services, a doll shop, a quaint tea room, antique store, and a community meeting place.

Our team, the San Diego Ghost Hunters, concentrates on the historical aspect of ghost-hunting, and Old Town is a treasure trove, full of the unexpected. Threading our way through streets and passageways, we arrive at the Machado-Stewart House.

In our search to provide readers with the most conclusive and concise historical facts we came across information that was conflicting and inconsistent. Who can say what is accurate? Realistically speaking - from our own experiences we are well aware that there are errors regarding names and dates on records, and so we strive to compile as much information as we can, comparing and cross-checking, until we come up with what we consider a fair assessment. We are not strangers to history and genealogy, and we always get excited when we are on the threshold of a new adventure. Each new scenario presents us with a challenge, and the treasure hunt is on! We dig, and then we dig deeper. Our "gold" after countless hours of research, is the satisfaction of a job well done, and we have enriched our lives with learning about those who have gone before us. It gives us the opportunity to pause and reflect on their courage, tenacity and strength. We are honored to feel that we know them a little better, and our promise is that they will not be forgotten. The past should be preserved - for how can we determine where we are going, unless we know where we came from?

Please keep in mind that the historical facts we offer are only as accurate as the information in the records we accessed. We can only rely on what is recorded, and we present you with the story that we have pieced together, to the best of our knowledge.

So, before we step into the welcoming coolness of the Machado Stewart adobe on a hot July afternoon in 2005, allow me to introduce you to the Machado and Stewart Families!

José Manuel Machado was born on November 28, 1781, at the San Gabriel Mission, California. His father, also named José Manuel Machado, was born in 1756 in La Villa De Sinaloa, Mexico, and married his mother in 1780 in Los Alamos, Mexico. Maria de la Luz Valenzuela Y Avilas was born in 1762, in Los Alamos, Sonora, Mexico. The elder José Machado was a poor muleteer who was looking for a better life, so he enlisted as a "soldado de cuera" or leather jacket soldier in the Spanish Army. Recruitment papers in Spain describe him as 5 feet, two inches tall, a Roman Catholic, with black hair, brown eyes, an olive complexion, wide nose, and a scar high on the left side of his forehead. Muleteers had poor reputations, and he had to wait to marry Maria until the church determined that he had no other "intended," or no other wife! In 1781, a year after they were married, José

Mission San Gabriel - Birthplace of Jose Machado Jr.

Manuel Machado, Sr. and his wife joined the expedition headed by Spanish Captain Fernando Javier de Rivera y Moncada. Captain Rivera was killed by Native Americans near Yuma, but other members of the party, including the Machados, reached the San Gabriel Mission. José Manuel Machado, Sr. was 25, and his wife, Maria, was 17. He served at the Santa Barbara Presidio and at the Mission la Purisma Concepcion. It was at the Mission in San Gabriel that José Manuel Machado, Jr. was born.

One document states that the Machado family arrived in San Diego around 1782, that the elder José Manuel Machado was a corporal in the Catalonian volunteers while stationed at San Diego Presidio in 1782. Their first-born, José Manuel, would have been about a year old at the time. As near as we can gather, the family lived within the protective walls of the Presidio for quite some time.

It is our belief that information on father and son, both named José Manuel Machado, has been innocently misunderstood, and therefore misapplied. What may have been facts concerning the father were documented to be those of the son and vice versa. Suffice it to say, the Machado family was indeed one of the earliest non-Native American families in San Diego.

As near as we can surmise, José Manuel Machado, born in 1781, married Maria Serafina de la Luz on September 26, 1805, at the Mission in San Diego (though another record states that the Machados did not arrive in San Diego until 1805, and that the marriage took place at the Mission in San Gabriel.)

Maria Serafina was born on September 1st, 1788. This can be verified in the book of baptisms of Our Lady of Sorrows Rectory in Santa Barbara, California. Maria Serafina was the daughter of Serafina Quintero and Eugenio Valdez of Real de Los Alamos, Sonoma. Eugenio Valdez was a native of El Fuerte de Los Alamos, Sonora, Mexico, and a member of the Los Angeles Leather Jackets. Maria Serafina is described as a petite, blue-eyed blonde. This was an arranged marriage, and although José Manuel was aware of the physical attributes of his bride-to-be, his first glimpse of her was at the marriage altar.

One source states that José Manuel, Jr., like his father, served in the Spanish military that protected the missions and presidios of Alta, California. José Jr. led a very rich life, which greatly influenced San Diego history. It is entirely possible that as soldiers, both José Machado, Jr. and his father, traveled back and forth between the missions with their families, living at the presidios.

Maria Serafina and José seemed happy in their marriage, and went on to have a large family. Different documents cite anywhere from ten to 15 children, eight daughters and seven sons, whose lives and futures were woven into the fabric of the history of California. The names of their children were: Juan, Maria Antonia Juliana, Maria Guadalupe Gegoria, Juanita, María, José Arcadio, Maríá Guadalupe Yldefonsa, Jesús, Rafael, Rosa Maria, Maria Antonia, Joaquin, Ignacio, Augustín, José Herculano and Dolores. It is said that the family lived within the walls of the presidio for 20 years. As the military personnel married and began raising their families, the living conditions within the presidio became progressively worse. When Indian attacks lessened, and people felt less threatened, some of them - in the hopes of improving their day-to-day lives - began to build homes in what is now known as Old Town, San Diego. This was located below the presidio. Houses began to populate the area as good, flat land and fertile soil was available. The earliest of these homes were built about 1820.

One of the early builders was José Manuel Machado, Jr. The exact date this home was built is not known, but it is presumed to have been around 1830. The site that he selected was a few blocks south and west of the Ruiz place, (one of the first homes built) and there he erected a small two-room, one-story adobe. This street address eventually became 2724 Congress Street. Originally, according to Pascoe's Map of 1870, it was located on parts of Lots I & 4, section 30, Block 436.

Again, it should be noted that there is a difference of opinion on the size of the Machado family.

One source states 15 children, yet another one lists ten and a genealogy source lists 12 children. We can only go with the information we can find, and hope that we are as correct as possible. At the time the new adobe was built around 1830 or so, it is more than likely that only the two youngest children, Rosa and Joaquín, were living with their parents. Several of the older children were already grown and married. It is with Rosa that the Stewart Family enters into the picture. We will explore that part of the story shortly.

INVESTIGATION #1
DATE: June 30, 2005
LOCATION: Machado-Stewart House
2724 Congress Street
Old Town, San Diego, CA

San Diego Ghost Hunters Team Members
Maritza Skandunas, Karen Ridens
Other Investigators: IPRO
Robert Wlordarski, Alex Sill, Lonnie Sill
Other Participants
Karen the archaeologist, park ranger Elizabeth Allancorte, and Ginnie McGovern

As a team, we approach and carry out our investigations from the psychic/intuitive side, balanced with scientific equipment. Several members of our team are intuitive, and we rely on our gifts during an investigation. Many times, this is and confirmed with what we capture on video, EVP and pictures, both digital and 35-mm. We do a historical and genealogical search after the investigation, and oftentimes our evidence is confirmed historically. We start and end our investigations with a prayer.

For this first official investigation, we carried minimal equipment with us. We had spent the day in Old Town, visiting many places and arrived at the Machado-Stewart House in the afternoon. Our intentions that day were to investigate the Machado-Stewart adobe and historically prove who had been there - and who was still there - via the questions that were proposed and answered, and what was felt by the team members. It is not our intent to be intrusive, and it is without question that we show respect. We also wanted to substantiate our findings with the Old Town Historical Society. Maritza subsequently followed the investigation with an extensive genealogy search to verify the team's findings and impressions.

The day was hot, a typical summer day in July in Old Town. Walking through the front gate, we could almost hear the slap-slap and sizzle of tortillas being prepared in the outdoor ovens, and the echo of children playing in the dusty roads. It felt as if the family was going about their everyday lives. As we entered the grounds, there was a tall growth of reeds on the left, and a clearing on the right. The home is often toured, and many field trips from schools are hosted here. There is a nice clearing, bordered by shade trees, where visitors can sit, relax and take in the view of this old adobe. One of the loveliest gardens in Old Town is behind the house. As mentioned, the front entry of the adobe is covered with mesh, through which visitors can see inside the home when it is closed.

Crossing the clearing, we went around to the back of the house. There are a couple of posts where horses had been tethered, and also the outdoor ovens, with the garden in back. We entered the home through that doorway, and as our eyes adjusted from the bright summer day to the dimmer interior of the adobe, we found ourselves transported back in time. On our left, there is a mannequin apparently busy working in the kitchen, which is filled with tools, herbs, buckets, gourds and other implements. On the right, there is a spinning wheel, a loom and more artifacts, with a small bed tucked against the wall, and several crucifixes gracing the old walls. The floor is adobe brick. The home is small, with the living area, and one bedroom. We were surrounded by old artifacts, representative of the bygone days of early Old Town. It is a museum, hushed and quiet, full of secrets. Not wishing to break the spell, we spoke in whispers.

We began our investigation in the bedroom, which is situated off to the right and to the rear. We felt female presence, and it seemed as if there was more than one woman in the room. We were picking up on a very sad woman, crying, and in pain. She was behind the bed, in the corner. There was also another woman who seemed to be helping her with her pain and sorrow. (Of note, there were countless births in the home). Maritza squeezed between the wall and the bed to talk to the woman. Several of the other investigators moved on into the main room of the adobe to continue with their own investigation,

while Maritza, Karen, and Ginnie remained behind in the bedroom to stay in touch with the female spirits they had contacted. Maritza and Karen felt much suffering and sadness, and Maritza felt such strong emotion that she was tearful.

We left the bedroom and joined the rest of the group in the main room, where we immediately felt a presence. The other investigators were trying to convince this presence to go outside. Karen was standing a little way back in the room, near the mesh door covering. Karen felt very strongly that this person did not want to go outside. She felt that he was frightened and overwhelmed, as there was a lot of activity going on around him, with all the investigators in the house. In addition, he may have been upset because the woman who cared for him wanted to be crossed over. Karen describes this presence that she was feeling as appearing absolutely frantic.

She felt at first that the presence was a child, but her senses told her that he was adult-size. She quickly realized that he was more child-like in his behavior, rather than being an actual child, and concluded that the presence we were encountering was mentally handicapped. Karen felt sure of this. She also sensed that he was in his 40s, and under the care of a woman. As a spirit, he did not venture outside. He did not like to leave the security of the home, or the woman who was taking care of him.

IPRO and the San Diego Ghost Hunters during the investigation

He wanted to stay where he felt safe and secure. He was coaxed to the doorway of the adobe, but never stepped through completely. Karen was taking pictures at the time because she felt his presence so strongly, never losing track of him, and was hoping to capture him in a photograph - and she did!

We also were able to capture EVP of this frantic spirit on tape recorders when we were asking questions. He was very upset, screaming "noooooo." (Of course, we did not hear this until the evidence review later).

In conversation with Ralph Mesa, Rob was using his divining rods, and Maritza and Alex were using digital recorders. (DR represents Rob's divining rods). We will present just a few highlights of our contact. It became obvious during the evidence that there were quite a few spirits at the Machado Stewart adobe, and several of them stepped up to speak. The divining rods and the EVP confirmed each other, as well as what the intuitives were sensing.

Right before this session, one of the investigators had picked up the name Maria.

Ginnie: "Were you related to Maria in the physical when you were here?"
DR: No.
Maritza: "Cousin? A distant cousin?"
Ginnie: "A distant relative?"
DR: Yes.
Rob: "Related, but not."
Ralph: "Yes."
Unknown Spirit #1: "HELP!"
Unknown Male Spirit: "Make it a distant."
Ginnie:" Did you actually want to go with her when she left?"
DR: No.
Ralph: "No."
Unknown Spirit #2:" Right now!"
Maritza: "Did you want to stay here?"

DR: Yes.

Ralph: "Yessss."

Rob: "Did you want her to stay?"

Unknown Female Spirit: "This is difficult."

DR: Yes.

Maritza: "Yes."

Ginnie: "Is there anything that we can help you with?"

Ralph:" No."

At this point we were trying to get him to venture outside, as Ginnie had picked up that Ralph had not been outside often. On EVP he would say "no" every few words. We got him by the door and Elizabeth Allancorte, the park ranger, was standing outside the door with her hand out.

This photograph is believed to have captured the spirit of Ralph Mesa on the left side of the doorway

Ginnie: "You are more than welcome to look outside."

Ralph: Noooooo.

Maritza: "They all like you, Elizabeth."

Ralph: "Yes."

Maritza: "How cute."

Ralph: "Yes."

Ginnie: "Elizabeth is going to remind you about going outside, okay?"

Ralph: "Yes, please."

Ginnie: "We really appreciate you communicating with us, Ralph."

Ralph: (very soft whisper) "Yesss."

While this was taking place, Karen, who was standing a little way back from the group, was picking up very strongly that Ralph was emphatic about not going outside, and that he was frightened and overwhelmed.

Ginnie and Rob were excited that Ralph stepped outside briefly.

Ginnie: "See, everything's okay - nothing happened."

Rob: "He is backing in again."

Maritza: "Yes, he's backing up."

Ralph: "Yes."

Upon evidence review later we learned that Ralph really did want to stay inside.

Ralph: "I CAN'T!"
Ginnie: "You'll be okay."

We also have an EVP of what sounds like a little girl kind of sticking up for Ralph. Right after Ralph says "I CAN'T" we hear an unknown spirit say, "I wouldn't do it!"

We also came across EVP of two other unknown spirits who sounded like little girls. They were speaking at the same time that we were trying to get Ralph outside.
Spirit #1: "Yes, he is. She is fine out there."
Spirit: #2: "You have to get her back in here."

Ginnie: "Do you ever leave the building?"
Ralph: "Nooooo. Sometime it isn't easy."

Right after that, we hear a little girl calling out:
Unknown Spirit: "Hannah!"
Unknown Male Spirit: "I want her back."

Note: When we were doing research after the investigation, we found that there was a Hannah Stewart, a daughter of John Stewart and Rosa Machado Stewart.

The investigators continued trying to get Ralph to go outside.
Ginnie: "Okay, just take three steps out and three steps in."
Unknown Spirit: "I feel sick."

Ginnie: "Thank you again for communicating with us. Ralph."
Ralph: "I'll be safe."

While in the home, we took many pictures, and used our audio recorders, as is our customary protocol. After this, we left the adobe as it was time for Elizabeth, the park ranger, to lock up the Machado-Stewart House. Karen felt this presence so completely and so strongly, she was anxious to get back to the house as soon as possible to see if she could make further contact with him, and perhaps learn more about him. She could not get this spirit out of her mind.

When Karen discussed her findings and feelings with Maritza, Maritza started her genealogy search on the house and its past occupants. Karen reviewed her pictures, and was rewarded with an incredible image near the door. Maritza poured over pictures, and listened to the audio tapes. Imagine our amazement when Maritza was able to actually find someone in the 1880 census, listing as Ralph Mesa, age 45, born in Mexico. He was entered as a "laborer," and there was a checkmark in the column labeled "Idiotic." (During this era the term "idiot" was very common to describe the mentally handicapped.) This would definitely explain why the presence, Ralph, would have been inside the adobe. Likely, his family felt that he was safe within the protective four walls of the home. Also, back then, there was a stigma attached to anyone who was not what society termed "normal." This information that Maritza was able to retrieve confirmed what Karen had sensed - a male, in his 40s, who seemed child-like.

We were so astounded by what we learned from our first investigation, we felt compelled to return and further investigate our findings to see if we could glean any more information on the inhabitants of this old adobe. We were determined to make contact with Ralph again, and to assure him that he was not alone. Karen, especially, feels very protective of Ralph. We have been back to the Machado Stewart home several times, as have other team members.

Karen communicating with the spirit of Ralph Mesa

VISIT #1
DATE: Aug. 4, 2005

San Diego Ghost Hunters Team Members
Maritza Skandunas, Karen Ridens

On August 4, 2005, just a few days later, we (Maritza and Karen) returned with our cameras, recorders and pendulums to chat with Ralph again and assure him that we would always return, and that he would never be forgotten. During that visit, while using our pendulums, we were able to make contact with Ralph, and we felt his presence. In one of the pictures that Maritza took of Karen using the pendulum to communicate with Ralph, there is a soft light in Karen's hand. We realized that Ralph felt very comfortable, safe and secure with us. Since that time, he comes out and joins us whenever we visit the Machado-Stewart House.

VISIT #2
DATE: March 25, 2007

San Diego Ghost Hunters Team Members
Maritza Skandunas

At another time, I (Maritza) returned for another visit with members of IPRO, and a friend, psychic, Alma Carey. As the home was closed at the time we were there we were only able to look through the mesh barrier. We told Alma about our initial investigation, and all the information we were able to verify on the census records. While sitting outside as a group in the yard, in a small clearing to the right side of the adobe, Maritza was talking quietly to Ralph, asking him to join her and her friends outside. It was then that Alma snapped a picture, capturing Ralph's energy, resting close to Maritza, who felt his warm and loving energy infused with the pure, trusting innocence of a child.

We visited Ralph in his home many times before we made another official, full-scale investigation of the Machado-Stewart Adobe. Ralph seems to enjoy our visits and our presence in his home and he now joins us outside. We feel protective of him, and also feel honored that he trusts us, and enjoys our presence in the safety of his home. We feel a very special connection with Ralph Mesa.

At this point, it's time to introduce you to the Stewart side of the Machado-Stewart family. As stated previously, it is felt that the two youngest children of José Manuel and Maria Serafina lived with them in the adobe - Rosa Maria Machado and Joaquin Aquilino Machado.

Rosa Maria Machado was born November 15, 1828 in Old Town, and Joaquin Aquilino was born about 1830. The house is believed to have been constructed between 1830 and 1835, so the children would have been very young when they moved from the presidio into their new 2-room adobe.

John Collins Stewart was born on September 2, 1811 in Hallowell, Maine. On the same document that lists his birth. There is a brother listed, also named John Collins Stewart, who was born October 3, 1810 and died September 26, 1811, when he was not quite one year old. (Although it was not unusual to name a child after another child who had died previously, especially in infancy, I cannot imagine that the parents named the younger John while the older John was still living. Therefore, I am assuming that our John Collins Stewart was born in September of 1812, which another record states.) John was the son of Solomon Freeman Stewart and Margaret Drew, who were both born in England in about 1790. Both of John's parents died in Hallowell, Maine, where John had been born - his father in September of 1817 and his mother in March of 1840. John was one of the youngest of seven children. He had a younger sister who only lived for about two years, and it seems that most of his siblings died during their youth.

During the early 1830s California and the New England states carried on a brisk trade. Trading vessels, sailing around the Horn, brought furniture, clothing, hardware, coffee, tea, etc., which they traded for hides. Oftentimes these vessels remained for months, visiting all the California ports - San Francisco, Monterey, Santa Barbara and San Diego, bartering for hides that made up the cargo for their return voyage.

It was one of these vessels that brought John Collins Stewart to San Diego. There has been some difference of opinion as to which vessel he sailed on, and new light on the subject is provided in the records at Hallowell, Maine, (John Stewart's birthplace). In the Vital Records, Vol. 8, p. 279, concerning John Collins Stewart and Family, may be found the following item, together with the genealogy of the Stewart family:

"Contrary to information now on file in San Diego, California, John C. Stewart was not aboard the ' Pilgrim' with Richard Henry Dana, when it left Boston, Massachusetts, to sail for California, August 14, 1834. He did sail on the 'Alert,' Edward H. Faucon, Master, bound for California from Boston, on November 26, 1834. On this trip he was a seaman, and of course he was with Dana when the latter returned after having transferred to the 'Alert,' when she sailed back from California on May 3, 1836, with Stewart once more aboard. However, this time he has been promoted to Second Mate. At this time he was 24 years of age; five feet eight inches tall, with dark hair and a light complexion."

Probably the best account of the hide trade, and of John Stewart's coming to San Diego, is contained in Richard Henry Dana's book, "*Two Years Before the Mast*," an account of a voyage he made in 1835-36. A subsequent book, "*Twenty Years After*," describes Stewart's marriage into the Machado family. In "Two Years Before the Mast," Dana described the San Diego that greeted him as, "a small settlement directly below the fort, composed of about forty dark brown-looking huts or houses, and two larger ones plastered, which belonged to two of the 'gente de razón'" (people of standing.)

Richard Henry Dana refers to John Stewart, who was his "messmate" as Jack. Dana stated that when they came ashore at San Diego, they "sailor like, steered for the first grog-shop." We wonder, when did he meet Rosa Machado? On his first trip to San Diego in about 1834, Rosa was only about six years old. It is said that John Stewart settled in San Diego in 1836.

John Collins Stewart and Rosa Machado were married on February 3, 1845 at the Mission. John was in his thirties and Rosa only seventeen at the time. Following their marriage, the newlyweds moved into the home of Rosa's parents - José Manuel, Jr. and Maria Serafina. The two families shared the house during José Manuel and María Serafina Machado's remaining years. Rosa's father passed away October 18, 1852, and her mother died March 12, 1861. After their deaths, Rosa bought out her brothers' and sisters' share of the home, and the Stewarts continued living in the Machado home for the rest of their married lives. All twelve of the Stewart children were born within those adobe walls, as were many of the grandchildren and several great grandchildren. (This fact may well explain the pain and sorrow Maritza and Karen had picked up during their July 30, 2005 investigation.)

In "*Twenty Years After,*" Dana wrote:

"The little town of San Diego had undergone no changes whatever. It is still like Santa Bartaara, a Mexican town. The four principal houses of the "gente de razón," of the Bandinis, Estudillos, Argüellos and Picos, are the chief houses now - but all the gentlemen - and their families too, I believe, are gone. I went into a familiar one-story adobe with its piazza and earthen floor, inhabited by a respectable lower class family by the name of Machado, and inquired if any of the family remained, when a bright eyed, middle-aged woman recognized me, for she had heard I was aboard the steamer, and she said she had married a shipmate of mine, Jack Stewart, who went as Second Mate the next voyage, but left the ship and married and settled here. She said he wished to see me. In a few minutes he came in and his sincere pleasure in meeting me was extremely grateful. We talked over old times, as long as I could afford to. I was glad to hear that he was sober and doing well...."

One document states that Rosita Stewart, Rosa and John's oldest child, was 14 years old when Dana called at her home to renew his acquaintance with her father. She remembered his coming in 1860 to the door and her mother, Rosa, telling him how glad her husband would be to see his old shipmate.

Other information we found states that John C. Stewart was a pilot, and was known as "el pilato" and that he served with the volunteer troops at San Diego during the Garra uprising in 1851, and saw service in the Mexican War. A record in Sacramento reveals that John Stewart was paid $220.00 for his services with The Fitzgerald Volunteers for the period from November 24, 1851 to January 7, 1852. This confirms his service (noted above during the Garra,)

Rosa and John had 12 children, with the oldest, Rosa Maria Elojia (Rosita) born in December of 1845, and the youngest, Maria Jesusa Elojia born in January of 1868. The Machado-Stewart family lived in the adobe until the mid-1960s, when the adobe was in such disrepair that it could no longer be inhabited. The state of California acquired the house in 1967. The adobe has been restored to its historical state as a house museum by the Park and Recreation Department and was furnished by the San Diego County Committee of the National Society of Colonial Dames of America.

After Rosa and John died, Frank J. "Pancho" Stewart, who was born in 1860 and raised in the old Machado-Stewart house, married and raised his own family there. Other members of the family who lived in the old place were Stewart's son, Manuel, his daughter, Margarita, and Rosita Stewart. Also a cousin, Rose Fournier, lived in the house for several years.

The last resident of the adobe was Carmen Meza, the daughter of Francisco Javier Stewart (Frank). Francisco was born in February of 1860. Carmen Meza was born in the house in 1912 and had lived there for over 50 years. She was forced to move out in 1966, when a leaky roof and crumbling walls made living conditions unbearable.

A descendent of the Machado-Stewart family remembers an outside oven that was still there when she was a little girl. And her mother told her that one of the chores assigned to her grandfather, John C. Stewart, by her grandmother, was to attend the oven while she went to mass almost every day. She also remembered her mother telling about a fireplace at one end of the building. She remembers a family altar in one of the bedrooms of the old house. The room had a red tile floor and in one corner was a small covered altar which was made by her grand-father. On the altar rested a religious figure. Here they gathered for family prayers.

She also has several mementos of the family including a rosary that belonged to her great-grandmother, Serafina Machado, and also her painted drinking cup, which was fashioned from a gourd. Among her treasures from the Stewart family is a camphor wood chest that belonged to her grandfather, John C. Stewart. There is also a crucifix, glass tumblers and bottles, and the Stewart family Bible. John Stewart's handwriting can be found in the bible, recording the dates of birth of most of the family and sometimes the dates of their deaths. It is unfortunate that no pictures of John C. Stewart or his wife have been found. Rosa Stewart has been described as short and dark-skinned and John Stewart was described as tall, slender and of light complexion. At one time he ran a lot of cattle and was something of a carpenter.

The Machado-Stewart adobe is remembered by one of the descendents as having had an orchard of pear, fig and pomegranate trees. The walls were white-washed about every six months.

John Collins Stewart's funeral is remembered as taking place on a rainy day in February. Eight black horses drew the hearse up the steep grade to the Mission Hills Cemetery. Below is his obituary:
The San Diego Union, San Diego, California, Thursday, February 4, 1892, page 5
Death of Jack Stewart
Jack Stewart, one of the truly historic characters of this region, died at Old Town Tuesday night at the age of 83. For a long time he had been utterly helpless and unable to speak or sit up, and was compelled to make his wants known by signs. He was an interesting character because of his early association with Richard H. Dana, author of "Two Years Before the Mast," he having been mate of the ship on which Dana made the voyage to this coast from Boston in the '30s. He knew Dana well and often said he was no account as a sailor but was popular because of his good fellowship. Stewart was at the battle of San Pasqual, and was active in other early incidents connected with this region.

And that of his wife, Rosa:
The San Diego Union, San Diego, California, Friday, May 6, 1898, page 2
An Old Resident Gone
Mrs. Rosa Marie Machado Stewart died Wednesday at her home in Old San Diego, aged 72. She was born in Old Town, near the site of the old Stockton fort, and all her life had been passed within a stone's throw of the place where she was born. In her young days she was married to John Stewart, one of the early American residents of Old San Diego, and the couple had several children, now all grown and married. Mrs. Stewart's funeral will be held at the Catholic church at Old Town tomorrow morning at 9 o'clock.

And the obituary of the Stewart's oldest child, "Rosita":
The San Diego Union, San Diego, California, Monday, September 18, 1933, page 1:4-5 and 2:5-6
Last San Diegan Born Before This State Was American Soil Passes In Death of Rosita Stewart Here

The last of those San Diegans born before the American era died Saturday night in the ancient adobe house on Congress Street in Old Town and in the same room where she was born Dec. 1, 1845. Miss Rosita Stewart represented the third generation of San Diego's oldest family, the Machados.

Her grandfather, Comandante José Manuel Machado was a corporal in the Catalonian volunteers while stationed at San Diego presidio in 1782, according to the historian H. H. Bancroft. Scattered throughout this vicinity and the southwest are representatives of the sixth generation of the Machado family, Miss Stewart's youngest sister, Mrs. B F. Parsons, lives at 2611 San Diego Avenue, and nearby live Miss Stewart's niece, Mrs. Leo Mustain, and her grandnieces the Misses Shirley, Adella and June Mustain. Other relatives in San Diego are Frank Connors of the police force and a sister-in-law, Mrs. Frank Stewart.

Married Dana's Shipmate
Don José Manuel Machado married Dona Serafina Valdez. They were the original owners of the great Rosario ranch below Tijuana, Lower California, a part of which is still owned by members of this family. Both of these pioneers are buried in the recently restored Campo Santo in Old Town. One of their daughters was Rosa Machado, who at the age of 17 married a Yankee John S. Stewart, shipmate of Richard Henry Dana, Jr., on the Pilgrim and afterwards on the Alert - a friend often mentioned as "S-" in "Two Years Before the Mast."
Jack Stewart was the companion of the future author on that memorable first day of liberty from the Pilgrim when they walked over the old playa trail on their way to town, and in the evening rode back on hired horses in 15 minutes, determined to have all the "go" possible out of their California mounts.

Served at San Pasqual!!!
Miss Rosita was the eldest child of Jack and Rosa Stewart. She was 14 when Dana called at her home to renew his acquaintance with her father. She remembered his coming in 1850 to the door and her mother telling him how glad her husband would be to see his old shipmate. Dana described Mrs. Stewart afterwards as "a bright-eyed middle-aged woman." She was then 31.
Mr. Stewart died in 1892. He had served at the battle of San Pasqual and later with the Fitzgerald volunteers. He was long known as "El Piloto" here. His wife died May 4, 1898. Both were buried in the old cemetery "on the mesa," a burial ground which Jack Stewart helped to lay out in 1875. Beside them Rosita will lie after a requiem mass in the Immaculate Conception church in Old Town at 8 o'clock Tuesday morning.

Gowned in Beef Hide
Though her life was passed in undisturbed tranquility in the village that is now part of a great metropolis, Rosita Stewart had witnessed more changes here than any other citizen. Before she was two, Fremont marched his battalion up from La Playa and quartered his offices at the Stewart house and the nearby house of Juanita Wrightington, Rosita's aunt. The child's life was despaired of when

someone remembered that it was good medical practice to wrap an ailing infant in a freshly killed beef hide. Every day they slaughtered a steer to feed the Americans; and after Rosita had been wrapped in a warm steer hide she began to improve immediately, it was said.

A group of little, old statues were for more than 50 years the special charge of Rosita Stewart. How old they were no one knew. They were called the "mission statues," and may well be the oldest sacred images in California. When they adorned the altar in the little adobe chapel across the road and after they were moved into the new church, Rosita dusted them and kept their surroundings beautifully neat.

When the traffic on San Diego Avenue became too bewildering for a tiny old lady of more than 80, she was induced to give up her beloved duty. It is fitting that during the last night of its earthly stay her body should lie near the scene of her long devotions. At 8 o'clock tomorrow evening relatives and friends will gather at the church to recite the rosary. Johnson & Saum have charge of funeral arrangements.

Both John Stewart and his wife Rosa are buried in the Calvary Cemetery in San Diego, (now a part of Calvary Pioneer Memorial Park), 1501 Washington Place, San Diego, CA 92103.

INVESTIGATION #2
DATE: Oct. 21, 2007
LOCATION: Machado-Stewart House
            2724 Congress Street
            Old Town, San Diego, CA

San Diego Ghost Hunters Team Members
Maritza Skandunas, Dawn Gaudette, Sharon Gaudette Hieserich, Sarah Ettelson, Matt Schulz
Other Investigators: IPRO
Robert Wlordarski, Nicci Sill, Alex Sill
Other Participants
Park ranger Elizabeth Allancorte and staff members from the department of parks and recreation

A crisp autumn evening finds us in Old Town, anticipating another investigation of Machado-Stewart adobe. As is our custom while in Old Town, we stopped by the Whaley House to say hello to the docents there. We had a few more of our San Diego Ghost Hunters team members with us, including Matt Schulz, our tech manager and web site designer, as well as the psychically gifted women. After a tasty dinner at one of the local Mexican restaurants we headed over to the Machado-Stewart House.

It was twilight, and the October night promised to be cool. Fall had sneaked in, stealing away the summer heat. The trees sighed and the winds whispered. Stars winked from darkened skies, like co-conspirators. What a great night for an adventure! We were meeting some of our friends from IPRO, along with the park ranger, Elizabeth Allancorte, who had been with us when we first met Ralph, along with one of the employees from parks and recreation and several of her friends. All in all, it was a large group, and the adobe is small, with only two rooms. We said our prayer, and thanked the Machado-Stewart family for sharing their home with us that evening. As we entered the home, it felt familiar. Our intentions were to make contact again with Ralph, and with the other spirits in the home.

Photographs from the investigation: (Above, Left) Rob and Nicci; (Above, Right) Sharon and Maritza; (Left, Top) Dawn's daughter, Sarah; (Left, Lower) Elizabeth and Matt

We had promised Ralph we would be back. Our team walked quietly around, snapping off picture after picture. Matt checked out the environment with EMF, Tri-Meter and the temperature probe. There didn't seem to be any anomalous readings, but he continued his monitoring throughout the investigation.

Rob made his way to the bedroom with his divining rods and recorder. We continued to take pictures, and then our team sat down in the outer living area to use a pendulum, divining rods, digital recorders and our senses. We sat quietly for a short time to see what we could feel before we started using our equipment. The women on the team are all intuitive, and usually tune in to the same thing. We were sensing that the spirits were feeling a bit crowded, and it wasn't until much later that we were able to make contact. Maritza, Dawn, Sharon and Sarah all sensed Ralph - he was glad we were there. Sharon sensed that there was a large family of cats that had lived in the yard and garden, and that Ralph played with them. We used divining rods, the pendulum, and recorders.

Several of the guests left our group and joined Rob in the back bedroom where he was making contact using divining rods. Rob was very successful in communicating with the spirits. He is patient and gentle. Shortly after, our guests left, and our team, along with IPRO and Elizabeth, remained to work for a while. We continued with EVP and our divining rods, with Matt monitoring for any spikes in temperature, or in EMF readings. It remained pretty

The team gathers during the investigation

benign. We enjoyed working with IPRO, and after they left we decided we would explore outside. We had made contact with Ralph, and we wanted to hold on to him. Sarah felt his presence strongly outside by the reeds. She shot a picture out the window, and caught a shadow man. Picture is below. We spent quite a bit of time outside, taking pictures, and Sarah, Dawn and Maritza were successful in capturing Ralph's essence. We all definitely felt his presence.

After listening to our audio, we confirmed that the Machado-Stewart House was active that night. As well as making contact with Ralph, we captured so many voices on our recorders. Again, just a few highlights of what were able to pick up via our recorders.

Maritza: "Ralph, are you here?"
Ralph: "You did come."
Maritza: "Do you want to say something?"

Maritza: "Do you remember me?"
Ralph: "Yes, I do."
Maritza: "Can you tap on the recorder?"

Maritza: "Ralph, are you here?"
Ralph: "These are tea cups." (Tin cups?)
Maritza: "Do you want to say something?"
Unknown female spirit: "Get down."

Maritza: "Do you remember me?"
Unknown male spirit: "Get down."

Maritza: "Can you tap on the recorder?"
Unknown male spirit: "Get down."

Maritza: "Can you flash the lights, Ralph?"
(We had a K2 light meter placed on the floor in front of us. The lights did not flash.)
Male Spirit: "Hold her back." (Roll her back?)

Maritza: "Can you touch that little machine and make the lights go off?"
Unknown Spirit: "Ranger." (Perhaps referring to Elizabeth, the park ranger who was with us?)
Maritza: "Can you the put the lights on?"
Unknown Spirit: "Get back!" (This sounded like a male.)

Maritza: "Is somebody in the back yard?"
Female Spirit: "That was me." (Her voice sounded young.)

Maritza: "Ralph, are you here?"
Male Spirit #1: "Help me."
Male Spirit #2: "Tell them."
Female Spirit: "Please help me."

Maritza: "Ralph, can we take a picture of you?"
Ralph: "Okay." (A whisper.)

Once again, it seems as if we have quite a few spirits in this realm. The following is some random EVP that was recorded at the adobe:

"Hit the light."
"I'm a gentleman."
"Give it some water."
"Too many people."
"Papa, there's lots of rain."
"The team was here."
"Get off grandma. (Or get off the ground.)
"Get out." (This sounded like a female voice.)

We also had some strange communications with the dowsing rods:

Maritza: "Ralph, can you moving the divining rods?"
Male Spirit: "Can you help him?"
Maritza: "Ralph, do you remember how to use the divining rods?"
DR: Yes.
Ralph: "Yes. Is this one okay? Same.....last.....year." (Some of the words were inaudible.)
Maritza: "Where are you?"
Ralph: "Here."
Maritza: "Are you between Dawn and me?"
Ralph: (inaudible)
Maritza: "Are you back over here again?"
DR: Yes.
Maritza: "Okay."
Male Spirit: "Richard!"

A VISIT
DATE: Jan. 11, 2008

While doing an investigation one night at the Racine and Laramie Cigar Shop in Old Town, Dawn

and Maritza scooted over to Machado-Stewart adobe to see if Ralph was there. As they felt his presence they took several pictures and talked to him, just letting him know they were there, and would return. Although they wanted to stay longer, they joined the team back at the cigar shop. Maritza and Dawn reviewed their pictures immediately, and were happy to see that once again they had captured Ralph.

The Machado-Stewart adobe continues to draw us in. We feel so fortunate to live in the birthplace of California, and most of our trips to Old Town include a stop at the house. We look forward to walking through those gates, and wandering around the garden. We peer through the mesh over the door and take our pictures, hoping to catch a glimpse of our friend, Ralph Mesa. We say hello, and spend a little time there. Many times we feel his gentle energy. After we say good-bye to Ralph, we leave, glancing back over our shoulders, still hoping to catch him in the yard, playing with his cats, and waving to us.

7. THE HAUNTING OF ALFRED'S VICTORIAN

BY KELLY AND JOHN WEAVER

The startled woman stumbled into the dining area with her pantyhose around her ankles. The room grew quiet and all eyes were upon her. This was not in my plans for the evening!

I was hosting a haunted dinner in October 2002 at Alfred's Victorian restaurant in Middletown, Pennsylvania, and I couldn't have planned a better entrance for a night of spooky tales. This elegantly dressed woman had excused herself to use the restroom during my presentation and Emma, the resident ghost, decided to make her presence known.

"The potpourri just flew off the toilet tank and hit the stall door with so much force - I high tailed it out of there. I can't believe it! I saw it with my own eyes. There is no way that should have happened." The frantic woman breathlessly told me and the 50 other guests who now sat with mouths wide open in awe. All of a sudden she realized how she must have looked with her pantyhose clutching her ankles. Her shirt was askew; her hair looked like she had survived a tornado!

"I'm not going back in there!" She firmly stated as she scurried down the hall tugging at her nylons. She disappeared into a vacant room to compose herself. I'm sure she was quite embarrassed at the scene she had just made.

I tried hard not to

laugh because I knew that Emma was a prankster. I've encountered her many times over the years.

HISTORY

Alfred's is a stately Victorian structure. Middletown is the oldest community in Dauphin County, Pennsylvania. It gained national attention in 1979 during the Three Mile Island nuclear plant accident. (TMI is still in operation, 30 years after the near disaster). The town was founded in 1755 on the site of a former Indian Village, as were many along the Susquehanna River. Union Street, where Alfred's is located, was once described as "the most fashionable boulevard west of Philadelphia" during the Victorian era. Built in 1888 by Charles Raymond, the house was full of luxuries. Raymond's extravagance was his own undoing and in 1896 the house went to the Middletown National Bank to pay off his creditors. In 1898, Redsecker Young purchased the dwelling for $6,600. Four years later, Simon Cameron Young bought it, eventually bequeathing it unto his daughter, Eliza, and his second wife, Mary Emma Sutton Young. In 1949, Herman and Sara Baum began their twenty-year residence in the home. Although it had been allowed to deteriorate, the original craftsmanship that made the house a showplace was still intact.

After purchasing the old mansion and undertaking extensive restoration, Alfred Pellegrini of Hershey, Pennsylvania, opened a restaurant on the premises in July of 1970. Today Alfred's is a regional landmark that has won countless awards for cuisine, service and ambiance.

Pellegrini's restoration efforts ensured the restaurant that bears his name would retain its former splendor. (It is on the National Register of Historic Places). Designed by architect Joséph Dise of Spring Glen, Pennsylvania, it was constructed of brownstone from the nearby Hummelstown brownstone quarries. Most of the exterior windows are crowned with leaded glass transoms. The irregularly shaped roof is accented by interesting peaks, dormers and wrought iron castings. Within the building you'll find distinctive ball and spindle grilles, carved wainscoting, and floors with inlaid ceramic. Fireplaces boast intricate woodwork, beveled mirrors and cubbyholes. Medieval minstrels grace the sides of the fireplace at the foot of the

stairs. A unique feature is found in the dining room where what appears to be floor-to-ceiling windows are actually doors which slide up into the ceiling to allow passage to the porch. All the windows can be completely covered by shutters, and most rooms are separated by massive pocket doors. Sparkling throughout the house are priceless chandeliers, many of them converted to electricity from gas fixtures. Dining at Alfred's is to some degree like dining in a museum, and even if there were no record of paranormal activity, one's first impression of the place would remain that of classic Victorian haunted house.

My favorite feature is the quiet tower window seat where John and I have had many romantic dinners. Alfred's has won numerous awards for its food, wine list and ambiance. It is a delightful place for a quiet dinner and the service is superior. There are many nooks and crannies offering a uniquely intimate dining experience, but remember: no matter how isolated you might be, someone could be watching!

I first ventured into Alfred's in the early 1990s when I worked in advertising. The restaurant was one of my clients. I met Pamm Yascavage, daughter of Fred Pellegrinni, who acquired the house in the early 1970s and turned it into the charming restaurant it is today. I mentioned to Pamm that I felt the place was haunted (I sensed this upon walking through the door). She smiled and began to rattle off a few of her own personal encounters with Emma.

"Do we have ghosts?" she laughed. "You wouldn't believe all of the stuff that goes on around here. When we were little and dad just opened the restaurant, we lived on the third floor. Many nights we would hear a party going on downstairs. When dad went downstairs to look, there was nothing out of place. Once he called the cops because it sounded like someone had broken in - we were so scared. Nothing was missing, no one was in the building and the alarm system was still activated. After a while we just got used to the strange encounters."

I suggested this would be a perfect place to do a haunted dinner presentation. Pamm readily agreed and our friendship – and a further business arrangement -- was formed.

Beginning in the mid 1990s, John and I have hosted "haunted dinners" every October and Alfred's packs them in. Over the years we've expanded the events beyond the Halloween season to include various theme dinners and even work with bus companies hosting haunted tours of the region, which includes Gettysburg, an hour away. As there is nothing negative about the activity here, Alfred's openly admits it is haunted and as its fame continues to grow; a good percentage of its customers cite this as their reason for dining there!

THE HAUNTINGS

Just about every type of paranormal activity – auditory, olfactory, levitating/moving objects, doors opening and closing by themselves, electrical/electronic interference, unexplained lights and apparitions – have been witnessed at Alfred's. Clearly, this is the scene of a classic "intelligent" haunting, and the culprit has long been said to be a woman named Emma.

Over the years, I've had the pleasure to interview many employees and guests who've had ghostly encounters here. For some time, there was a rumor that Emma committed suicide after being jilted by a lover. Another version claims that her fiancée died in World War I and she was so despondent that she took her own life; She is said to have thrown herself into the furnace. It turns out all of these are just colorful rumors -- the truth is Mary Emma Sutton Young was Simon Cameron Young's second wife. She lived to be almost 90, dying in 1948. Her grave can be visited a few blocks away in Middletown Cemetery. It is unclear if it was the Baums – who lived here from 1949 to 1969 – who first

A photograph of Emma Sutton Young

Emma's grave in the Middletown Cemetery

claimed that a female ghost was haunting the place or if they even noted anything strange. However, during Alfred Pellegrini's restoration efforts, while his family lived in the third floor apartment prior to opening the restaurant in 1970, Emma began to make her presence known, and this presence has grown over the years.

A dark basement, be a structure haunted or not, is not the most welcoming place and Alfred's basement has quite a reputation. No one likes to go down there to use the employees' restroom or to visit the wine cellar. One server told me that of being mysteriously locked in the wine cellar by an unseen force. Thank Goodness another employee came down to gather some supplies and heard her screaming for help! Frankly, I'm not too fond of the basement myself and I suppose the very clear "Get out!" EVP I recorded here several years ago supports my feeling that someone does not like living souls in that part of the house!

While filming a segment for Fox's *Pennsylvania Ghost Project* in 1999, I was able to chat with one of Alfred's chefs, the late Chuck Liskey. This gentle giant (he looked more like an outlaw biker than a gourmet chef) had many stories about Emma and her mischievous antics. Chuck told me how Emma loved to throw his pots and pans around the kitchen. She also was fond of knocking on the kitchen door. Many times the door would be shut and dead bolted, only to swing open, pushed by unseen hands. He said that all he'd have to do would be to tell her he was busy and to go bother someone else and she would comply. (All this clearly supports our feeling this is a classic intelligent haunting). Chuck said he never believed in ghosts before coming to Alfred's, but after working there for a while he was a firm believer. Sadly, Chuck passed on several years ago. As a medium I've never sensed that he, too, stuck around the place, but had he chosen to do so, one must wonder what mischief he and Emma together could have stirred up!

One Saturday morning, Fred Pellegrini, Jr. (Alfred's son) and an assistant were in the kitchen making a crab stuffing. They were the only two people in the restaurant. Both men went into the basement for supplies and upon returning, their large bowl of crab filling was missing. Where did it go? Were they going crazy? They checked and rechecked the refrigerator; opened up cupboard doors and checked under the counter. No crab. No very expensive huge bowl of crab. They walked around the restaurant and finally found it – in the UPSTAIRS dining room. Was Emma trying to make a statement?

Alfred's chef, the late Chuck Liskey

Jeannie Dunaway is a housekeeper at the restaurant. While running the vacuum cleaner, she hears conversations when no one else is around. (As many know, white noise, such as the humming sound produced by a vacuum cleaner, is considered to be a conduit for spirit communication. Many times Dunaway hears a woman calling out to her. Nikki, a server, also hears Emma calling her name late at night when all of the patrons have gone. It seems that Emma likes to play in the early morning and late at night when all of the guests have gone home. It likewise appears that new employees are fair game to her. Perhaps that is her way of welcoming them to the family.

On one occasion, Jeannie was told the upstairs dining room was empty the night before and didn't need to be cleaned, but she decided to just take a quick look. Upon entering the Flammette Room on the second floor (which Emma loves to frequent) she noticed a table setting was moved around: silverware was on the plate, the wine glasses were tilted, the salt and pepper shakers were out of order and the napkin was draped on the seat as if someone had just finished a meal! This has happened more than once. During a haunted dining event in this same room, Emma didn't let me down. Everyone seated along the wall felt a sudden gust of cold air shoot around their ankles. That got their attention! There is no heat or air conditioning duct by these seats. It added to the ambiance of the event. I silently thanked Emma for showing up.

Jeannie was checking the upstairs kitchen recently and found two coffee pots on the floor turned upside down. When she asked the supervisor if anything had happened, she was told that everything was fine a few minutes ago. Thinking she was losing her mind, Jeannie just shook her head and walked away. Emma had more up her sleeve for Jeannie that day. She had placed her cleaning supplies on a bench outside the ladies room and quickly checked the bar area; In a matter of seconds all of her supplies were missing! She once again asked her supervisor if she had moved them only to be told that she was downstairs the entire time. After 45 minutes, the cleaning supplies were found – back in the supply closet.

Emma loves to play with the radio. Years ago, Alfred's would play easy listening music or classical music from local FM stations during the dinner hour. Image you're in this romantic restaurant, getting ready to propose marriage only to have AC-DC or Motley Crue suddenly blaring from the speakers! Many times the radio would tune itself up and down the dial. The advent of CDs has evidently put a halt to the musical manipulation. Telephones and credit card machines are not immune to Emma's antics. After one haunted dining, Pamm told me that her phones wouldn't work, or when they did, they'd ring and no one was on the line. The credit card machines went haywire. Repairmen could find no earthly explanation.

Fred Pellegrini, Jr. related how Emma likes to change his drink orders. Years ago, he was the floor manager as well as a waiter. He made his drink orders and placed them on the bar. When he turned around the drinks were totally different from what he had just poured.

Many times when the morning staff show up for work the front door will be ajar and the alarm system still on. Emma – or someone unseen – appears to have a thing for various doors in the place.

After climbing the beautifully curved staircase to the second floor, you'll notice a human-sized doll holding a tray. There is something strange about this figure that I can't quite figure out. Pamm told me servers have seen it move. Jeannie said that more than once when walking by the mannequin it would be turned totally around facing the opposite direction than it had been a few minutes before. When she asked another worker if they had moved it, they shook their head "no" and looked at her like she had two heads. I'm sure Emma was having a good laugh.

Her bathroom antics are not limited to tossing potpourri at female diners. Twice in the past year a cloud was noticed spewing from the men's room. Somehow, the air freshener kept in the men's stall set itself off. Pamm, who was alone in the building and working in her adjacent second floor office, found the canister just sitting on the back of the tank in its normal position with the button depressed.

After Christmas every year, Alfred's Victorian closes down for a complete cleaning following the hectic holiday season. On one occasion, Jeannie was in the parlor. Turning towards the wall, she noticed a small dark silhouette from the waist up. It appeared to be a woman of small stature wearing a dark coat with the collar turned up. The silhouette quickly moved to the kitchen from the dining room. Thinking it was someone who needed help or someone to sign an invoice she followed the shadow into the kitchen area only to find no one there but the cook. He hadn't noticed anything at all. Thinking once more she was going crazy, she asked the supervisor if any delivery men had just come in the building. She didn't think so, and they both checked out the windows and could see no sign of a truck or car in the parking lot or on the street. A rare light anomaly was also witnessed by Jeannie near the front desk: A vertical column of bright light shot up from near the register to the second floor. This is in the same area where an unexplained brilliant streak of blue light moving on the stairs manifested on a 35mm shot Pamm was taking from the landing in the late 1990s.

At the entrance to the La Flammette Room on the second floor, there is a heavy wooden sliding door that can be closed for a private party. More than once, employees setting tables for the following day at the end of the night have reported that the door had closed on its own before they could finish their job. John has debunked any chance of traffic on the street nearby or people walking on the floor as an explanation.

The delightful scent of lavender often wafts through the hallways, announcing Emma's presence. Both patrons and employees have encountered it. Another odor, a quite unpleasant one, has been noticed above the first floor organ. At one time there was an elevator here which took Emma and her stepdaughter up and down stairs; Rumor has it one of them was quite sickly. Jeannie described this smell as that of an infected sore. They must burn scented candles and incense to cover up the offensive odor. No one can detect where or how this smell is formed.

From my perspective as a medium, I've always sensed a strong female presence here. I feel Emma – if that is indeed her name – has a deep love for this lovely restaurant and loves the good energy brought by generations of happy customers. I must say I have detected a less strong presence – that of a male – whose domain seems limited to the small second-floor bar and adjacent Magnolia Room. His demeanor suggests someone who was in banking or finance, and I suspect he may have been involved with the bank that originally acquired the place when original owner Charles Raymond could not keep up with his payments. We have recorded a couple of EVPs in the Magnolia Room that are decidedly masculine.

My husband, John, is not immune to Emma's antics. After a night of filming with a local TV station, he had his own frightening encounter with her.

"It was around 11:30 p.m. Kelly's late great-uncle, Cecil Downing, the master dowser who lived nearby and also knew Emma well, had just finished his interview and I accompanied him downstairs, to let him out. The only others left inside were all upstairs - the cameraman, Kelly and Pamm. After seeing Cecil off and locking the outer door, I then began to shut the inner vestibule door when a raspy female voice was heard, imploring 'Don't shut the door!' This intrepid ghost hunter felt pretty damn silly running upstairs to be greeted by Kelly and Pamm asking why I looked so frightened. I did gather some equipment and returned to the area but did not get any evidence. It is one thing to hear ghostly EVP that you have recorded but when you actually are spoken to and there is no living person anywhere nearby it is really quite unnerving!"

INVESTIGATIONS AND EVIDENCE

At many times over the past fifteen years, John and I, as well as members of our SSP investigation team, have had the place to ourselves during midday and late night hours. As a medium and investigator, I think Emma is comfortable with us and feels unthreatened by our presence; after all, between events, investigations and just dining there ourselves, we're there once monthly – sometimes more. These investigations have yielded some solid evidence – mainly in the form of Electronic Voice Phenomenon – that support the contention that Alfred's is haunted.

One of these, recorded while we were alone in the restaurant

Spirit Society of Pennsylvania team members at Alfred's during an investigation

(Left) More investigations with the SSP team

(Above) Kelly Weaver attempts to communicate with the spirits present at Alfred's. A Tri-Field Natural EM meter is placed on the table to pick up any disturbances in the energy of the room.

on Oct. 13, 2004, actually mentions Emma's name. In response to John's question "Is anyone here?" a clearly male voice was captured saying "Emma is here!" This was in the upstairs Magnolia Room that Kelly feels is the domain of the "banker." Alone in the same room, John also had the very rare experience of audibly hearing a response to his prompt for EVP that also was captured on his digital recorder. Prior to this EVP capture, John noticed a bright streak of vertical light high on the wall – similar to what Jeannie saw downstairs. One of my personal favorites was recorded in the ladies room where mocking laughter responds to my question, "Emma, are you here?" Upon capturing the "Get out!" in the basement and playing it for John, he gave me a strange look and said "That sounds like the same voice that told me, 'Don't shut the door.'" (These and other EVPs captured at Alfred's can be heard at www.spiritsocietyofpa.com)

Several EM and Thermal anomalies have been documented in Alfred's over the years, and a recent (Nov. 2008) investigation yielded infrared camcorder footage of a shadowy figure moving into the wall along the staircase, but John feels one of the best pieces of evidence remains the photo taken by Pamm in the late 1990s:

"There is one photo that I feel -- and Troy Taylor agrees -- makes a strong case for being Emma. It is a 35mm image taken by Pamm late one evening while standing on the landing of the main staircase. The staff is assembled below and a translucent blue streak is seen following the path of the stairs. The anomaly in this photo is no more easily explained that the disembodied voice I heard!"

John also discovered something very unusual while helping me prepare a presentation in 2005.

"When preparing video to use for Kelly's talk on haunted places she has investigated at a conference in Baltimore during July 2005, one of the clips we decided to use was a dramatic candle-lit piece filmed by the local ABC affiliate several years ago. Kelly was speaking about encounters with Emma in the upstairs "La Flamette" Room. For the first time, I discovered what certainly seems to be a female face suddenly appearing in a mirror off to and above Kelly's left.

This amazing photograph, taken by Pamm Yascavage in the late 1990s, remains truly unexplained to this day.

When this was filmed, the large sliding doors were shut (there is no other entrance to this room), and the only people inside it were Kelly and Dave Edwards, the cameraman from WHTM. Dave, of course, was behind the camera, understandably secured on a tripod. The room was lit only with candles. Looking at the mirror, the image moves in slowly from the right, is stationary for perhaps a second, then disappears. It is seen in only 50 to 55 frames of video (there are 30 frames per second), thus the "apparition" lasts slightly less than two seconds.

Since the photo included with this story was taken of an individual video frame on a TV, it is nowhere near as compelling as what can be seen when actually viewing the video on a decent-sized screen. Still, they clearly show that something moves into the mirror, and that something appears to be a female face. With the camera and its operator stationary, no one else in the room except Kelly and the doors tightly closed to block light, there is no rational explanation for anything appearing in that mirror. The original footage was filmed in the late 1990s, and attempts to contact Dave Edwards – who had long since moved on – have been futile. I cannot fully rule out some sort of creative editing, but as the piece was shown the evening after it was filmed, I wonder if there was sufficient time to do so. The book is still open on this one."

OUR MOST RECENT INVESTIGATION

Perhaps the most complete investigation of Alfred's took place in November 2008, when John and I, along with several members of our investigative team, joined housekeeper Jeannie Dunaway at 10 p.m. on a Saturday evening. Typically working alone, she has probably had more experiences than anyone but the Pellegrinis themselves and was a useful tour guide into the paranormal world of Alfred's.

We were given the run of the place from the basement to the upstairs dining rooms. Some of the evidence captured that evening came from an IR camcorder John had set up on the bottom of the very active main stairway. It recorded some dramatic footage of what appears to be a shadowy figure going into the wall. A strange sound which may be EVP was also captured as the shadow entered the wall. I also recorded an EVP while I was alone in the kitchen and asked if anyone wanted my help or wanted to speak to me. A very eerie "Yeeeessssss" can be heard. It sounded like it was from a place far, far away. I can assure you that it was no one on the investigative team. Matt Wood recorded a voice answering him while he was upstairs and also may have captured some phantom footsteps; John recorded another voice while he and Jack Thomas were in the La Flamette Room.

We broke up into three groups to work the basement, first and second floors, changing locations at appointed times so all areas were covered by all investigators. As is typical with our group, at least one sensitive is assigned to each group. Along with myself, Laura Shank and Matt Wood -- who have proven competent and reliable investigators, not only as sensitives but using technology -- were split between the groups. After our individual team investigations were completed, we all met at the stairs, sat down, turned on our recorders and began asking questions to any of the spirits that may haunt the restaurant.

At one point of questioning we all heard the men's bathroom door open and shut. No one was upstairs at the time. Matt's face was priceless when this happened. He dashed up the stairs to investigate, and indeed found the door ajar, with no rational explanation. Regrettably, in anticipation of leaving after this last group EVP session, no one had left any camcorders running upstairs, or the antics with the men's room door may have been captured.

John offers some of his own observations of this investigation:

Prior to this, any time we had been in Alfred's alone it was just Kelly and me. Having three groups this time certainly afforded coverage of this very large old home, but the downside was learning how easily sound travelled here - even muted voices could be heard one floor below. While this to some degree compromised attempts to gather audible evidence, I still feel some credible EVPs were captured. However, some of the experiences we had support the steady accounts of strange activity in certain locations here over the years.

One of these seems easy to debunk, but just too weird to ignore – the woman's room toilet running... evidently on command! The staff say they've had this checked (you don't have to be a paranormal plumber to know what running toilets do to water bills) and Jeannie told us it is sporadic, but is often heard when she is there by herself cleaning. It began happening that evening and upon entering the ladies room and asking, "Who's making the water run - is that you Emma?" the toilet did just that! (This was, of course, recorded). Wondering what role the old floorboards might play, I then walked out and came back in again at different times in an attempt to see if my weight on the floor had any effect. It did not. When we began our group EVP session with everyone downstairs, Jeannie asked the same question and seconds later got the same response: The toilet again ran! Perhaps a coincidence, but it certainly confirmed that the presence of any living forms upstairs played no role in making it flush on its own.

I'm still kicking myself for not following through with a thought to keep my one camcorder upstairs during our final session. By not leaving at least one of the several camcorders focused on the upstairs bathroom areas, we likely missed a great view of the men's room door opening and closing. This was clearly heard by all and then confirmed visually by Matt. With all of us downstairs and no exterior doors or windows being open, no rational explanation such as a draft can be made for this event.

During my earlier walk through in the downstairs front dining room, I encountered a lady who I perceived was dressed in old Victorian garb that included a fur muff and white ice skates. She told me how she loved to skate on the river. This was Not Emma – I've sensed her presence many times but this was someone different. There was also a small boy tied to this part of town who appeared to me in the same room. He said that he came from "down the street." Who he was, I cannot tell you. I don't think these other spirits really have anything to do with the old mansion itself but may have just sensed my presence and attempted to contact me. Many times when I'm "in the zone" or "open," spirits can sense this and gravitate toward me, even if it is not their usual domain.

I once again sensed the man whom I call George in the upstairs bar area. He was involved in banking in Middletown and seems to keep to himself in the adjacent Magnolia Room and the back bar. I suspect his is the clearly male voice that appears to say "Emma is here" recorded by John in the Magnolia Room several years ago. It was an interesting, eventful evening and we look forward to returning again in the near future and continue our quest to find out who or what haunts this lovely restaurant and former mansion in Middletown, Pennsylvania.

VISITING ALFRED'S

Anyone with an interest in ghosts and the paranormal would certainly relish a visit to Alfreds's. Even if you encounter nothing unusual during your meal, the quality of the food and service combine with Victorian charm to build a memorable experience. If considering attending one of the several haunted dining and other events John and I host throughout the year, we recommend making a reservation early as most of these sell out quickly. As Gettysburg, the site of the largest battle ever fought on the North American continent and a magnet for ghost hunters is only an hour away, anyone traveling to the region may want to include Alfred's on their list. As she has done for nearly the past 40 years, Emma will be glad to share her former earthly home with you for a few hours.

Alfred's Victorian is located at 38 North Union Street Middletown, PA 17057. The phone number is 717-944-5373 and their website is: www.alfredsvictorian.com

8. AN INVESTIGATION AT THE JEROME GRAND HOTEL

BY CHAD PATTERSON

In my 19 years as an active paranormal investigator I have investigated and researched well over one hundred cases involving claims of paranormal phenomena. As President, of the California Society for Ghost Research (CSGR), I have investigated a variety of haunted locations over the past seven years. Those places have included private residences, museums, ghost towns, cemeteries, theaters, hotels, other types of businesses throughout Southern California, Nevada, Arizona and a very small percentage south of the border in Mexico.

In the most recent seven years haunted hotels have emerged as one of my personal favorite locations to investigate for numerous reasons. Although being far from the easiest type of site to investigate, haunted hotels and motels have presented me unique opportunities to conduct research. Given the individual circumstances of the haunts themselves these locations will typically offer a variety of witnesses to paranormal activity. These witnesses can be employees of the location and include hotel maintenance workers and housekeepers, security guards, front desk clerks, cooks or chefs, gift shop workers, bar tenders and management. Often times, the accounts of patrons, claiming

a paranormal experience are documented online. Also, most often haunted hotels will offer historical value and are usually quiet in the wee hours of the morning after hotel restaurants and bars have closed. An investigator has a high probability of finding evidence of residual energy due to the large number of people checking in and out over the years for different purposes. Sometimes historical hotels where not always functioning as a hotel and were built for another purpose. For example, the *Queen Mary* in Long Beach served as fully functioning sea-going vessel before eventually being dry docked and becoming a hotel. There were claims of haunted activity existing on board before it became a hotel.

Fifty percent of the locations I have previously investigated with CSGR, had existing reputations for being haunted, but did not always turn out to be. Thus far, in my career as a paranormal investigator I have established top five lists for each type of location mentioned above where I have found paranormal activity to possibly exist. For hotels and bed and breakfasts, these locations have presented paranormal activity and a specific uniqueness to the type of activity within them. In no particular order these locations are as follows: In California, the Bella Maggiore B&B in Ventura, and of course the Hotel Queen Mary in Long Beach. In Nevada, the Gold Hill Hotel in Gold Hill and, in Arizona, the Hotel Lee in Yuma and the Jerome Grand Hotel, in Jerome Arizona.

Of these above-mentioned hotels, the Jerome Grand stands out as a unique location for paranormal research for reasons specific to the site. For one thing, the site had more than one public identity and was a former hospital before it became a hotel. For another, the site exists within one of the United State's largest and currently inhabited ghost towns. Third, the Jerome attracted a wide variety of human inhabitants while it was a booming mining town. Finally, more than one type of haunt exists within its walls.

On Friday April 24, 2009, members and officers of the CSGR ventured out of state to investigate claims of paranormal activity at the historic Jerome Grand Hotel. We came across the hotel in February of 2009 on the world-wide web and approached its paranormal claims, as we do all web-reported sites, with great skepticism. During this time we had no previous knowledge of the hotel itself and little information on the historic mining town. In the past I've spent quality time in numerous historical towns, both still inhabited and ghost towns alike, but did not recall any previous knowledge of the immense mining town Jerome had been. The more research we did on the location the more it intrigued us, but for the next two months of preparation we were unaware of the wealth of historical data and paranormal activity we had in store for us.

At an elevation of 5240 feet, the Jerome Grand Hotel, as previously noted, overlooks the largest inhabited ghost town in the western United States. At one point Jerome was claimed to have been the fourth-largest city in Arizona and now has a present day population of roughly 400 living residents. Today this hotel has much to offer potential guests, with comfortable accommodations, a spectacular view of the Verde Valley, a very hospitable and courteous staff, great steaks served in its Asylum restaurant and a wealth of Western U.S. history. For the modern day ghost hunter/researcher or paranormal enthusiast the hotel, of course, offers much more: an elevated probability of a paranormal experience.

Jerome, Arizona, began in 1883 like many Southwestern towns of the late nineteenth century, as a mining camp. It was named after Eugene M. Jerome, a New York investor who owned a majority of the mineral rights in the area during this time. The nearby United Verde Mine was the life's-blood of the fledgling town and would produce well over one billion dollars worth of precious ore over the span of several decades. By 1900 Jerome's population reached nearly 2,900. The United Verde Mine

Extension, an extension of the original mine would later be discovered and help propel the town's local economy through the year 1932. The United Verde Mine's body of ore was largely massive quantities of copper. Other precious metals such as gold and silver were also extracted from these sites.

During Jerome's prime the seeds of commerce were planted early like other successful mining camps that became towns. Entrepreneurs were establishing businesses offering goods and services. Prosperity boomed rapidly in Jerome and with little government resources available to manage the town's rapid growth Jerome became infested with crime. Prostitution and gambling were daily rituals for many of the miners and other inhabitants and Jerome became arguably known as "the wickedest town of the West."

The building that is today known as the Jerome Grand Hotel began construction as the United Verde Hospital in 1926, when the town's population approached nearly 15,000 inhabitants. The hospital opened its doors in 1927 and was considered state of the art for its time period. Many of the patients checking in to the hospital never checked out. Many tuberculosis patients went to Arizona seeking a dryer climate to ease their symptoms. It is said there were a great deal of TB patients treated at the hospital. It officially closed its doors in 1950, just before the last mine closed and Jerome's population declined rapidly to under 100 residents.

After its run as a functioning medical facility the United Verde Hospital sat vacant for the next 44 years. The building was maintained until 1971 in case it was needed again by the town. Its restoration began when it was purchased in 1994 and in 1996 it reopened as the Jerome Grand Hotel.

Since its construction this structure has housed and arguably stored a great deal of spent human energy within its walls. Examples of this energy, one may consider, would be the physical and emotional pain of hospital patients. One must remember medical procedures and treatments were far less painless at the time the hospital was in operation than they are designed to be today. Another form of considerable "spent human energy" would be the over-worked hospital staff tirelessly circulating the corridors attempting to maintain patient care. Also, once it became a hotel, one cannot exclude the continuous physical activity of hotel guests and staff.

CSGR members investigate the third floor of the Jerome Grand Hotel

During our CSGR pre-investigation research period I had read numerous reports of ghostly activity at the hotel. People have reported hearing the sounds of disembodied speech, coughing and yelling or screams from unoccupied rooms and corridors in the hotel. Also, there were reports of visual encounters with some of the hotel's ghostly inhabitants. One story in particular intrigued me: the famous lady in white who was said to circulate the halls of the upper levels of the building when it was a hospital. The origin of this individual was a little gray for the lack of a better term. Some reports read there had been apparitional encounters or sightings of the lady dating back to when the hospital was in business. These reports stated sightings were prevalent on the upper level where the hotel balconies are now located. Other reports claimed that the white-clad woman was a nurse from the former hospital. It is said that sightings of this entity ceased when the building reopened as a hotel in 1996 but some still claimed to see the apparition of a woman dressed in white near the elevator, which is original to the hospital's construction in 1926. This elevator is an area of particular interest since it was reported to be directly related to another ghostly inhabitant of the hotel, namely Claude Harvey, known as Scotty, a hospital maintenance worker in the mid-1930s, whose body was found pinned beneath this same elevator. His death was officially ruled an accident; however, there is speculation it may have been a homicide. It is speculated that Harvey was killed before his body came to rest at the bottom of this elevator shaft and that his accidental death was staged. His neck was said to have been broken and the only other physical injury to his body was a small scrape behind one ear. There was another report that Harvey had had jumped to his death. Reports of ghost lights in the elevator shaft, feelings of angry presences and audible phenomena have been said to have been witnessed on all levels of the hotel within proximity of this elevator.

Other deaths reportedly taking place at the hotel were of a man in a wheelchair reportedly falling from one of the balconies, a shooting, and a suicide by hanging. The hotel seemed to offer a great deal of potential for the possibility of capturing paranormal phenomena on video or still frame. Also, other paranormal research groups had claimed to have obtained evidence in the form of EVP from this location.

Members of CSGR scheduled to attend the investigation were CSGR vice president and web-master Don Neudecker, his wife and active member Virginia Neudecker, secretary Nancy Richling and active members Alma Engelsman and Lily Aragon. Also, attending the investigation was renowned psychic-medium Virginia Marco.

On the morning of Friday April 24, Don and Virginia Neudecker were the first to arrive at the Jerome Grand Hotel. Don would later describe to me that upon entering the hotel he felt an overwhelming or sickening sensation. This sensation was followed by slight dizziness and nausea. Don said he felt fine previous to his arrival at the hotel. For the record, Don is one of our most skeptical CSGR members. His approach to the paranormal has always been very scientific and cautious. I was certainly not going to take this information from him lightly -- especially when he felt he could not explain the physical symptoms he had experienced shortly after entering the hotel.

Psychic-medium Virginia Marco, accompanied by her husband, would be the next to arrive. Also, for the record, I would like to mention that Virginia knew nothing of the hotel's history or details of its ghostly lore. She was only aware the hotel had been reported as haunted, or why else would we have driven out from California? I have worked with Virginia Marco for almost ten years and can say she is absolutely the most gifted psychic-medium I have ever worked with. With a specialization in spirit releasing and communicating with the dead, Virginia's psychic gifts have helped to shed much light on cases with leads she has provided. The following is derived from her official psychic evaluation and report:

"...Inside the hotel we could feel, breathe in and, as a result, smell the energy from the past. I could immediately see why, when, right away, I noticed a lady in the lobby of the hotel. I could see her greeting all of us. She was curious about our presence there. I told this female spirit I would be

happy to listen to her story soon enough. She smiled at me..."

Virginia called me on my cell phone to confirm the hotel was haunted by multiple intelligent entities. She stated there were four spirit entities in addition to the residual energy haunting the location. Hearing this in addition to Don's previous testimony excited me as I approached Phoenix on my way to the hotel. Also, Don would later warn me, the road to the hotel itself, was very easy to miss in the dark. This was absolutely true as we passed it and had to double back in the dark.

Next to arrive that Friday evening was Nancy Richling, a member of CSGR for nearly eight years, and her nephew, Christian, our guest that weekend. Members Alma Engelsman, Lily Aragon and I would not end up arriving until around 1 a.m. on Saturday, April 25. Our official investigation was to be that Saturday evening.

Upon my arrival, I was eager to unpack my equipment and take in the hotel. I made two trips to our truck before settling in the room. I would like to confirm that staying at this hotel was like taking a step back in time. I personally enjoyed the décor and the numerous historical objects, such as an old switchboard and organ, posted stationary in the hallways of the place. While walking through the corridors to our rooms I felt a slight headache and very faint nausea and I remembered what Don Neudecker had told me. Once officially unpacked I spoke with the Neudeckers briefly about the rounds they had made that evening around the hotel. Nancy and her nephew had already gone to sleep in the adjoining room for the evening. We had reserved rooms 23 and 25, which were adjoining rooms, sharing a bathroom, on the second floor. The Marcoses were staying in Room 12 one level below. Alma, Lily and I did not wish to disturb Nancy, already asleep in Room 25, so we proceeded to lay sleeping bags on the floor, in the hallway, connecting the two rooms. The lights went out. About an hour into sleep I awoke and stared immediately down the hallway toward Nancy's room, which I was facing. For a brief moment I thought I may have seen a male silhouette standing there staring at me. The silhouette was similar to that of a shadow. I could barely make it out in the dark. The rest of the early morning I did not sleep well and would awaken on two more occasions before 6 a.m., but saw nothing but darkness and experienced nothing of the ordinary.

At dawn I awoke and prepared myself to meet the other CSGR members downstairs. It was about 10 a.m. by the time we all met for coffee and pastries, which the hotel provides free of charge in the mornings. Virginia Marco was sitting on a bench in front of the hotel waiting for me. It was then she began to describe the four resident spirits haunting the hotel.

Virginia described first the spirit of a thirty-nine-year-old male mainly occupying the second floor. He went by the name of Walsh. Walsh had blond hair, blue eyes and a long beard. His pants appeared to be beige and he was wearing some sort of long johns. Also, he wore suspenders and appeared to fit the physical description of a miner. His face was some-what dirty and, despite his relatively young age, it appeared weathered, causing him to look older. He had, what appeared to be, crow's feet in the corner of his eyes, which tended to squint. Walsh's demeanor was very serious and was not polite. Virginia stated he was impolite. When Virginia asked him what year it was Walsh's response was arrogant as he leaned his faced in close to hers and spelled out each number individually "1-8-9-9," he replied. He was very stand-offish as if we had no business being there. Virginia Marco showed no interruption of her professional exterior. She had communicated with countless entities, if not more over her life. It was going to take a lot more than a spirit's blatant rudeness to shake her demeanor.

The second spirit was that of another male. His name was Paul. According to Virginia Paul was also a miner, but dressed much better then Walsh. Paul wore dark pants and a long black blazer. Paul was 54 years old and his hair was white. He had a short white beard to compliment his already-white hair. Paul was the more polite of the two males. When asked, what year it was Paul replied, "1912."

As we finished our coffee Virginia gave me a briefing on the other two entities she had witnessed there at the hotel. She stated that the third and fourth entities were both female. The third spirit gave her full name as Maribel Garcia. Maribel was 35 years old and dressed in a long pink dress.

Chad Patterson and Virginia Marco share findings on the third floor of the Jerome Grand Hotel.

She was very feminine and very pretty. Virginia described her complexion as being very light colored with reddish-brown hair. Maribel did not tell Virginia what year it was at that present time.

The last and final entity was that of an older woman dressed in a white gown, a hospital gown with some sort of buttons at the top. She had been a patient at the hospital for some time, but Virginia did not have a year at this particular point in time. She stated her name was Patricia. She seemed very demoralized and very sad. She was the woman Virginia had seen downstairs in the lobby area.

After walking the entire hotel I had an idea of how we would approach the investigation. Since we had never actually set foot inside the location, I had to decide our actual approach onsite. The investigation would begin at roughly 930 p.m. We would break down into four pairs: Don and Virginia Neudecker, Virginia Marco and I, Nancy Richling accompanied by her nephew Christian, and Alma Engelsman and Lily Aragon. We would spread ourselves out on different floors. The areas under observation at this time would be our set of adjoining rooms 23 and 25, the hallway on the second level, the hallway on the third level and the top level. We would proceed to the bottom level at a much later hour due to many people still going to and from and making purchases from the gift shop, etc. Each group would switch levels at 15-minute intervals and give each team an equal opportunity to examine each area for evidence. During this phase of the investigation we would be taking still photos with Cannon Rebel Xti digital camera and hand-held Sony and Samsung digital cameras. We planned to take video with a handheld Sony Hi 8 and Sony digital handy cams with night shot. We would take EMF readings using the Tri-Field Natural EMF detector and the Fieldtester 200A, taking temperature readings with IR Thermometers, and recording infrared footage with a RAZ-R PRO thermo infrared camera recorder by FLIR. Also, during the night Don and Virginia Neudecker would be running surveillance of the hotel room with a surveillance camera system and laptop computer, of which they would review footage later. These cameras were strategically placed by Don to fully monitor both rooms 23 and 25 while we were away and throughout the night. After the first hour we would reconvene in Room 23 and decide where we should focus based on any possible similarities or distinguishable patterns we could determine based on readings, observations and photos that our pairs of CSGR members would collect. Also, during this first hour Virginia Marco would see what additional leads she might discover.

Beginning phase two we would look at what we had based on our present analysis and attempt to shift our direct focus to potential paranormal hot spots we experienced during phase one, taking additional camera footage in addition to EMF and temperature readings. At midnight we were to venture back to Room 23 and settle down for an EVP session. During our EVP session we would have cameras ready for video and still footage while I attempted to communicate verbally with the spirits. Also, at this time Virginia would call out to the spirits and ask them to be present as I attempted to ask a series of questions.

Upon ending the EVP session we would see where we were and make adjustments of where to take it from there.

The rest of the mid-afternoon on April 25 we spent venturing out to see Jerome during the daytime and visit nearby Sedona. During our time in Jerome we came to discover other businesses that were reported to be haunted. One was the Haunted Hamburger Restaurant, which I highly recommend to anyone who enjoys a quality hamburger.

Upon returning to the hotel around 7 that evening we begin preparing our equipment and spent some down time wandering about the hotel. Nancy Richling, Lily Aragon, Alma Engelsman and Virginia Neudecker went down to the front desk and gift shop. The gentleman at the front desk was very approachable and was very open about the history and haunted claims of the hotel. He told us he had not had many experiences himself, but did recall a night when the switchboard to an unoccupied room unexplainably lit up as though someone inside was making a call. Another gentleman at the front desk told us of one quiet evening he was working when the front doors had blown open as though heavy winds had pushed them apart. Those visiting the hotel will note the front doors are heavy and would not be blown open with ease. This gentleman was very hospitable and stated the doors stayed open a few seconds before they closed on their own. He noted that in his considerable time working at the hotel this was the only occasion this phenomenon happened.

Time passed and it was eventually 930 p.m. as we started our initial investigation. Virginia and I began in Room 23 while the others synchronized their watches and ventured out to the floors where they were scheduled to begin their analysis. I began taking EMF readings with the Tri-Field Natural EMF detector. While sitting stationary by the bed in Room 23, setting my meter to the sum setting, I did note two separate occasions the needle spiked in the 15 minutes I was watching it before our scheduled rotation. On one of those occasions the needle of the held at "3" for above five seconds before returning to "0." I noted this and prepared to move on to the outside hallway that awaited us on level three.

Between 9:45 and 10:00 p.m. I took EMF measurements in the hallway outside our hotel room at three separate points. Before group rotation would take effect and we would begin transition to the fourth level Virginia and I briefly discussed our present findings. Virginia stated to me that the spirits were all active and moving about the third and fourth levels of the hotel. According to her they were all aware of the fact we were there for them.

As Virginia and I walked to the stairs that led upward to the top floor of the building I was hit in the face with an overpowering whiff of urine. The phantom odor was strong and did not last long. The scent was within close proximity between the elevator and stairwell. It lasted about 15 seconds, dissolved and was gone. Shortly after this we were met by Lily and Alma who had been taking temperatures, still photos and video on the floor below. They told us there were still a few people going to and from the hotel restaurant and bar. Lily showed me a few suspect orb shots and her hand-held Sony digital camera, but it was tough to tell if the shots were dust or not.

A little after 10 p.m., we were on the fourth and top level of the hotel. I started taking random EMF measurements at different points. I did not notice any strange scents on this level. Virginia had detected there was not a great deal of patient activity on this floor. Also, there was something significant with the medical staff. The question that came to my mind was it possible the hospital doctors had their offices on this top floor level? This would have been the level with the most spectacular view. We made a side note of the observation, but later, after asking one hotel employee on duty, we could not determine if there was any truth behind this observation or not.

When phase one had ended we determined that the third level had the greatest amount of potential paranormal activity. It was on this level from which we had 90 percent of any potential EMF readings we gathered, and the Thermal Camera had read a few potential cold spots here, but none on the rest of the hotel during phase one. We continued to evaluate the third and fourth floor during phase two until midnight approached. We all proceeded back to Room 23 and found a quiet place to sit and make observations while I conducted our EVP session. Virginia called out to the four spirits and asked them to enter our hotel room. I would proceed to ask a series of questions as we would record with digital and analog audio recording devices. We would also have camera footage rolling. We turned out most of the lights and let the room settle into silence for the next two minutes. Then I began asking questions.

The following is derived from the report of Virginia Marco and represents an actual portion of the EVP session that took place during this investigation. The following questions were those that, according to Virginia's psychic evaluation, elicited a direct response from our ghostly subjects. They include the faint responses of the all four spirits in the room.

Question 1:"What is your name?"
 According to Virginia's report the Paul was the only spirit speaking right away.
Paul: "My name is Paul."

Question 2:"What year is it?"
 According to Virginia's report both male entities addressed this question. She told me Walsh stood very close from where I was standing, only a few feet away at this point.
Walsh (In a fast an authoritative manner):"1899!"
Paul (In a more calm tone): "1912."
Patricia (Speaking in a very sad and confused demeanor): "1921."

Question 3: "Are you here and if so why are you here?"
 Virginia stated Patricia, Walsh and Maribel spoke out.
Patricia: "Yes! I am here!"
Walsh: "Yep, Yep!"

Maribel G.:(Beginning to sob) "I have nowhere to go! I cannot get out!"

Question 4: "Can you tell me what year it is?"
According to Virginia she heard Maribel speak with concern in her voice.
Maribel G.: "I don't know what year it is."

Question 5: "Do you know where you are?"
 Virginia Marco stated all spirits responded.
Paul: "Yes! Yes! I was working for them."
Walsh: "Not for me."

Question 6: "Are you sick?"
 Virginia Marco stated the spirit Patricia, the hospital patient, began to speak in a sobbing voice.
Patricia: "I am sick, I am sick!"

Question 7: "Do you need a doctor?"
 Virginia noted only Patricia's response.
Patricia: "Up..Up! Upstairs...doctors..left after work...I saw them leave!"

Question 8: "Do you know you're dead?"
Maribel G.: "Yes, I am...It's been so long."
Walsh: "That's what you think!"
 (Virginia noted Walsh laughing out loud as he said this)
Paul: "Yes. I died here."

 Question 9: "Do you feel pain?"
Patricia: "I can't feel anything anymore...treatments...bad treatments."

Question 10: "Is there something you want to say to me right now?"
Patricia: "No medicine!"
Maribel G.: "I don't know."
Paul: "I miss my life."
Walsh: (Laughing hysterically) "How?"

Upon concluding the EVP session, the room felt slightly colder, as though the temperature had dropped a few degrees. We knew, when this night was over, we'd have much footage to view. After conversing with one another Nancy had stated she thought she was not alone in Room 25 where she had gone to station herself during the EVP session. I had stated there was one point when I was halfway through asking questions I felt I had someone standing directly in front of me. Virginia had told me it was Walsh who had approached me. Virginia also stated Paul had selected Don and was draining his energy in a sense. The sickening feeling Don was experiencing was due to the fact that Paul was close by.

After finishing with additional video footage and EMF and temp readings everyone had finally turned in between 1:30 and 2 a.m. We all left with the impression and belief this location was haunted. I, myself, was fully convinced. Virginia Marco's psychic evaluation and the handful of suspect EMF readings had me personally convinced based on my experience as a paranormal investigator. We only wished we had more time to spend gathering corroborative evidence. We examined the evidence for weeks after and were able to come up with a few potential orb shots, and possible EVP of feminine-sounding mumbling, but actual words were unclear. An example of this might be comparable to hearing a living person speaking through a wall and unable to tell exactly what they are saying. All I can say is no one in our group was speaking, but me during this EVP session. I would certainly welcome a follow up investigation to the Jerome Grand Hotel to revisit our newly acquainted ghostly inhabitants. Until then, I would recommend this location to the experienced and novice ghost hunter alike. I would recommend making sure one has at least two days to gather evidence. In addition, I would recommend running footage in one's hotel room while sleeping as one may be able to capture Paul or Walsh standing motionless in the dark room. Or perhaps one might hear the sobbing of Maribel or Patricia as they aimlessly roam the corridors of this historical hotel.

9. CAMP CASSADEGA
A TOWN FULL OF SPIRITS AND THE RESIDENTS WHO LIKE IT THAT WAY

BY DUSTY SMITH

When most people think of Florida, they see sunshine, beautiful beaches, fishing, NASCAR racing, vacation destinations such as Sea World, Disney World and Cypress Gardens, Spring Break festivities, Bike Week and lots of cool drinks and relaxation. There is however a good deal more to the state of Florida than those diversions. Being home to this country's first city, St. Augustine, there is more history and tragedy here than most people know or can even imagine. It all started with the Spanish crossing the Atlantic Ocean and building a fort in St. Augustine that they named the Castillo de San Marco.

Many brave soldiers and innocent civilians lost their lives in and around the Castillo throughout several different occupations of the fort. It changed hands from the Spanish to the English several times and now is a part of the National Parks Service where a guided tour -- or self-guided tour will take you back in time as workers dressed in period clothing reenact battles from days gone by and the daily 3:00 p.m. firing of the cannons.

Things have come a long way from those bygone days of musket balls, men patrolling the ramparts and cannon fire between two countries battling for ownership of the new land. Eventually the droves of people moving to the Americas would eventually spread far and wide into this great land we now know as the United States. While Florida is all of the aforementioned things, it is also home to a sleepy small town known as Cassadega.

Cassadega sits between Daytona Beach and Orlando along the I-4 corridor and those driving by who have never heard of it keep right on going either to the beach or the land of the famous mouse without thinking twice. Little do they know that this sleepy little town attracts millions of visitors each year from all over the world and is home to many spirits What's more, the residents prefer it that way. You see, Camp Cassadega is home to spiritualists who are trained to speak with those who have passed on and can communicate information from those on the other side to their still-living relatives.

The History of how it all Began:

The founder of Southern Cassadega Spiritualist Camp Meeting Association, George P. Colby, was born to Baptist parents in Pike, New York, on January 6, 1848. When Colby was eight years old, his family moved to Minnesota where, at the age of 12, he was baptized. This event changed the course of his life in an unusual and unexpected way. Once baptized, Colby began to show aspects of having

(Left) Photo taken of George P. Colby taken circa 1919 est. Photo courtesy of the Florida Memory Project. (Right) Photo of George P. Colby's headstone located in the Lake Helen/Cassadega Cemetery in Lake Helen, FL on Kicklighter Road. Photo by Dusty Smith

psychic abilities. He quickly became locally known for his clairvoyant and healing abilities. However his first experience with his newfound psychic abilities was the reception of a message that he would one day found a Spiritualist camp somewhere in the southern United States. In 1867 he formally left the Baptist church and became an itinerant medium visiting various Spiritualist centers. He made a living demonstrating his psychic skills. Like many mediums, he had several spirit guides who would channel knowledge to him; among them was a Native American who called himself Seneca.

In 1875 Senaca directed Colby to go to Wisconsin, where he would meet T.D. Giddings, another medium. The pair travelled by rail to Jacksonville, Florida, where they searched out a location that Senaca had described. Colby settled there, near a natural spring, and named the place Cassadenga after a small town near the Spiritualist community of Lily Dale, New York. Cassadenga is a Senaca Indian word meaning "rocks beneath the water." Some say this name was told to Colby by his spirit guide Senaca.

Colby's abilities became renowned so quickly that by the early 1900s people would flock from all over the country seeking advice and healing from this human wonder. He eventually set aside 43 acres of land for the camp so other mediums and psychics could live alongside the healing spring. He then built his own home near the spring. He had been told by his spirit guide to drink the water from this spring and inhale the smoke from small fires made of lighter knot (a pine sap-like substance) to cure his tuberculosis. He did this and lived to be 85.

Colby held regular camp meetings where he would minister to camp members and teach them how to "tap into" their spiritual side so that they would be able to communicate with the dead and heal others as he could. He is credited with writing several books, hymnals and courses on these methods. He also loved children. While he never fathered any, he and his longtime girlfriend had many children stay with them and adopted several over the years. The camp began to grow so quickly that Colby felt he needed some room to himself. He built a home some distance from the camp and had a hotel built for those visiting the area for healing or seeking their own spiritual path.

INVESTIGATION OF LOCATION ONE

The team for our initial investigation would consist of me, Chris Petry, D.J. Torres, Kevin Hare, John Diamond, Stacie Melewski, Kourtnie James and Frank Perrick. While Kourtnie and Frank could not join us on our first night, they would be with us for the remainder of the investigation. When we begin every investigation, we start by interviewing any witnesses to any purported activity. Then we take baseline readings of the area we are about to investigate and then decide what equipment is to be set up and who will be using and/or monitoring it. Logs are also kept either on an audio recorder or on hard copy to compare notes and findings once we are through. Then we're off to see what we can find.

Our initial investigation was at the foundation where George P. Colby's home once stood. The structure itself burned down twice but the foundation is still there. Kevin, John, Stacie, D.J., Chris and I climbed over the gate and walked down the long, dark, wooded pathway where we finally found the remains of what was Colby's home. We broke out our equipment and began taking photos, EMF readings, temperature readings and running audio. Since we had no power supply we were only able to use battery-operated equipment. There were a couple of EMF spikes that seemed to be connected to the location; as it is in the middle of the woods with no power lines, phone lines or any other modern day sources nearby that would make the EMF meter fluctuate in such a way. We would find out later that one of the EMF spikes corresponded to an EVP that Kevin captured on his audio recorder, as well as photos that produced a mist and shadows. The temperature and humidity remained a constant 74 degrees F and 22 percent humidity. We all felt as though we were not alone and upon examining her photos, Stacie would find that we indeed were not alone. As we were deciding who would climb the gate first, Stacie took a photo that produced a shadowy figure off to the right of us and the gate.

After Kevin listened to his audio recordings he discovered something very interesting. Kevin is about six feet, two inches and wears a size 3X shirt; he is no small man by any means. He asked, "Is there anyone here that would like to say anything to us?" A male voice immediately answered, "You're

(Left) This is a photo of an old metal building that sits on what was George P. Colby's property. Photo by John Diamond.

(Above) This is the original concrete slab marked with the date the foundation was poured: 2/28/1885. The odd coincidence was we did our initial investigation on 2/28/09.
Photo by John Diamond.

These are the series of photos taken in the one time home of George P. Colby while Kevin was using the dowsing rods and getting answers to his questions, DJ Torres was photographing the dowsing session and these unusual shadows formed. There also appears to me a small mist in the upper right hand corner of the first photo. (Note: we were asked by the current owners of this location not to disclose the exact address due to past incidents with vandals.)

fat!" To date this has to be the funniest and most interesting EVP we've captured. If that is not proof of an intelligent haunting, I don't know what is. It would later be noted that at the same time this EVP was recorded and an EMF spike occurred, Stacie took a photo containing a shadow by Kevin's right lower leg.

It was a nice night; not too cold and not too hot. Since Florida is famous for fog in the early morning and at dusk during the fall and spring people who live here are used to it. As a paranormal investigator you need to be aware of this fact as well. Since the temperature that night was only 74 degrees F and the humidity levels were only at 22 percent we all knew we had nothing to worry about as far as fog was concerned. So when we went through our photos and discovered several orbs -- generally associated with high humidity levels in Florida, and a strange mist that also corresponded with EMF spikes, battery drains and the EVP that Kevin captured, we were intrigued.

The only other evidence of note directly connected to George P. Colby was a group of photos taken at the home he built for his sister. This home also eventually became the home Colby shared with his longtime girlfriend, Pearl. These photos contained odd shadows between the camera and the investigator. They didn't have human forms, just odd shapes.

The dowsing rod session produced several answers to yes and no questions. At the end of every question we say, "If yes, please cross the rods." I will leave you with that knowledge so it is not repeated at the end of every question below:

Kevin: "Is there someone here that would like to make your presence known to us?"
Rods: Crossed for yes.
Kevin: "Are you the spirit of someone who used to live in this house?"
Rods: No response.
Kevin: "Are you one of the children that used to visit this house?"
Rods: Crossed for yes.

Kevin: "Do you know that your physical body is dead?"
Rods: Crossed for yes.
D.J. interrupts Kevin to let him know about the shadow she has seen on her LCD screen.
Kevin: "Do you know if there is someone else here with us now?"
Rods: Crossed for yes.
Kevin: "Do you know who it is?"
Rods: Crossed for yes.
Kevin: "Are you afraid of this person?"
Rods: Crossed for yes.

D.J. notes that the temperature around Kevin is dropping significantly. We are using a dual thermometer with a stationary base reading 78 degrees F and the 16 foot lead thermometer, placed near Kevin's feet, is now reading only 19 degrees F. Kevin feels the cold but continues asking questions.

Kevin: "Are you still here with us?"
Rods: no response.
Kevin: "Did the other person that was here scare you away?"
Rods: quickly cross, uncross and cross again.
Kevin: "It's okay, we're not here to harm you. We just want to communicate with you. Can you still cross the rods for us?"
Rods: no response.

After several more attempts by Kevin, the rods went cold and we decided it was time to move on. This was the end of night one in a three-night-long investigation.

HISTORY OF LOCATION TWO

When the Cassadaga Hotel opened in 1894 to be a home away from home for visiting spiritualists, psychics and mediums no one knew at that time that the hotel would eventually become home to several restless spirits. It does make sense that since mediums, psychics and spiritualists live, work and visit the area as well as tourists hoping to connect with departed loved ones on the "other side" that some of these spirits would find the Cassadaga Hotel to be a welcoming place. Some believe that the town of Cassadaga also sits directly over a vortex of energy that attracts and sometimes holds spirits to this plane. Until science can come up with a way to prove or disprove that theory we will just have to go by the fact that the Cassadaga Hotel and surrounding spiritualist camp have plenty of otherworldly residents.

The hotel is in need of renovation; it is not a four star hostelry by any stretch of the word. People who visit need to understand this fact. This is a place for people to go who want to get in touch with their spiritual selves, make contact with deceased loved or get away from it all. When I state "get away from it all" I do mean all. Each small room in the hotel gives visitors a good glimpse into the past -- the antique furniture, small beds, and the lack of televisions, radios or telephones brings guests from the present into the past very quickly. The management leaves at 8:00 p.m. and if you are staying there, you'd better not forget your room key. Once the doors are locked to the outside veranda, you cannot get back in without it. There is also no Internet service and cell phone service is

The Cassadega Hotel: Then & Now. Photo on left courtesy of the Florida Memory Project. Photo above by Dusty Smith.

intermittent at best. The bathrooms were added after a fire nearly consumed the entire hotel. Prior to indoor plumbing there were shared lavatories and an outdoor community shower. Many of the newly added bathroom facilities are very small with barely enough room to fit your knees between the toilet and wall. Most of the rooms have only a shower. The few that have tubs are a bit more pricey but if you enjoy a long hot bath as opposed to a standing shower where you need to bend down to get your head under the shower head it's well worth the extra money to spend leisurely time soaking in the old cast iron, claw foot tubs. There are no sinks in these small bathrooms; the sink is located in the main hotel room with a small medicine cabinet above it.

Almost every room in the Cassadaga Hotel boasts of having spirit activity in one form or another. There are the spirits of Alice Myers and her brother Arthur, Gentleman Jack, young sisters Sarah and Katlin, a cat that was a longtime resident of the hotel and reports of several other unknown and unnamed spirits. Some of these spirits have existed in the hotel for so long that many of the employees know their daily or nightly routines and can almost set their watches by their spirited activity.

While many visitors to the Cassadaga Hotel come to find their own family spirits--a few guests come to find the resident spirits of the hotel. The staff is generally open about the ghosts and doesn't mind sharing their own personal experiences if time permits; which was lucky for us when we began our investigation into the hotel's famous spirits.

One such worker was a dishwasher at the hotel several years ago. Prior to her employment there, she knew of a brother and sister who were employed at the hotel. Alice was a maid and her brother Arthur was a maintenance man. They were both hard workers and enjoyed their jobs. They also had the added benefit of being given room and board as part of their salary, which was a definite plus. They each had a small room on the second floor of the hotel in the staff wing, which they shared with many long time resident mediums. During this time it was rare to have overnight or weekend guests renting rooms on the second floor. Alice and Arthur would go about their daily work assignments and at the end of the day finish things off by having a good hot meal in the dining room. Arthur would cap off his night by having a couple of shots of gin from a bottle that he kept well hidden in his room as he knew his sister did not approve of drinking alcohol. After his nightcap, he would then descend the stairway into the lobby of the hotel and begin to play the piano for his sister, other workers and hotel guests. It was a nightly routine that made Arthur an almost famous fixture at the hotel.

No one seems to remember when or how Alice passed away, but they do know that she died before her brother Arthur. Since spiritualists believe that death is not an end but only a transition to another sphere of consciousness these kinds of details may not warrant remembering. But, whenever and however Alice passed away, she did die while still working and residing at the Cassadaga Hotel. Alice used to live in Room 19 and several guests reported while unpacking their belongings hearing a woman's voice say, "My name is Alice and I belong here." Some guests would become so unnerved that they wouldn't finish unpacking. They would stuff their belongings back into their suitcases and race down the steps and out the front door, never to return to the Cassadaga Hotel. It is said by many of the mediums at the hotel that Alice's spirit has since moved on and is now at rest but some guests claim differently. They say that Alice is still residing in Room 19 and she lets hotel guests know that she is present every chance she gets.

INVESTIGATION OF LOCATION TWO
PART A

The team members on site for the rest of the investigation of the hotel and surrounding area would consist of John, Stacie, Chris, D.J., Kevin, Frank, Kourtnie and myself. We would split up into groups and investigate as many locations in the hotel as we could since there were so many reports from so many different areas. We were hoping to get to all of them in the two nights we had in the hotel. John, Stacie, Kourtnie and I would head up to Room 19 where the reports of Alice were, while Chris, D.J., Kevin and Frank would remain downstairs in the hallway and see what they could find. There had been so many reports of Alice interacting with hotel guests that the hotel finally closed

Room 19; also known as Alice's room. Now used for storage. Photo by John Diamond.

The upstairs hallway of the staff wing at the Cassadega Hotel. Photo by John Diamond.

Room 19 to guests and it is and now it is used only for storage.

When we investigated Room 19 we found some interesting activity that may be related to the long-since departed Alice -- or not. EMF fluctuations were minimal. We got no temperature variations, but we did get a woman's voice on our audio recorders that seemed to say, "Alice." We didn't spend too much time in Room 19 as we had other spirits to find on our search this night. Our time was limited and the other spirits we would seek out on this night had produced many more numerous reports of recent activity. One final note on Alice, as we left the room one of my researchers, Stacie, had her shoulder touched, and since she was the last one leaving the room, I doubt she touched her own shoulder for fun.

As we were leaving the second floor, John noticed an entryway to the attic. He asked if it would be okay if he went up there. I told him that the owner gave us full reign of the hotel so I assumed it would be all right. John jumped at the chance and pulled the ladder down and climbed up into the dark and very musty attic. It was very noisy up there too. The combination air conditioning and heating unit was making a horrible racket. I got about half-way up the ladder when John started complaining about how hot it was up there. This being Florida, that would normally make sense, but, it was only 54 degrees F outside at this time as a minor cold front had moved through and the heat was running in the hotel. We also took into account the fact that heat rises. John pulled out his IR thermometer to find that it was 96 degrees F and climbing. He began asking questions with his voice recorder in hand. "Is there anyone here that would like to say something to us?" He then said to me, "Dusty, I feel like something is circling around me in almost a predatory way." I climbed a little bit farther up the ladder and poked my head into the attic. It was very dark, musty and hot. I could see the sweat pouring off of John. I told him he needed to get out of the attic and he did.

Upon listening to his voice recorder later that night he would discover that after he asked the one question a voice came back saying, "Get out! Get out! Get out!" It went on for a full two minutes and just as John had stated that he felt it was circling him, you could hear the voice moving farther away and then closer and again farther away and closer. It was a bit unnerving. None of the staff of the hotel ever mentioned anything about spirits being in the attic so we had no clue who it might have been. One thing is for sure, John is a retired professional wrestler and fit as a fiddle, for something to unnerve him to the point of not minding to leave an area was a first.

INVESTIGATION OF LOCATION TWO
PART B

Sarah and Katlin are two young sister spirits that reportedly reside at the Cassadaga Hotel. These active spirit girls still roam the halls of the hotel; playing, running and laughing their way through the afterlife. We were told that the girls are quite friendly with hotel guests and are always in a playful mood. Many hotel guests have reported seeing the girls dancing and running down the halls. They have been heard laughing and singing and on the rare occasion that another child is present in the hotel it seems they like to share that child's toys.

One of the hotel rules is that no children under the age of 18 are allowed to stay at the hotel unless accompanied by an adult. Even when accompanied by an adult, having children around is frowned upon. No children are allowed to stay overnight; at least that was the rule at the time of this investigation. Remember, this is a place for getting in touch with your spiritual side or for contacting the dead. Young children may not understand these concepts unless raised around them and the thought of actually speaking with the dead may not be a good experience for some children. With that stated, it is unclear why Sarah and Katlin were once residents of the hotel. It may be that their parents were part of the staff or they may have been a part of a spiritualist family that lived at or visited the camp in the early years. What is known is that the girls seem to have no idea that they are no longer among the living and they continue interacting with the living every chance they get.

As we were gathering up our equipment to head downstairs I decided to ask if the spirits of either of the young girls that are reported to still be lingering in the hallways of the hotel might be hanging around. I grabbed my dowsing rods and began to ask a few questions. At first I didn't get much, but then the rods started going crazy.

Dusty: "Is this the spirit of Katlin or Sarah?"
Rods: crossed for yes.
Dusty: "Is it Katlin?"
Rods: no response.
Dusty: "Is it Sarah?"
Rods: crossed for yes.
Dusty: "Is your sister here with us too?"
Rods: no response.
Dusty: "Is she somewhere else in the hotel?"
Rods: crossed for yes.
Dusty: "Is she in the lobby with Arthur?"
Rods: no response.
Dusty: "Is she in one of the guest rooms downstairs?"
Rods: crossed for yes.
Dusty: "Is she near our friends?"
Rods: crossed for yes.

Photo of bright orb in upstairs hallway. Taken by Stacie Melewski.

Dusty: "Is she trying to communicate with them?"
Rods: crossed for yes.
Dusty: "Is she with them now?"
Rods: crossed for yes.

The EMF meter began to get a reading of 3.2 mg and Stacie took a photo down the length of the long upstairs hallway. She got a very bright orb that we would later learn was directly above our members downstairs.

Just then Chris called us on the two-way radio and said they were using the dowsing rods in the downstairs hallway and were getting great results from Katlin! He proceeded to inform me that he just asked where her sister was and got the response of "On the second floor." He continued, "Then I asked if she could get her sister to come downstairs and talk with us too. How are you guys making out?"

"Well, we're up here talking to Sarah now," John informed him.

Dusty: "Sarah, are you still here with us?"

Rods: Crossed for yes.

Dusty: "Do you want to go downstairs and see your sister?"

Rods: Crossed for yes.

Right at that point the two rods went cold and Chris reported that they were getting answers using their dowsing rods from both Katlin and Sarah now. We rushed downstairs to meet up with the other half of the team and sure enough, the dowsing rods again were very active; as well as several other pieces of equipment. Our EMF detectors were jumping between 3.5 mg to 5.8 mg. The air in the long hallway suddenly went cold. It dropped from 81 degrees F to 63 degrees F in under two minutes.

The hallway on the first floor of the hotel is odd. It is very long and narrow and the floor is off center. When you are standing at the lobby end looking down towards the opposing end, it's almost like looking into a fun house. It makes many people queasy and some even hold onto the wall as they walk down it to their room. I wondered if this optical illusion might have something to do with the sightings; at least in this section of the hotel.

Chris was still asking questions with the dowsing rods while Frank had the parabolic dish set up and his headphones on. Frank said, "Did anyone just hear the heavy footsteps?" We all looked at him and shook our heads no. At that moment the dowsing rods stopped responding to Chris, the temperature returned to normal, the EMF detector went silent and all of us heard what sounded like heavy boots coming down the hallway. We started snapping photos, but got no results. Frank did capture the sound on his audio recorder that was also hooked up to his parabolic dish.

I was odd. It seemed like whoever made the heavy footstep sound frightened the young spirit girls away. We never did make further contact with them during the rest of the time of our investigation.

INVESTIGATION OF LOCATION TWO PART C

Our next investigation would lead us to search for Arthur and his famous piano playing. Arthur died shortly after his sister Alice; some say of a broken heart. But while there are disagreements over the fact of whether Alice's spirit is still present or not, there is no arguing that Arthur is still residing, working and playing the piano at the Cassadaga Hotel. Every evening, just as the kitchen staff is finishing up their final duties of the night, footsteps can be heard coming down the main staircase. Several years ago the dishwasher would

This photo was taken as the EMF meter was spiking. Photo by Frank Perrick.

Three different views of the hotel lobby. Photos by Stacie Melewski and John Diamond.

hear the footsteps coming down the staircase and purportedly met the spirit of Arthur, who was kind enough to bring her a shot of gin each night. She would always remind Arthur to be careful on the stairs and not to fall. This may be how Arthur died. It is said by some that he had gotten so drunk in his room one night after his sister's death that when he descended the stairs to get more liquor he lost his footing and upon tumbled down the stairway, broke his neck and died.

The claims of Arthur continuing his nightly routine intrigued our research group. We hoped to document his nightly ritual -- just as the dishwashers are finishing up their nightly duties -- hearing those footsteps coming down the main staircase. Possibly even seeing Arthur standing at the foot of the stairs with a shot glass of gin in his hand would be phenomenal. Or better still, if we could record the piano that still sits in the lobby of the beginning to play all by itself! Could it be the spirit of Arthur still entertaining the employees, guests and other spirits of the Cassadaga Hotel? We were about to find out.

Not only did this bright blue moving orb show up at the same time that Stacie took the photo after hearing the sound of a chair being moved, but the chair closest to the lobby was pulled away from the table and there appears to be a shadow on the upper right hand side of the photograph.
Photo by Stacie Melewski.

Frank, Kourtnie, Stacie, John, D.J., Chris, Kevin and I set up the equipment. We had two video cameras; one pointing up that infamous stairway and the other aimed across the lobby at the piano. We were armed with our standard equipment: EMF meters, thermometers, dowsing rods, voice recorders, cameras and I thought we'd try an old trick or two of mine. I laid out black plastic garbage bags sprinkled with flour to try to get the imprint of footprints in if Arthur actually did walk down the stairway. I also set out the anomometer to see if there was any wind source that may account for the sound of someone coming down the stairs. The fact that the outside doors are locked gave us the added security of no one being able to tamper with our equipment or evidence.

As we sat there quietly, snapping a photo here and there, we suddenly heard a sound coming from the stairway area. John jumped up and grabbed his EMF meter but found it was just noise coming from the kitchen which sat directly behind the wall to the stairs. The ice machine was chugging away and it sounded sort of like footsteps. Stacie also heard a sound like someone moving a chair in the small meeting room. She walked over and snapped a photo. Her EMF meter hit 4.1 mg and the thermometer we left in that area indicated the temperature dropped to 56 degrees F.

One of our team using dowsing rods near Arthur's infamous piano. Photo by Frank Perrick.

There were few guests in the hotel that night so we pretty much had the place to ourselves. It also made it nice that we didn't have to worry about people coming and going up and down the stairs or in and out of the door to the main lobby. We checked the flour and found no results but would leave it there and see if anything came of it later in the night. After what seemed like days we finally decided that we may have missed Arthur or that he was still upstairs drinking his own brand of spirits and that we should move on to the next location in the hotel.

I left Kevin, Kourtnie and Frank in the lobby to monitor the equipment there and keep an eye on things just in case a guest did manage to come in or go out this late. That way we would have a record of it.

INVESTIGATION OF LOCATION TWO
PART D

The spirit of a ghost that everyone calls "Gentleman Jack" apparently still resides at the Cassadega Hotel. Gentleman Jack's origins are a mystery. Some claim that he was a traveling salesman who frequented the hotel on his trips from the North through central Florida. Others claim that he was a gambler who traveled all over the South playing high stakes poker games. Others say he was just a man trying to get away from his nagging wife and who liked the solitude of the Cassadega Hotel. One thing that we do know is that Gentleman Jack is one of the most active spirits at the Cassadega Hotel and he is definitely a ladies' man! Gentleman Jack always rented the same room on the first floor. The room is now Room 10. During Jack's time the hotel wasn't as long as it is now. A fire destroyed most of the original structure and when it was rebuilt, the building was nearly doubled in length. The demand for rooms in the Spiritualist camp at that time were on the rise and the owners decided they would expand the building. When visitors of today rent Jack's room and encounter his spirit, he is only experienced through about half of Room 10. It is believed that this is because the rest of the room never existed in Jack's time. Could this be a sign or even proof of another intelligent haunting? We hoped to catch Jack on film or video and prove this claim.

Being the true ladies' man that he is, whenever women stay in Room 10 or even enter the room he makes his presence known. He will make a cold chill go through the part of the room he used to occupy and produce the smell of bay run aftershave, and even cigar smoke. But when women are not present, Gentleman Jack is nowhere to be found. Gentleman Jack is in no way threatening. He simply prefers the company of the ladies and besides making his presence known in the aforementioned ways it is reported that he also physically interacts with women by touching their hair, tugging on their clothing or even lightly touching their arms or shoulders. He is also reported to prefer blondes. Since we had enough female team members with varying shades of hair color, we would put this report to the test as well.

Gentleman Jack likes to hang out in the bathroom area of what is now Room 10 - one of the largest rooms in the hotel complete with a full sized bathroom and living room area. The bathroom in Room 10 used to be the bedroom before the fire that consumed the hotel. Since most of the bedroom area and all of the living room area were not in the original hotel, Gentleman Jack never passes that imaginary halfway point. While no one is sure of why Gentleman Jack is stuck here or chooses to remain behind at the Cassadaga Hotel, everyone who has experienced his presence agrees that he will remain an otherworldly resident for a very long time; or, at least as long as the ladies will keep him company from time to time. We were about to find out.

We began our investigation into Room 10 by having Stacie and myself sitting in the bathroom. John, Chris and Kourtnie would remain in the bedroom/living room area and we would all see if we could coax him out. We left Kevin and Frank watching over our equipment and flour scattered in the lobby/stairway area to make sure that no one staying in the hotel that night tampered with it.

We set a video camera up in the closet, which gave us the best wide and long shot of the entire room. The only portion of the room we couldn't get into the frame was where the hotel room door was. We didn't think this mattered as Gentleman Jack was said to never go that far into the room. We set up audio recorders in three locations: on the dresser, on the bed and in the bathroom on the small shelf above the sink. We placed EMF detectors next to each audio recorder and each of us was armed with a camera and thermometer. I also had a set of dowsing rods with me. I set my camera on the shelf over the sink next to the audio recorder and proceeded to begin the dowsing rod session. I sat on the toilet, lid closed of course, and while I asked questions, Stacie took photos and recorded the session.

Dusty: "Is there anyone here that would like to communicate with us?"
Rods: No Response.
Dusty: "Is the person known as Gentleman Jack here with us?"
Rods: No Response.
Dusty: "We are told that you like the ladies. There are two of us here. Can you make your presence know to us by crossing the rods I'm holding?"
Rods: Crossed for yes.
Dusty: "Is it Gentleman Jack that I'm speaking with now?"
Rods: Crossed for yes.
Dusty: "Do you know what year it is?"
Rods: Crossed for yes.
Dusty: "Is it 2009?"
Rods: No response.
Dusty: "Is it the early 1900s?"
Rods: Crossed for yes.

Dusty: "Is it 1939?"
Rods: Crossed for yes.
Dusty: "Is this when you stayed in this hotel as a guest?"
Rods: Crossed for yes.

Stacie stopped me at that point to tell me the temperature in the room was going up. We both thought that odd as the reports of interactions with Gentleman Jack always mentioned cold spots. The temperature in the room when we arrived and took our initial baseline readings was 78 degrees F and now it was going upwards of 89 degrees. I started back at asking questions and was getting no response whatsoever. I kept at it and began provoking Jack a little bit to see if I could get him to come back. I asked what brand of cigars he smoked were and if he could light one up so we could smell it. I asked about his cologne and if he wouldn't mind letting us smell that. I got nowhere. I finally said, "Well, if you're not going to continue speaking with us, then we're just going to leave." and something shoved my left shoulder making the dowsing rod fly out of my hand and almost into the next room. Stacie's audio recorder shut itself off, my camera fell off the shelf and into the sink and Stacie was shoved so hard that she almost fell onto the bathroom floor.

It was clear to me that it was not Gentleman Jack that we were now dealing with. I wondered if whatever or whomever it was that had made John feel so uncomfortable in the attic had followed us downstairs. The temperature continued to rise to 96 degrees F; the same exact temperature John had experienced in the attic. Chris informed me that the dowsing rod flying out of my hand were caught on video as she had been monitoring it. John and Chris were snapping photos the whole time but they produced no evidence of anything usable. When Stacie and John listened to their audio, both of them got two EVP's of the same voice. It sounded like the same voice from the attic and it again said, "Get out! Get out! Get out!" However this time instead of it sounding like it was circling it sounded like it was standing only inches from John and Stacie. I wondered why the two other voice recorders and the audio portion of the video didn't pick up the voice as it was so clear and loud on John and Stacie's recorders.

As some of us began to pack up and leave Room 10--John and Chris would be spending the night there along with Stacie on the pullout couch -- we decided that we needed to give Jack one last chance to make his presence know to us. I stood at that imaginary line and asked as sweetly and innocently as I could manage, "Jack, would you please come and at least say 'good-night' to me?" Just as I finished speaking the smell of cigar smoke permeated the room. The temperature began falling and when the audio tapes were reviewed a male voice replied just seconds after I asked the question, saying, "Shoe sweet lady." It was so clear it took my breath away.

We decided that since it was now 4:00 a.m. and we had been investigating since 7:00 p.m. the night before that we should get some badly needed sleep. We packed up the equipment and headed to the lobby to get Kevin, Kourtnie and Frank and check on what equipment we had left there. As we started down the corridor towards the lobby, Kevin met up with us. He said, "Dusty, I was just coming to get you. I was sitting in the lobby taking some photos and monitoring the equipment we left there when I heard footsteps coming down the stairway. I waited to see if it was one of the staff or guests staying upstairs and it wasn't. I heard the second floor door open and listened as the footsteps came down the stairs, across the hardwood floor into the lobby and stop right next to the piano! I waited a minute to see if it would start playing, but then the footsteps moved across the lobby and in front of me by the rocking chair. Then the rocking chair started rocking back & forth all by itself."

A photo of the rocking chair that Kevin saw rocking in the lobby. Stacie is taking temperature readings, while I am pointing out the EMF meter making noise on the opposing chair. Photo by John diamond.

I asked him if he checked the flour we left on the garbage bags on the stairs and he told me he didn't. He was so excited about hearing what he assumed to be Arthur that he didn't even think about it. He did leave Frank there to make sure no one touched anything until Kevin returned with me.

We all quickly headed to the lobby and began rewinding audio recorders and video footage. I was the first one to the stairway and noticed that there was what appeared to be shoe prints in the flour. They were not clear enough to come out in the photos we took of them, but, it did appear that Kevin had had an experience with Arthur. The shoe prints were about a size 11 man's shoe. I guess I had been a bit over zealous and used a bit too much flour. We could all physically see the definite imprints but none of the still cameras would pick the prints up. I was very disappointed with myself.

We packed up the equipment and headed to our rooms for the night. We hoped our next night would bring us some more definitive evidence than we had gotten that night. We still had a couple of locations to investigate and we were eager to do so.

INVESTIGATION LOCATION TWO
PART E

After a very short and restless night's sleep we all met up in the late morning for coffee and donuts. Frank who is used to being up at 5:00 a.m. was up at the crack of dawn. It wasn't because he has an internal alarm clock, though. It seems that during the night the spirit cat that is claimed to be roaming the hotel jumped up in the bed with him. Since Frank has a pet cat he knows the feeling of when they carefully get into bed and curl up in the small of your back. He said that it bothered him so much that he couldn't get back to sleep and just thought he'd stay up and ask the desk clerk about when she arrived at 8:00 a.m.

The desk clerk began to tell Frank that Room 3 is host to another interesting and longtime resident spirit. Many years ago a stray cat showed up and took up residence at the hotel. No one seemed to mind and the cat quickly became a fixture of the hotel. He would wander through the hotel meeting and greeting guests--all to get a good petting and possibly a free bite to eat. He would lazily sleep in the sun on the veranda when he wanted warmth and when the weather turned sour, he would find a cozy place to rest in the lobby.

She continued that there have been many reports from guests over the years seeing this phantom feline in several locations throughout the hotel. Many people see him lying on the ledge of the veranda in the bright morning sunlight when they are exiting their hotel rooms on the veranda side. Once they turn and lock their door and turn back to see the sweet kitty blissfully resting on the ledge, he is no longer there. When they ask one of the hotel employees where the cat has gotten off to they are always told that the cat is no longer among the living. Similar sightings have been reported in the dining area, lobby, second floor hallway and front porch, all with the same results; the kitty is not really there; he's only there in spirit.

There have also been reports similar to Frank's experience of couples sleeping in Room 3 that are woken in the middle of the night to the feeling of a cat jumping up onto the bed. He will walk across the mattress and curl up between the two people, snuggling into the small of their backs. When one or the other person wakes up to see what just happened, there is no cat or anything else in the bed. In the morning when they ask the staff about a cat being in Room 3, they are told that the spirit cat frequents that room and likes to cuddle up with the living while they sleep. This phantom feline and Room 3 would be our next hunt for our investigation.

There have also been numerous reports of the doors on both sides of that room unlocking, locking and opening by themselves. This includes the screen door on the veranda side of the room. There is one exterior door on the veranda side and the other opens up into the hallway. People will leave the room, pull the door closed tightly and turn the handle to make sure it is locked and when they return they find it is now either unlocked or completely open. The screen door closes so tightly that you almost have to fight with it to get it to open. Some guests don't mind this type of activity as it is like playing a game with a spirit that seems to enjoy doing it. However others are not so amused by it; Frank was one of them. I guess I can agree with the fact that if you have $3,000 worth of equipment sitting in your room, you expect some measure of security. If this class clown ghost does away with that comfort zone I can see where someone could get upset about it.

We set up infrared cameras in Room 3 and video on the veranda side of the hotel in hopes of catching the kitty and the class clown ghost opening the door. I badly needed coffee, which I had given up drinking, but because I had such a restless night of sleep I decided it was time to begin drinking it again. Apparently no one bothered to warn us that in Room 9 there is also activity. Kourtnie and I shared the room that night and just as I was about to fall asleep, my blanket slowly pulled back from across my body. I opened my eyes just in time to see it slipping down to around my knees. I whispered, "Kourtnie, are you still awake?"

"Of course I am. What are you doing over there?"

"I'm not doing anything. Something or someone just pulled my blanket down."

"All I hear is heavy, wheezing breath sounds. That's not you?"

"No, it's not me. I haven't fallen asleep yet. I used my asthma inhaler and I don't snore. Do me a favor, lay there and pretend you're sleeping and watch my blanket for me."

"Sure."

We both lay there patiently for what seemed like an hour and then it happened again. My blanket started slowly pulling back off my body from my shoulders down to my knees. I asked Kourtnie, "Okay, did you see that?"

"Oh my god dude, that was so cool! Let me get the camera out."

It happened twice more over the course of the next hour or so. Every time I would lay down and just start dozing off to sleep, my blanket would be slowly pulled down.

Kourtnie continued to take photos but got no evidence of whatever it was that was messing with me and my blanket. I even tried tucking it under the mattress and it would still happen. Around 6:45

Frank caught the screen door to room three opening by itself while he sat on the veranda early in the morning. Photo by Frank Perrick.

a.m. I finally gave up and said, "Look, if you want my blanket so badly, take it, just let me get a little sleep." I tossed the blanket to the end of my bed and laid back down. Kourtnie sat up watching me for a while but she also finally fell asleep. When I woke up, my blanket was up around my shoulders once again. I don't know if I did it in my sleep, or, if my blanket thief decided to put it back.

One other thing that bothered me about our room was there was a creepy-looking small door under the sink. It looked like the troll door in Stephan King's movie, "Cat's Eye." Kourtnie and I tried to figure out what this little door was for and discussed it at length on our drive to get coffee, but we never did figure it out. We opened it and it smelled musty and was dark, but there was nothing in there that we could see--even using a flashlight.

After reviewing the video tapes from Room 3 and the veranda, we didn't catch our phantom feline but we did manage to catch the class clown ghost as we had come to call him--or her. Three different times the door to the room would slowly open about a foot and then slowly close again. Not all the way, but just enough so that you could see the door had been tampered with. The bathroom door also opened at one point on the video in the same exact manner. Frank was sitting on the veranda at one point when he looked over and watched as the screen door opened by itself.

We walked around the town a little in the late afternoon before having dinner and starting our final investigation. There are many quaint small houses from the Victorian era, a bookstore, and the church--which boasts a séance room. The mail is still delivered by a postal worker on horseback. We

Spirit Pond as it looked while we were investigating Camp Cassadega. Photo by Frank Perrick.

visited the area known locally as Spirit Pond. Many spiritualists over the years have had their ashes thrown into the pond after being cremated and that may explain part of the reason why it looks more like a mud hole than a pond now. It is claimed that many, many spirits hang out near Spirit Pond and during the early evenings it is one of the most active places in the camp.

As we came back up the street on the veranda side of the hotel, I noticed a cat sitting on the ledge of the veranda right in front of us. Frank quickly broke out his camera and took several photos. Kourtnie said, "Here kitty-kitty. Meow." The cat raised its head, flicked its tail, turned and jumped off the ledge. We walked as fast as we could to the direction in which the cat had gone but when we got there it was nowhere in sight. After developing the photographs I was shocked--the cat that we all saw was not in them!

After eating dinner we took a short nap and got ready for the long night ahead of us. Our final investigation would be of portions of the camp itself and we would close out the night by doing a table tipping session to see if we could communicate with any of the spirits that way. We grabbed

This photo was taken of the veranda where we saw the cat sitting on the ledge. Notice that there is no cat in the photograph.
Photo by Frank Perrick.

our hand-held equipment and headed down to Spirit Pond first. Upon arriving we noticed several things that would make our investigation difficult to say the least. While the 'pond' had some water in it, it was way below its usual level and we would have to be careful where we walked as the mud-- better known as marl in Florida--is like quicksand. The other problem was the humidity was up higher that night--it was about 38 percent-- and the proximity of a water source always gives the possibility of moisture orbs on our photographs.

We stayed for about two hours and got no results. Nothing on audio, video or EMF. No temperature fluctuations and the only photos we managed to get were either mosquitoes, moths, moisture droplets or other questionable sources. We decided it was time to head to the Meditation Garden. This is a small area directly across from the hotel and down a stairway. There were benches, a water fountain and plenty of landscaping to make even the most stressed-out person able to relax. Frank and I sat next to one another on a bench--Frank, ever armed with his parabolic dish, me with my camera and dowsing rods and I began to ask questions.

Dusty: "Is there anyone here that would like to communicate with us?"
Rods: Crossed for yes.
Dusty: "Are you a man?"
Rods: Crossed for yes.
Dusty: "Did you once live in this town?"
Rods: No response.
Dusty: "Are you here to communicate something to a loved one?"

Rods: Crossed for yes.
Dusty: "Do they know you're here?"
Rods: No response.
Dusty: "Is there someone here that can help you?"
Rods: Crossed for yes.
Dusty: "Is it one of the readers at the hotel?"
Rods: No response.
Dusty: "Is it one of the readers who live here in town?"
Rods: No response.
Dusty: "Is it someone here with me?"
Rods: Crossed for yes.
Dusty: "Is it Frank?"
Rods: No response.
Dusty: "Is it Kevin?"
Rods: No response.
Dusty: "Is it me?"
Rods: Crossed for yes.
Dusty: "Do I know you?"
Rods: Crossed for yes.
Dusty: "Are you one of my family members that have passed?"
Rods: No response.
Dusty: "Are you one of my friends that have passed?"
Rods: Crossed for yes.
Dusty: "Did you pass within the last five years?"
Rods: No response.
Dusty: "Did you pass within the last ten years?"
Rods: No response
Dusty: "Did you pass within the last fifteen years?"
Rods: No response.
Dusty: "Did you pass within the last twenty years?"
Rods: No response.
Dusty: "Did you pass within the last twenty-five years?"
Rods: Crossed for yes.
Dusty: "Did I know you when I was growing up in New York?"
Rods: Crossed for yes.
Dusty: "Will you come with us to the hotel and speak with me more during a table tipping session?"
Rods: Crossed for yes.

Frank and I grabbed our equipment and headed across the street as quickly as we could. We sat at the heavy oak table in the lobby with the other team members. John, D.J., Kevin, Chris and Kourtnie would monitor the video camera and audio equipment.

We started the session by each of us protecting ourselves in our own way and then meditating for several moments. We hooked our feet behind the chair legs with our knees bent in so no one would accidentally move or bump the table. We then envisioned energy going from one to the other around the table and from us into the table. We began by asking if anyone was with us to please move the table. We told them they could move it from side to side, back and forth or in a circular motion--whatever they were most comfortable with. It took only a matter of seconds before the table began moving. It started out relatively slowing, rocking back and forth between John and me. (We were sitting opposite of one another) I asked, "Is this the same person that was speaking with me outside? If so move the table towards me for yes and toward John for no." The table moved towards me.

"Is there some way you can tell me who you are?"

The table moved towards me again for yes. "Thank you. Please move the table back to the center."

Kourtnie brought over a pencil and piece of paper and handed it to me. "Can you help me by using me to write a message?"

The table again moved towards me for yes. "Thank you. Please move the table back to the center." I held the pencil lightly in my right hand while Kourtnie held the paper. I began writing a name: Salzburg. At first I couldn't think of where I knew that name from and then it hit me. Frankie Salzburg lived down the street from me when I was a child growing up on Long Island. "Is this you Frankie?"

The table moved towards me for yes. "Thank you. Please move the table back to the center. I didn't know you had passed on. Was it after I left home?"

The table moved towards me for yes. "Thank you. Please move the table back to the center. I know you were in the service. Did you pass that way?"

The table moved towards me for yes. "Thank you. Please move the table back to the center. "Was it during the end of the Vietnam War?"

The table moved towards me for yes. "Thank you. Please move the table back to the center." Just then John said he heard someone whispering in his ear. Stacie said she felt someone touch her and Kevin was getting a headache and felt nauseous. "Are more than one spirits here with us now?" I asked. The table rocked back and forth almost violently for nearly three minutes. John asked if it was the girls playing with the table and when he played his audio back he got an EVP that said in a female child's voice, "Hi, John."

We kept at the table tipping session for nearly four hours and by the time we were done we were all exhausted. It seems that spirits really do use our energy to manifest themselves. We closed the circle protecting ourselves once again and headed off to our rooms for what was left of a long night.

After reviewing all of our evidence from our investigation we had little to show on still photos, dozens of EVPs that corresponded with temperature fluctuations, EMF spikes or physical interactions. We had some evidence on video that cannot be explained and as with most investigations, our personal experiences were nearly too many to list. We had a wonderful time investigating the hotel, town and founder's home and hope to do so again soon as the spirits of the Spiritualist camp never seem to disappoint.

 No matter what your reason for visiting the beautiful sleepy little town of Cassadaga--whether it be to get in touch with your spiritual side, speak to a departed loved one or just relax in the peaceful atmosphere--one thing is certain, you won't be disappointed by the hosts and ghosts who greet you, entertain you, and keep you on your toes, at the Cassadaga Hotel.

10. A QUIET COURAGE
DEATH IN GOLIAD

BY PETER JAMES HAVILAND
A.C.C.H.

Growing up in Texas has brought me a lot of understanding to the words of pride and honor. I was too young to understand those words when I lived in Maryland, and having walked the humbling Civil War battlefields of Manassas and Gettysburg these were just history lessons for a young kid. Then in 1979 things changed and I moved to Texas. The only thing I really knew about this state was that it was the land of cowboys, Indians, the Alamo, and Roger Staubach. I also remember carrying my Texas history book with my right arm in a sling when I started class, but not only did I learn a lot about what makes The Lone Star State so BIG, but I had a hell of a bicep growing from toting that fifty-pound monster of a book to and from class. Years later I had the unique honor of walking on true hallowed ground on an investigation in 2000 at a small town named Goliad, and at a mission called Presidio Nuestra Senora De Loreto De La Bahia, The Presidio La Bahia. Some call it Fannin's Folly, some call it Santa Ana's Blood Bath, but a truer measure of courage could not have shown so brightly, and added to the legends that Texans talk of.

On October 17, 1835, defiant Texans in the tiny hamlet of Gonzales, east of San Antonio, fired a small cannon at the advancing Mexican forces hell bent on retrieving the weapon that had been

loaned to the village by the Mexican army in 1831 for use against Indian attacks. Santa Anna had proclaimed himself dictator of all Mexico in 1832, and he decreed that all foreigners be removed from Mexican soil. With the increasing unrest running through the countryside, Gonzales residents weren't about to surrender the cannon. "Come and take it," they taunted, as they set off a charge of old rusty chains, scrap iron and nails that would lead to blood-soaked battles of the Alamo on March 6,

1836, and to the inhumane Goliad massacre two weeks later. Ironically, it would also lead Francisca "Panchita" Alavez, a Mexican army captain's wife to rise up and become the "Angel of Goliad," the only recognized Mexican heroine in the Texas Revolution.

The last three months of 1835 and the early part of 1836 were times of great triumph and horrific tragedy for Texas. The Texan army had captured the great stone presidio of La Bahia at Goliad in October, ousting more than 160 Mexican soldiers in the process, and right after this important military victory; the capture of San Antonio

La Bahia at Goliad

in December hit the Texan forces like a bucking mule to the gut. February's cold winds found Colonel William Travis laboring to make the Alamo defensible, while Colonel James Fannin and his volunteer army, made up mostly of farmers from Georgia, worked to improve La Bahia. It was no secret that time was not on their side, as Santa Anna was on the march with more than 8,000 men at his command, an agenda that would scare the most seasoned of men.

General Antonio Miguel de Lopez de Santa Anna de Perez de Lebron wasn't worried about the 400 men commanded by Fannin at La Bahia because he was more concerned about regaining San Antonio, as that city was he considered the gateway to America. Taking most of his army northward, he sent General José Urrea, with infantry and cavalry brigades numbering approximately 1,200 men, to march south along the Texas coast to quell the insurgents of La Bahia. One of the officers in General Urrea's command was a handsome young captain from Toluca named Telesforo Alavez. Captain Alavez, as was the custom of Mexican soldiers of the time, took his wife Francisca to war with him.

Francisca Alavez, or Panchita as she was affectionately called, first came to the attention of Texans four days after the Alamo fell to the Mexican army. As General Urrea marched along the seacoast conquering all pockets of resistance, he stopped his progress in San Patricio, west of Corpus Christi, on March 10th to rest his troops and bury the dead.

He still sent out patrols, just to be cautious, and when they returned with prisoners, he'd have them sent off to Matamoros as prisoners of war.....until a scout rode up with orders straight from Santa Anna: All prisoners would be executed!

Father John Thomas Molloy, the presiding official over the burial of both the Mexican and Texan dead at San Patricio, warned Urrea that it would be an un-Christian act to murder the men, thus he threatened to hold no more Masses if the barbaric orders were carried out. Panchita joined in, the argument urging her husband to intercede. Reuben Brown, who was captured in an ambush at Agua Dulce Creek on March 2, wrote that his life was spared only because of the intervention "of a priest and a Mexican lady named Alvarez." Brown's account, published in the 1859 *Texas Almanac,* is

Colonel William Travis

probably the reason Panchita Alavez's name has always been misspelled and is still spelled Alvarez.

Eight days after the Alamo battle, Urrea's forces swarmed the half-ruined walls of Mission Nuestra Senora del Refugio, just 25 miles south of Goliad. The Texan army fought till they exhausted their ammunition and were forced to retreat into the woods under cover of darkness, Urrea's army managed to hunt down and kill nearly all the hundred-odd Texans, men who were Fannin's front line of defense for La Bahia. Several survived and made it to Goliad to warn Colonel Fannin that the Mexican army was on the move from the south.

The great stone presidio of Nuestra Senora de Loreto along with the mission of Nuestra Senora del Espiritu Santo de Zuniga were called La Bahia, meaning the bay or harbor because they were originally built in 1722 on Espiritu Santo Bay, which is now modern Matagorda Bay. Although having moved 25 miles inland in 1749 to their present site on the south bank of the San Antonio River in Goliad, they retained the name and were the strongest defenses ever built by the Spanish in Texas. The fortress had walls ten feet high and three feet thick, enclosing more than three acres of ground atop a rocky hill. Eight cannons, shipped up from Veracruz, covering every possible direction From its defensible hilltop location, it was a key military structure, and whoever held it controlled the supply lines to San Antonio.

General Sam Houston sent Colonel Fannin orders on March 11 to fall back to Victoria, 25 miles east of Goliad, but Fannin made the fatal mistake of awaiting the return of many soldiers in scouting parties, men who had already been captured by Mexican troops and were unable to escape their captures. March 18 came and Urrea's cavalry was now on the horizon.

Colonel Fannin planned a retreat that night, but the movement didn't commence until the next day, disregarding General Houston's orders to sink the surplus artillery in the river, Fannin insisted on taking the nine brass cannons and 500 spare muskets with him, and unfortunately. no rations of any kind for his men.

On a beautiful, open prairie about ten miles east of Goliad, the Colonel halted his men. If he had continued on a few more miles, he would have found water and the protection of trees, and it didn't take long for General Urrea's seasoned troops to surround the inexperienced band of Texan volunteers.

By all accounts, it was a long afternoon, and the smell of gunpowder and blood weighed heavy in the air, at nightfall, nine Texans lay dead and 51 were wounded. Many of the uninjured could have escaped, but their pride and resolve made them remain with their fallen comrades, not trusting the mercy of the

Colonel James Fannin

Mexican army after what had happened at the Alamo. The punishing March heat dehydrated them, and all night long the wounded cried for water that was just not there. At daybreak Urrea ordered a shelling of the shallow, makeshift trenches with 12-pound cannon fire. Fannin and his men then contemplated surrender.

Under a white flag of truce, Fannin sent for parley; if they were to be executed like the defenders of the Alamo, then they would fight to the last man, but if they were granted honorable treatment as prisoners of war, they would lay down their weapons. Urrea told Fannin that he felt sure he could convince Santa Anna to grant the Texan command the honorable terms of war, which meant transporting them to New Orleans with a warning to never to return to Texas. He presented Fannin with a surrender document, which Fannin then signed. Fannin surrendered at discretion, to use the term of the day, with the understanding that his men would not be executed. The Texans reluctantly laid down their arms and marched back to Goliad where they were confined as prisoners in La Bahia, believing they would soon be going home to work the fields and rejoin their families.

For one week they languished as prisoners while Urrea continued his march eastward, being joined by more and more prisoners captured by Urrea's campaign. They were also joined by some 80 Tennessee volunteers under Major William Parsons Miller, who were captured at Copano Bay while they were celebrating the end of a voyage on the ship William and Frances from New Orleans. Having been cooped up for 21 days, the Tennesseans jumped into the bay and as they were swimming ashore, the Mexicans snagged them.

Since they were not carrying any weapons, they were not violating the Mexican decree that any foreigners found bearing arms would be treated as pirates and executed. Colonel José Nicolas de la Portilla used this reasoning to avoid killing them, but bound them tightly with rawhide thongs for good measure.

The thongs soon dried and tightened, cutting off circulation; causing great pain and suffering to the captives as they were left for hours in the heat without food or water. The men suffered immeasurably, as they marched to La Bahia. Panchita, taking every opportunity to aid the prisoners, was absolutely horrified when she saw their condition. She ordered their bonds cut and food and water to be given to them immediately. She felt compassion for the stricken men and fussed over the captives as if they were part of her family.

La Bahia was to be a nightmare for all prisoners. In one room of the presidio, more than 400 men were crammed together so tightly that there was no space in which to lie down. Modern visitors can still see the room as it was then. It was Panchita, however, who persuaded Colonel Portilla to let the captives out into the courtyard for exercise and fresh air, and she also persuaded the Mexican commander to provide food and medical treatment. When the Tennessee prisoners arrived, she convinced Portilla to send them on to Matamoros, since they had arrived on Texas soil without weapons and had not fired a shot against the Mexican army. Panchita's compassion is credited with sparing the Tennessee regiment from the slaughter that followed.

Urrea, still marching east, had written Santa Anna about the terms of the honorable surrender he offered Fannin, but in answer to Urrea's letter, Santa Anna ordered immediate death to the "perfidious foreigners." Reading Santa Anna's response, Urrea ignored the orders and intended to honor his agreement with Fannin. He then sent Colonel Portilla instructions to treat the captives with consideration. Unknown to Urrea, Santa Anna had sent Portilla another order to "execute the prisoners in your hands at dawn." So, on Palm Sunday, March 27, 1836, when the prisoners at La Bahia were roused from sleep and ordered outside to form three columns, they all believed they were going home. When she learned what was about to take place, Panchita managed to smuggle several captives through the lines to the river before being stopped. She then pleaded so effectively with Colonel Francisco Garay that he spared 20 of the men who were doctors, interpreters, nurses, and mechanics. Garay, who would later become a great man in Mexico, was so revolted at the barbarous orders that he had resolved, at great personal risk to himself, to save all that he could.

Panchita didn't stop her pleas to Colonel Garay. Sneaking Texans by ones and twos, she managed to hide about two dozen on a parapet of the fortress. She pulled fifteen-year-old Benjamin Franklin Hughes, a young boy already in the ranks, into her care, and when a Mexican soldier objected, she said she needed the youth for only a few moments, and then spirited him out of sight. Hughes, who had been Fannin's drummer boy, tried to return, but Panchita wouldn't let him. He lived to become a prominent citizen of Dallas. It was he who called Panchita the "Angel of Goliad."

The men were marched out in separate divisions, under different pretexts. Some were told that they were to be taken to Copano, in order to be sent home; others that they were going out to slaughter cattle; and others that they were being removed to make room in the fort for Santa Anna. Dr. Shackleford, who had been invited by Colonel Guerrier to his tent, about a hundred yards southeastwardly from the fort, wrote: "In about half an hour, we heard the report of a volley of small-arms, toward the river, and to the east of the fort. I immediately inquired the cause of the firing, and was assured by the officer that ' he did not know, but supposed it was the guard firing off their guns.' In about fifteen or twenty minutes thereafter, another such volley was fired, directly south of us, and in front.

At the same time I could distinguish the heads of some of the men through the boughs of some peach-trees, and could hear their screams. It was then, for the first time, the awful conviction seized upon our minds that treachery and murder had begun their work! Shortly afterward, Colonel Guerrier appeared at the mouth of the tent. I asked him if it could be possible they were murdering our men. He replied that ' it was so; but he had not given the order, neither had he executed it.' "

In about an hour more, the wounded were dragged out and butchered. Colonel Fannin was the last to suffer. When informed of his fate, he met it like a soldier. He handed his watch to the officer whose business it was to murder him, and requested him to have him shot in the breast and not in the head, and likewise to see that his remains should be decently buried. These natural and proper requirements the officer promised should be fulfilled. So Fannin seated himself in a chair, tied the hand-kerchief over his eyes, and bared his bosom to receive the fire of the soldiers. Later it was found out he was shot in the head and left in the open field.

As the different divisions were brought to the place of execution, they were ordered to sit down with their backs to the guard. In one instance, a man named Fenner rose to his feet, and exclaimed, "Boys, they are going to kill us—die with your faces to them, like men!' At same moment, two other young men, flourishing their caps over their heads, shouted at the top of their voices, ' Hurrah for Texas!' "

Many attempted to escape; but most of those who survived the first fire were either cut down by the pursuing cavalry or afterward shot. It is believed that, in all, 27 of those who were marched out to be slaughtered made their escape; leaving 330 who suffered death on that Sunday morning.

When Urrea learned of the slaughter, he was greatly outraged and mortified, placing in his diary that `I never thought that the horrible spectacle of that massacre could take place in cold blood....' Shackelford later escaped and returned to his home in Alabama. His account is probably the most complete and most reliable of the Goliad massacre.

When Panchita found William Hunter, a volunteer from Missouri, left for dead with bullet and bayonet holes in his body, she dragged him to the San Antonio riverbank, concealing him among the grasses and reeds while she dressed his wounds. Mexican soldiers later came upon seven other men who escaped the massacre, killed three, and took the other four prisoners to Victoria, where Captain Alavez had been reassigned. While lining them up before a firing squad, Panchita dashed out and placed her body in front of the doomed men. Her bravery prompted another Mexican woman to join her. Refusing to move, the two women forced the execution to be canceled.

The Lone Star State would never be the same after Goliad. The slaughter outraged Americans everywhere, and it was Santa Anna's Waterloo. Although he had executed American invaders at Tampico in 1835, and Americans didn't react, his brutal executions of these men who had surrendered as prisoners of war only encouraged American support. If the Alamo was cruel and heartless, La Bahia was barbaric. All across the United States, volunteers and money headed for Texas.

"Remember the Alamo! Remember Goliad!" Was now the battle cry that the defiant Texans would be heard yelling going into The Battle of San Jacinto. The Texas armies were resolved that as their brethren received now quarter and no mercy, they were going to show the same to their Mexican opponents.

At the start of the campaign Santa Anna had amazed his subordinates with his attention to detail and micro-management. That day, though, he could not be bothered, and left the army leaderless in the afternoon while he (legend has it) retired to his tent with his personal opium chest and an attractive biracial hotel housekeeper named Emily West, later to become famous as the "Yellow Rose of Texas." Emily is sometimes erroneously called Emily Morgan by those who assumed she was a slave belonging to James Morgan. In reality, she was born a free black in New Haven, Connecticut. She signed a contract on Oct. 25, 1835 to work for Morgan for a year at his New Washington Association's hotel in Morgan's Point, Texas.

On April 16, 1836, Mexican cavalrymen seized Emily and a number of other workers and residents at Morgan's Point and forced them to accompany the Mexican army. Among the captives was a boy called Turner. Santa Ana convinced him to lead his scouts to Houston's camp but Emily persuaded the boy to escape and warn Houston of the Mexican general's arrival.

Unaware that the Texans were on the way, the Mexicans settled into a siesta. And then the Texans struck. Santa Anna was captured the next day, still, the old stories say, clad in silk pajamas. Emily West remained in Texas until early 1837, when she received a passport allowing her to return home.

One of his captors, Freemason James Sylvester claimed that Santa Anna had given the Masonic sign of grief and distress directly to him and then later to Sam Houston. This

Mexican General Santa Anna

story is also related by another Mason, John Stiles, a soldier from Red River, who was also guarding Santa Anna. Allegedly, Santa Anna later presented his Masonic apron to Stiles in gratitude for interceding on his behalf.

Brought before Houston, Santa Anna is said to have given the secret distress signal of the Master Mason. He denied having done anything wrong at the Alamo or Goliad but offered to make an example of Gen. Urrea, who carried out the executions. (Two years later, Urrea would launch a coup against Santa Anna, briefly controlling two states in northern Mexico.) Feeling edgy, Santa Anna asked for -- and got -- some of that familiar pain-killer he saw being administered to the wounded Houston.

And so they had a mellow conversation for the rest of the afternoon, the two men basically dividing up North America while stoned on opium. Santa Anna agreed to have the Mexican army retreat, and recognize an independent Texas with its border at the Rio Grande. (The Nueces River would have been more logical, having long been the Mexican state border for Coahuila y Texas. It may simply have been harder to find on a map.) Finding him so useful, Houston defied popular opinion, complied with his Masonic oath, and let Santa Anna live. Deposed and back in the Mexican army in 1838, Santa Anna lost a leg defending Veracruz against a French attack.

GHOSTS OF GOLIAD
THE SIGHTINGS

When the team arrived we went into the gift shop and with no prompting from us, the woman who runs it told us that La Bahia is haunted with ghosts, and proceeded to give us this account:

- Strange lights have been seen on the grounds at night
- Friars in black hooded robes have been seen wandering the grounds
- A woman in white sometimes floats through the graveyard while babies cry from their graves
- A woman in black sobs in the chapel then disappears before anyone can console her
- Mysterious singing can be heard in the chapel.
- Doors unlock themselves
- Invisible hands pull the ponytails of unsuspecting tourists

She said she believed none of this when she began working there until one day, alone in the gift shop, she heard voices, and was unable to find the source of those voices. Another time, while parking her car she saw a man in nineteenth century garb seated on one of the benches. She glanced away, then a moment later looked back and he had vanished.

But the strangest apparition, she claimed was the face of General Antonio Lopez de Santa Anna that appeared in the fireplace one day. "It's still there if you want to see it," she offered and led us to the fireplace. "There," she said, pointing." The smudges she pointed to was one of those patterns that were not as haphazard as they seemed on first glance. If you looked very carefully you could see the epaulets on a uniformed man's shoulder, and his profile. "It looks exactly like the portrait of Santa Anna in the other room," she insisted. We smiled and shook our heads, but it looked like a clear case of pareidolia, a psychological phenomenon that allows a vague or random stimulus such as an image or a sound being perceived as significant. An example is seeing animal shapes in clouds.

We have also had re-enactors experience the feeling of not being alone on the field during a re-enactment and one even claimed to have seen a soldier loading a cannon mounted on one of the turrets during their campfire gatherings.

THE INVESTIGATIONS

We arrived at 1:00 pm on January 1, 2000, giddy as school kids at the thought of having the run of such a significant structure for the night. The museum and grounds had been closed all day for the New Year's holiday and would not reopen until 9 the next morning. We took EMF readings of the entire grounds and found nothing abnormal since most of the readings fell into the .1-.2 milligauss range with nothing above .7. Pete reported the smell of death in the southeast corner. During a short trip to the grocery store for supplies we set up EVP. Before the sun set completely we took a short drive to the site where Col. Fannin and the other victims of the Goliad Massacre were buried to pay our respects.

After sunset we set up EVP again on the grounds. Although the chapel was locked, we were able to set a microphone inside the large old lock. As the microphone was being placed inside, Joe Perez was taking video and apparently he picked up a voice saying, "It don't fit." Some of the sounds caught on tape are furniture being moved inside the church, and the lock being fastened.

At 11 p.m. Pete and Dean were outside, and as they looked out of the chapel courtyard into the quadrangle they noticed a strange, thick mist gathering in the southeast corner of the quadrangle (where Pete had smelled death earlier). Dean reported a sense of something building, and predicted that in about 30 minutes, something would happen. At 11:30 all team members were in the chapel courtyard again gathering EVP equipment when Pete happened to look into the quadrangle. Katie felt a need to NOT look into the quadrangle. Suddenly Pete froze and just stared. We returned to the quarters and Pete was visibly affected by something he didn't want to discuss. Dean, Katie and Joe entered the quadrangle to retrieve the IR video camera, and Katie had the distinct impression that there were bodies on the ground. When they returned, Pete informed them that what he had seen was the aftermath of the Goliad Massacre. He gave details on some of what he'd seen, such as, "Some of them weren't old enough to shave." All of the bodies had been decaying for a few days, and he also mentioned that he could smell the gunpowder of the rifles as the soldiers fired into the injured captives. Pete also made mention of the faces of the prisoners and the look of sheer terror as the firing of the guns started. He said he saw them run for the walls and try to climb out, and heard the screams of the men as they were bayoneted. The whole time Pete had said the scene was daytime, and he was visibly shaken as he described that he felt the anguish and overwhelming fear of the men, as if the past was broadcasting the pain and suffering all at once.

PRESIDIO LA BAHIA

Pete caught on film the bright outline of a woman in the courtyard. While he was outside and after his "time slip," he said that he saw a moving fog. He snapped his 35 mm Canon T-40 and to his amazement this is what he captured. Could it be the Angel of Goliad? There was no one but him outside at the time of this shot.

While Dean was walking the walls he came upon this area and right away felt that there was someone there. As he continued to watch and take notes he snapped off this shot. We all know how we feel about orbs, but when you can couple it with a sensation and a fluctuation of an EMF meter as he did, then you may have something. We don't feel it's "ghostly" but we do feel it was significant to the confirmations of a personal experience. The EMF and the photograph made it worth the post.

At about 1 a.m. we all tried to get some sleep. Dean and Katie slept in the first room, which has a door that leads to the courtyard. Not five minutes after they lay down, the door began banging. The wind was blowing that night, but this was a solid wood door, very heavy, with very little play. Dean continued to try to sleep and Katie went to the other bedroom where Pete, Carolyn and Joe were discussing the evening's findings. She informed them about the door in her room. We were exhausted at this point and needed some sleep. We were done with the investigation, but the ghosts weren't done with us. When we heard the sound of horses' hooves approaching the door from the living room to the courtyard we determined that there was only one way any of us were going to get any rest. The door in Dean and Katie's room had calmed down, but as Joe approached it, it banged again. At 2 a.m. all five paranormal investigators were sound asleep... in their cars.

Other experiences that night included strange mumblings in the guest quarters and a human-shaped shadow moving behind the well in the quadrangle.

ANALYSIS

This haunting is both intelligent and residual. The banging on Katie and Dean Phillips' door was in response to the living, the voice heard on Joe's tape was commenting on activity as it was happening, and past reports indicate that the friar that was seen becomes aggressive, which indicates intelligent interaction with the living. The vision that Pete saw, the horses' hooves in the courtyard, and some of the EVP captured that night indicate that there is also a residual haunting in effect, or place memory. This means that so much emotional energy has been expended that when the conditions are right, the events play over again like a recording for those who can perceive them. There is no intelligence behind those aspects of the haunting; it's more like watching a movie.

That was the first time the team went to this place and to say it's not overwhelming both in size and emotion is an understatement. When later looking at the footage Joe had, the sound of a clear voice stating, "It don't fit," was clearly distinguishable.

COLLECTION OF THE NEXT THREE INVESTIGATIONS

In subsequent investigations we set up some prototype equipment in the priest's quarters. It's called The EVP Precipitator designed by AVR Technologies. Engineer Steve Quest and I had been talking a lot and wanted to test this piece of equipment in La Bahia to see if the pulse mode would attract the subtle energies that he seemed to be getting in his lab. We charged the area for a couple hours and I don't know if it was the pulsed white noise that unnerved us or just exhaustion, but you could start to hear voices in the room and the atmosphere did seem like it shifted and made the air heavier. We set up a security VTR (video tape recorder) in the gift shop and ran it for 12 hours. On the sound track you can clearly hear footfalls like in a pair of heavy boots, but there was no visual. We then had a documentarian working with us for a pilot and he captured on digital video the appearance of a mass moving around his power cord and then going into the church. We then set up an array of EMF detectors behind the church on another investigation and it can be clearly seen on video that as the visual of the friar came from behind the church, it triggered each EMF detector as it made its way to the tower directly behind the church. It seems that at 11:45 p.m. the EMF fields had a drastic buildup from .4 mg to 10 mg.

At about midnight we had a higher reading of 24 mg and at this time we had a visual of a clearly formed humanoid-looking shape in the tower moving up and down appearing to be watching or standing guard. We later read in one of the books about the site that there were some friars who became ill but would still walk the perimeter on the lookout for Indians or dangers, until they became too weak and died. We did notice there are a lot of locals who try to sneak a peek at the "ghosts" so we had to be on guard for folks trying to scale the wall. As you look at the tower to the southeast it's so close to the ground that you can see an occasional person jumping up to look in. A bobbing head is a weird sight to see when you're concentrating on running an investigation.

In conclusion, we are planning to return and bring our thermal imaging camera, and our camera arrays to build on the EMF readings and time trends to either confirm or explain the past investigations. The Presidio La Bahia has always been a place of honor for us, and we hold the personal sacrifices that were made there very sacred. We look forward to spending more time in this grand structure.

11. NIGHTS AT THE GAITHER PLANTATION

BY BOB HUNNICUTT

Compared to any other region of the United States, hauntings in the South are unlike any you may find anywhere else in the country. Warm weather throughout most of the year provides favorable conditions, especially when visiting the remaining Southern plantations. Beautifully manicured grounds, full of pine, oak and of course, magnolia trees, all seeming to add a frame to complete the picture of Southern tradition at its best. But those visiting will see a real change when the sun sets and the tragic history of the property are dramatically revealed in the moonlight.

HISTORY

Nestled deep in the heart of Newton County, Georgia you'll find the Gaither Plantation. Originally built in the 1840s by William Hulbert Gaither for his young bride. Cecilia Wood, this once-proud plantation encompassed 900 acres with approximately 130 slaves to work the property, with cotton being the primary crop.

In 1888, the eldest son Henry killed a neighboring tenant farmer named George Smith. Smith had started a brush fire and destroyed the nests of Henry's turkeys, in a rage Henry struck Smith fatally in the head. Henry fled to Colorado, never to return and his father died two years later.

In the 1900s, the cotton crop was wiped out due to infestation by the boll weevil and in 1906

Gaither Plantation

Cecilia moved to Conyers Street in Covington, Georgia with her son, William H. Gaither, Jr. and his wife.

Even though the family moved their permanent residence to Covington, the plantation house was host to many a house party. Unfortunately, in 1921 the Gaither family was forced to declare bankruptcy and lost the plantation.

In 1996, the Newton County Board of Commissioners acquired the Gaither home place for its historical significance but the main house was in need of major renovation.

Now the plantation house is used for weddings, receptions and has also appeared in several major

(Left) A rear view of the plantation house (Right) The Gaither house prior to the renovations

motion pictures including Tyler Perry's "*Madea's Family Reunion.*"

During the filming of one motion picture, the director, cast and crew were reported to have numerous experiences that could not be easily explained, with the most notable occurring during a scene in the great room that had been set up as the kitchen. The scene was set and the camera was rolling when footsteps coming from upstairs were heard by everyone. The director stopped the scene and asked for someone to please tell whoever was walking upstairs to stop and be quiet.

Upon checking, no one could be found upstairs so they set up to begin shooting again. This time the footsteps could be heard coming down the staircase, and again the scene was stopped. The increasingly frustrated director requested once again for whoever was walking on the stairs to stop and be quite. As before, no culprit could be found. Naturally perplexed and more than a little aggravated, the director called out; "Whoever is walking around making noise, would you please stop so we could finish?" Reportedly, after this, no other activity was experienced for the remainder of the movie company's stay.

Over the years, many visitors have seen the apparition of Confederate soldiers both outside and inside the house. Notably, a misty figure wearing gray has been seen on numerous occasions at the foot of the basement stairs.

The main staircase is also a focal point for phantom footsteps sometimes accompanied with whispers, singing and a whistling. Tales of the Gaither family offering aid and comfort to Confederate soldiers provide the background for activity in the attic. Stories tell of Union troops searching for Confederate hideaways in the attic by sending goats up the steep stairs in hopes of panicking the soldiers to reveal themselves. Now, the only evidence

The staircase where the phantom footsteps were heard during the filming of "Madea's Family Reunion."

The team assembled for the first investigation at Gaither Plantation

of their being there are the strange sounds of footsteps when visitors stop by.

INVESTIGATION #1
AUGUST 25, 2001

In 2001 we became the first paranormal investigative team allowed access to the plantation. Though dozens of visits would take place over the next eight years, this first event proved the old adage, be careful what you wish for; you just might get it! One of our newest members, Don, accompanied us for his very first ghost hunt and before the night was over it became clear it would be his last. His example is a good lesson for those who simply dismiss the supernatural as an overactive imagination or foolishly decide to jump headfirst into a field with little experience and no understanding on the reality of ghosts, spirits and haunted locations.

The request for an investigation came from Jerry Love to another paranormal outfit, Georgia Paranormal Research Team, founded by Andy Calder. Love did not have the resources to take on an investigation of this size, so he contacted us to take assist. The team consisted of Shaun Brehm, Julie Dye, Don Martin, Drew Hester, Kelly Calhoun, Caulder and I. After receiving the full tour of the house and property, we got underway setting up our equipment.

It would be fair to say we take a little bit different approach to our methods and way of thinking when it comes to our initial workup of a location. While I think it is safe to say the Gaither Plantation is haunted, we always take the approach of not drawing any conclusions one way or another until every possible explanation for the activity can be looked into. Rather than using the "debunking" method often used today, we choose to see if there are any natural explanations for any reported activity. Once those have been evaluated, we can move on to other explanations through careful review and examination of the photographs, video and audio collected. This review is a painstaking evaluation of documentation to prevent false positives from being identified as either paranormal or supernatural activity. At times it is awfully tempting to simply take each and every piece of apparent evidence at face value. But it's important to remember the ultimate goal for this field is finding the truth and looking for corresponding evidence for the activity. Unfortunately, some will accept the easy route for notoriety and don't understand the importance of careful scrutiny of their own work.

During this investigation, Calder took a photograph that at first glance resembles a person carrying a candle or oil lamp in the dark. All of the power was turned off and everyone in attendance was outside when this photo was taken. The "light" appears to be over the original well that is now sealed but still visible in that area. I must admit at first glance it was a truly amazing photograph and it captured the attention of many.

However, using our approach to evidence review, it was possible to rule out a paranormal explanation and prove it was little more than a street light reflecting off the glass. The "movement" of the light is actually the camera being indivertibly moved at the moment the photograph was taken. Thus the light source seems to move and there is no blurring usually associated with unintentional movement of the camera.

To prove this point, a photograph was taken from the handicap ramp at the rear entrance of the main house in the approximate location of the original photo. Although the "light" is longer, you can clearly see how moving the camera even slightly can produce the same effect with no blurring of the surrounding area.

Part of the normal routine for our investigations involves taking baseline reading for electromagnetic fields, temperature and humidity, weather conditions including lunar and solar activity. As the night progresses, additional readings are recorded and compared to original readings while we notate any radical changes for the area.

The investigation provided practically nothing in environmental or atmospheric phenomena for our first visit, temperature was a comfortable 72 degrees F, relative humidity was 48 percent. The moon was waxing crescent, solar/geomagnetic activity was normal/quiet. Baseline readings for EMFs, temperature, humidity, background radiation were atypical and during the rest of the night no abnormal readings were detected. Video recorded failed to provide any material for review but one EVP session provided an unexpected extra.

In order to communicate with resident spirits, we use two tried and true methods for collecting electronic voice phenomena. Using both analog and digital audio recorders depending on the location amounts of ambient noise and foot traffic; we either record in a static mode where the recorder is left on throughout the time we're on location or during multiple 10-minute increments asking specific questions in hopes of obtaining a response.

To ensure some measure of results, we request verbal responses but also give the option of knocking on any solid surface to respond; one knock for "yes," two for "no."

When we begin a session, the audio recorder is started at least 10 seconds prior to any questions. The recorder is placed on a solid surface to help prevent added noise from being picked up by the sensitive built-in microphone. On this occasion, before any questions could be asked or words spoken, we picked up a wispy voice saying, "someone's trying to kill me." Unfortunately, we weren't able to obtain additional responses to the question of who was trying to kill whom, but apparently other spirits seemed willing to communicate.

Over the years, numerous reports of footsteps, knocking, whispers, singing and whispers abound from visitors to the upstairs bedroom that belonged to Cecelia Gaither. It is said Cecelia has been seen either in her rocking chair or standing in front of one of the bedroom windows. Though activity has been experienced throughout the house, many feel Cecelia's former bedroom is a major hot spot worthy of intense study and scrutiny. Using a Sony ICD-B7 digital audio recorder in conjunction with a Sony analog Hi-8 camcorder, we made numerous attempts at spirit communication with the fourth session yielding the most promising results for the evening.

In preparation for all of our EVP sessions, we notify our tech station as well as other teams on location of our intention to begin recording. Once everyone has responded, our two-way communications are silenced until completion to prevent the possibility of any recording devices accidentally picking up radio communication. Once the recorders have been activated, someone will verbally explain our intentions and ask for the spirits' cooperation.

BH (Bob Hunnicutt): "I am speaking to the spirits believed to continue to occupy this home; will you come forward and speak with us?"

BH: "If you are unable or unwilling to speak with us, would you respond by making a audible noise such as knocking on a wall, table or anything available, once for yes, twice for no?"

Response: One knock; everyone verified they also heard it.

BH: "If that was an attempt to communicate an answer, would you please do it again?"

Response: One knock.
BH: "Are you a member of the Gaither family?"
Response: Two knocks.
BH: "Did you work on the plantation?"
Response: Two knocks.
BH: "Will you tell us your name?"
Response: Two knocks.
BH: "Are you able to tell us your name?"
Response: One knock.
BH: "Were you a slave here?"
Response: Two knocks.
BH: "Were you a soldier?"
Response: A whistle came from the hallway
BH: "Was that you whistling?"
No response.
BH "Are you still here with us?"
Response: Noises from the downstairs foyer

This is the first time we experienced what quickly became a common occurrence in the house: auditory phenomena that seemed to instantly change locations. When you're upstairs voices are heard downstairs move downstairs and the voices move upstairs. It's puzzled us for quite some time, primarily due to our inability to record the voices.

The only other activity experienced was noted in the basement during our fifth rotation (teams are given the opportunity to switch locations every 60 to 90 minutes to prevent fatigue.) Julie Dye was overcome by what she described as a strong, foul odor while sitting in a chair at the base of the stairs. The odor dissipated almost as quickly as it arrived and a search of the area failed to provide any evidence of natural causes that could have produced such a smell.

Even though it was our first visit and we obtained minimal data and documentation, the plantation had made its mark on us all, especially Don. While the rest of us were very impressed with its beauty and history, the experience had been entirely too much for him. At the completion of the investigation, Don got into his vehicle and drove away, never to be heard from again. No one knew for sure had happened but he obviously got a lot more than he bargained for that night.

INVESTIGATION #12
SEPTEMBER 17, 2005

Team members for this evening included Drew Hester, Julie Dye, LeAnne Boggs, Shaun Brehm, Matt Brinkley and I. At this point, we had all become very comfortable at the plantation house and each of us had our own personal experiences from our visits. While there was nothing to collaborate these, the fact that many of them shared certain characteristics proved to help make them a memorable experience and something to share amongst ourselves.

Now we began branching out to some of the other buildings on the property, primarily the cabin and a period church building. None of these buildings are original to the plantation but were donated to Newton County from surrounding areas. Having enough personnel available to set up two teams

(Left) The old cabin that was rebuilt on the Gaither Plantation property.
(Right) The old Harris Springs church building.

made it possible to cover both locations at once and allowed me to rotate between the two buildings as needed.

Though the cabin is often thought of as an old slave shack as it was portrayed in Tyler Perry's "*Madea's Family Reunion,*" it originally was an old homestead that was moved to the property and rebuilt.

The Harris Springs church building was constructed in 1916 and a murder-suicide tragically ended its use as an active house of worship. The building was deeded to the Newton County Historical Society in 1985 and has remained at the plantation since 1991. It was soon discovered that both structures have haunting activity associated with them.

Baseline readings for both structures varied as the church had electricity while the cabin did not. We did obtain minor fluctuations in the electromagnetic field around the stone hearth and fireplace in the cabin, which remained intermittent throughout the night. The church had no abnormal readings. Temperature was in the mid-80s, humidity was 72 percent, and no background radiation was noted at any time. Sunset was at 6:41 p.m. The lunar phase was full and solar/geomagnetic was normal/quiet. Video cameras were set up in both buildings and were activated at 9:30 p.m. and maintained throughout the night.

On several occasions, significant spikes in the electromagnetic field were noted inside the cabin in the area of the fireplace. Using a stationary Natural Tri-Field meter placed on the fireplace mantel, there were readings of 2.0 to 5.0 occurring at irregular intervals. Though no audio was recorded during several EVP sessions, unexplained footsteps were picked up on video using a Sony Analog Hi-8 Camcorder. The footsteps were very reminiscent of someone walking either up or down the staircase leading to the upstairs of the cabin.

Cold spots were detected on three separate occasions; twice in the cabin, (once upstairs, once downstairs) once on the front porch and another time in the yard near the wooden fence. Using a combination of Oregon Scientific digital temperature probes and a Fluke hand-held IR thermometer, significant temperature drops in upstairs area of the cabin (12 degrees) cabin downstairs (11 degrees) and outside of the cabin near the wooden fence (15 degrees) the only corresponding documentation to these temperature drops was a single photograph of an unexplained mist. Ambient temperature at

The strange photo taken near the wooden fence

the time the photo was taken was 74 degrees F, no one present was smoking and there were no fires in the immediate area.

At approximately 12:45 a.m. I joined the team already set up in the church. Inside in the dark, it's difficult to judge the exact size of the interior and space between the aisles. This wasn't our first investigation of a church, but it is the first church we visited that also happened to be a murder scene. The story we were told involved the murder – suicide of the pastor and his wife, apparently part of a love triangle gone awry, and it is believed the activity was the catalyst for the haunting.

Baseline readings except for electromagnetic field readings and temperature were virtually the same as the cabin. The interior temperature was approximately 5 degrees warmer with no cold spots registered throughout the night. With video cameras set up to cover the entire interior, digital thermometer probes and passive IR motion detectors located on the pulpit and front entrance at the back of the church.

Right from the start, sounds of footsteps and knocking throughout the building with no obvious focal point were heard. Multiple attempts to communicate using the Olympus VN-3100 PC did not produce any positive results so a decision was made to use a Natural Tri-Field Meter in conjunction with an Olympic VN-3100 PC digital audio recorder. We were unable to pick up discernable voices but using a stationary Natural Tri-field meter did provide some interesting results on four specific questions during an EVP session at the pulpit.

The interior of the church building

BH: "Pastor, are you here?"
Response: Sudden spike on the analog meter
BH: "Is your wife here with us too?"
No response
BH: "Pastor, are you still here?"
Second spike on the analog meter
BH: "Pastor, do you regret killing your wife?"
Response: Sustained spike on the analog meter
BH: "Do you still love her?"
No response

Subsequent questions failed to elicit any response or spikes on the meter's analog display. It is difficult to say for sure, but this method of spirit communication does seem to hold some promise and more research should and will be conducted in the field again in the future.

INVESTIGATION #20
OCTOBER 31, 2008

We were granted access to the entire property for the purpose of conducting a sizeable investigation as well as having our work documented on film. Working with Ron McEllen of Southlan-Films, and Drew Hester and Aubrey Bailey of the Wormwood Project, Tim Beach and I set out to gather as much documentation of the activity as possible. This would encompass the main house, the cabin and church over a weekend and would provide some of the best evidence ever collected by our team.

To start off, we focused on the cabin by setting up 2 Sony Digital Hi-8 camcorders and an Olympus VN-5100 PC digital audio recorder. To ensure that the results would not be tainted by our presence, we left the cabin for approximately an hour. Upon return and review of the recordings, we would be amazed at what we discovered.

The noises recorded sounded very much like metal being dragged over gravel. Inspection of the fireplace and hearth provided a probable source of the peculiar noises recorded. The cabin contains several antiques, notably a cast iron skillet that is placed on the fireplace's stone hearth. Sliding the skillet over the hearth produced sounds similar to those recorded. Review of video shot during the same period failed to pick up the same noise recorded on audio, but had something truly amazing. One of the video cameras placed at the back of the cabin

One of the video cameras that was aimed at the window from inside apparently picked up a face looking through the glass. There were no lights in the building, which could have caused a reflection and the window is seven feet from the ground, which ruled out an intruder or curiosity-seeker.

was facing to the left of the fireplace and also covered one of the windows. This particular window is approximately seven feet from the ground, making it extremely difficult for anyone to peer in from the outside. Also, it is important to note that the cabin has no electrical power or artificial light installed.

The main house became our next focus, our tech station was set up downstairs in the great room at the back of the house, and video cameras were set up in the upstairs bedrooms, the attic, and downstairs in the parlor, dining room and bride's room. During the next few hours the activity began extremely slowly but did seem to increase after 11 p.m. On two occasions, muffled voices were heard in the downstairs hallway during our EVP sessions in the dining room. As always, we began our sessions by announcing our intentions and asking for the spirits help and cooperation as well as giving them alternative methods of responding:

BH: "Are any of the Gaither family here with us tonight?"

Response: One knock.
BH: "Is this William, Sr?"
Response: Two knocks.
BH: "Is this William, Jr?"
Response: Two knocks.
BH: "Is this Henry?"
Response: One knock.
BH: "Are you glad to be home?"
Response: One knock.
BH: Henry, we're here just to communicate with you, not pass judgment, did you ever get to return home to see your mama?
No response.
BH: "Henry, I know you regret what happened and we're sad you had to leave. Did you ever get to talk to your family after you left?"
Response: Two knocks.
BH: "I'm sorry Henry, thank you for speaking with us."

It was plainly obvious I had struck a nerve with Henry; my impression was he is still sad about the entire situation especially about not seeing his parents again. Strangely, while we recorded this session, the Olympus picked up a series of noises unlike any I've heard during EVP sessions. They were a series of clicks and quick whistles that seemed to come from different locations in the room as if something was moving around us.

Upstairs in Cecilia's room our video cameras picked up a sudden sharp movement of the bed which is a difficult task to be sure. The bed's head- and footboards are part of the Victorian bedroom furniture purchased especially for this room. It was made in England and shipped to Savannah, Georgia. When it arrived it was carried to the plantation by wagon. On only one occasion did any of us attempt to move this bed, it is very solid and extremely heavy. Also, the clearance underneath was so low that only a child could crawl under it.

Interestingly enough, later the video captured the rocking chair rocking on its own for 17 seconds. This is the same rocking chair several witnesses admit having seen an older woman sitting in. Some visitors to the property have stated they have seen her holding a baby or small child, either standing

The rocking chair in Cecilia Gaither's room

Cecilia Gaither

in front of the window or in the chair.

Attempts to communicate with Cecilia are a hit or miss endeavor, mainly depending on her mood at the time and the person's patience when asking the questions.

BH: "Ms. Cecilia, will you please come speak with us tonight? We've come to visit again."
Response: "Company coming."
BH: "We love coming here."
No response.
BH: "Does our being here please you Ms. Cecilia?"
No response.
BH: "Is there anyone else here with you tonight?"
No response

No further auditory responses were recorded but soon after, everyone heard footsteps on the staircase going down. When we followed to the top of the stairs, everyone heard what sounded like someone humming a single musical note.　But true to form, after we descended downstairs, intermittent whispers could be heard coming from upstairs.

At approximately 2:45 a,m., Drew and I rotated out to the church to wrap things up.　We spent the last 45 minutes shifting the camera positions and participating in a final EVP session with Ron McEllen. Apparently, the spirits present didn't want to communicate at that moment but were feeling frisky and mischievous. Before our arrival to the church on two separate occasions, Ron's cap was knocked off his head giving everyone the impression someone didn't like Ron being there and it didn't take long to figure out why.

For years, Ron has produced and directed award-winning independent horror and mystery movies. So it wasn't that far a jump for him to think about doing something dealing with the real side of the paranormal and supernatural. However, the main difference is when the director calls cut, the action on the movie set ceases. Not so when you're at a haunted location. To compensate for his increasing uneasiness, Ron would resort to making sarcastic and provoking statements hoping to stir up paranormal activity so he could film it. It didn't quite work out the way he was hoping and he was dished up a lesson in spiritual politics. Not wanting to admit his mistake, he continued with the provocation and the spirit would respond in kind by knocking off his hat. After two more retaliatory strikes against Ron, he was ready to call it a night.

Fortunately, during Ron's spiritual etiquette lesson, one of our video camera aimed at the front of the church picked up a mist moving slowly towards the pulpit. It appeared suddenly and dissipated just as quickly, but not before being recorded on infrared video.

One thing my years of experience have taught me is that communicating with the spirit world is not that different than our corporeal existence. It doesn't always require verbal communication; sometimes they can be telepathic while others communicate in a matter very much like code.

While other situations require actions rather than mere words, it really depends on how perceptive people are and whether they realize when it's time to stop talking and start listening.

12. A HAUNTING MYSTERY
SEARCHING FOR THE GHOSTS OF THE VILLISCA AX MURDER HOUSE
BY TROY TAYLOR

Nearly lost among the rolling hills and fields of southwestern Iowa is the tiny town of Villisca, a quiet, peaceful place of only a few hundred people and one tragic and enduring mystery. It was here, in June 1912, that a horrific mass murder took place that wiped out an entire family. The murder was never solved, casting a pall over Villisca that still lingers today. And this dark cloud may not be the only thing still lingering here. There are many who believe that the spirits of the murdered family may remain here as well, their ghosts haunting the old house where they once lived and tragically died.

I happen to be among the believers and if you had the chance to experience what several investigators and I did at this house in May 2005 you might become one, too.

Villisca is located in a remote corner of Iowa, far off the modern interstate and a good distance from any town that might have a population of more than a couple of thousand souls. It's an isolated place, accessible by only an old, two-lane highway and believe it or not, this is in great contrast to how it was back in the early 1900s. In those days, Villisca, which means "pleasant view," was a booming town of more than 2,500 residents. The streets were lined with flourishing businesses and several dozen trains pulled into town every day. It was a popular spot in Montgomery County in those days, offering not only shops of just about every kind but restaurants and a theater as well.

Villisca was a close-knit community but the peacefulness was shattered on June 10, 1912 with the discovery of eight bloody corpses in a house along one of the town's tree-lined streets. The J.B. Moore family, respected and well-liked members of the community, along with two young overnight guests, were founded murdered in their beds. And still, more than 90 years later, the crimes remain unsolved.

What happened on that dark night in Villisca? And what occurred to cause at least some of the spirits of the slaughtered to stay behind in this world?

BLOODY MURDER

It was a warm evening in southwestern Iowa and the town of Villisca stirred quietly in the gloom of the setting sun. The dinner hour had long since passed and many residents escaped to the cool of their front porches after the heat of the day started to settle. Stores locked up for the evening and lights began to appear in the windows of homes along the darkening streets. At the Presbyterian church, music filtered to the street outside, along with laughter and polite applause. The Children's

Day Program came to an end around 9:30 p.m. and soon the parishioners began trickling out into the street, heading home for the night.

Sarah Moore, who had coordinated the program, gathered her family around her as they started walking home. She was joined by her husband Josiah, known popularly in town as J.B., and her children, Herman, Catherine, Boyd and Paul. Two young girls, friends of the Moore children who had also been in the evening's program, Lena and Ina Stillinger, came home with the Moore's to spend the night. The children were excited after the evening's festivities and

A vintage view of the J.B. Moore Home

Sarah knew that she would have trouble settling them for the night. She couldn't help but laugh at their antics and jokes however, especially after J.B. joined in with them. The sound of their laughter could be plainly heard as the small group walked along and they waved happily at the other families and friends they passed.

Everyone like the Moores --- and no one who saw them that night could have imagined that this would be the last time the family would be seen alive.

The following morning, June 10, Mary Peckham, the Moores next door neighbor, stepped out of the back door of her home to hang some laundry on the line. The sun was barely peeking into the sky but it was better to finish the outdoor chores early and avoid the heat that came later in the day. Mary went about her business, wringing water from the wash and hanging the wet clothes on the line that stretched across her backyard. As she worked, she had a clear view of the Moore house next door but thought little about how quiet the place was until she finished with the clothes and realized that the clock in her kitchen now read 7:00 a.m.

She suddenly realized that not only had the Moores not been outside to start their own chores that morning but that the house itself seemed unusually still. This was very strange as J.B. Moore always left early for work and Sarah was always up at dawn to start breakfast and the day's work. The Moore house was full of young children and so the morning hours were always loud and boisterous. Could the Moores be sick? Mary waited for a few more minutes and then finally decided to go next door and check on her friend Sarah and the rest of the family. Mary approached the house and knocked on the door. It was still eerily quiet inside. She waited for a few moments and then knocked again. Once more, there was no answer and so she tried to open the door, thinking that she could poke her head inside and call for Sarah. She pulled on the door handle and found that it was locked from the inside. She found it hard to believe that this was the case but apparently the Moores had

THE VILLISCA MURDER VICTIMS

(Left) J.B. Moore, one of Villisca's most prominent residents and (Right) his wife, Sarah. Both were murdered in their beds during the early morning hours of June 10, 1912.

(Left to Right) Herman, the oldest of the Moore children; Kathrine, a close friend of the Stillinger girls; Boyd and Paul were the youngest children, ages 7 and 5 at the time of the murders. These photos, taken when they were much younger are the only existing photographs of the two boys.

(Left) Lena Stillinger and (Right) Ina Stillinger. The two girls were close friends of Katherine Moore and had been present at the church activities with the Moores on June 9. Tragically, they returned home with their friend on the night of the murders.

All Photos courtesy of Olson-Linn Museum / Villisca Ax Murder House

decided to sleep late.

Mary walked back through the yard, deep in thought. It seemed so unlike the family but who was she to pry? Mary went out to the small barn behind the Moore house and let out the chickens into the yard. She felt it was the least she could do to help Sarah, who she was convinced must be under the weather. After she let out the chickens, Mary went back into her own house but the more she thought about the silent home next door, the more that she worried. Finally, when she could stand it no more, she placed a telephone call to J.B.'s brother, Ross Moore, and he promised to come over as soon as he could. This was the first step in what would turn out to be one of the most bungled criminal investigations of the era.

When Ross Moore arrived at the home of his brother, he was met by Mary Peckham, who had continued to try and raise someone in the neighboring home. Ross tried the door himself and then leaned up to peer into a bedroom window. It was too dark to see anything and so he returned to the door, banging on it and shouting for his brother and sister-in-law. There was still no answer and so he produced his own set of keys and looked through the ring until he found one that opened the front door. As he pushed open the door, Moore stepped into the parlor with Mary Peckham behind him. She stopped at the entryway however, and did not go any farther into the house. Moore looked around, seeing no one in the kitchen. He called out but there was no answer. On the opposite side of the parlor was a doorway that led into one of the children's bedrooms. He carefully opened the door and looked into the room. He nearly cried out when he saw two bloody bodies on the bed and dark stains on the sheets. Moore never even looked to see who was lying there. He ran back to the porch and shouted for Mary Peckham to call the sheriff --- someone had been murdered!

The City Marshall, Hank Horton, arrived a short time later and searched the house. The two bodies in the downstairs bedroom were Lena Stillinger, age 12, and her sister, Ina, 8. The girls were houseguests of the Moore children. They had come with them after the church program the night before. The remaining members of the Moore family were found in the upstairs bedrooms. Every person in the house had been brutally murdered, their skulls crushed with an ax. The victims included Josiah Moore, 43, Sarah Montgomery Moore, 44, Herman, 11, Catherine, 10, Boyd, 7, Paul, 5, and the Stillinger sisters.

Almost as soon as the murders were discovered, the news of the massacre traveled quickly throughout Villisca. As friends, neighbors and curiosity seekers descended on the Moore house, the town's small police force quickly lost control of the crime scene. It has been said that literally hundreds of people walked through the house, staring at the bodies, touching everything and even taking souvenirs before the Villisca National Guard unit arrived at noon to close off the scene and secure the home for state police investigators. It's easy for us now to blame this disastrous mismanagement on local police officers but in 1912, such a crime still would have been much more difficult to solve than it would be today. At that time, fingerprinting was still a new idea, crime scene photographs were rarely taken and DNA testing would be unimaginable for decades to come. In short, investigators in rural areas like this simply did not see crimes of this magnitude in 1912. In spite of this, the investigators did manage to make some notes of the scene or all of the clues would have been completely lost. As it was, any evidence the killer left in the house was likely destroyed.

The detectives did manage to put together a list of clues but at that time, little of it made sense and combined, it managed to make the mystery even more perplexing. What was known for a fact was that all eight people in the Moore house had been bludgeoned to death in their sleep, sometime between midnight at 5:00 a.m. A doctor that examined the bodies guessed that the murders had

A reproduction of the Moore's kitchen, as it would have looked in 1912. The house today has been restored with great attention to detail.

The Moore's front parlor

J.B. & Sarah's bedroom, where marks were found on the ceiling, left by the upswing of the ax

occurred closer to midnight. The murder weapon was presumed to be the bloody ax that had been left behind at the scene. The ax, which belonged to J.B. Moore was found in the downstairs bedroom that had been occupied by the Stillinger girls. The ax was covered with blood but the killer had made an effort to wipe it off.

A kerosene lamp was found sitting on the floor at the foot of J.B. and Sarah's bed. The glass chimney had been removed and placed under the dresser and the wick had been turned down almost all the way. Another lamp, with the chimney also removed, was found at the foot of the bed where the Stillinger girls had been sleeping. With the wicks turned down the way that they were, the lamps would have provided only a very small amount of light; perhaps just enough for the killer to carry out the murders.

As mentioned, the Stillinger girls had been murdered downstairs but the bodies of the six members of the Moore family had been found in two upstairs bedrooms. The ceilings in the bedrooms of the parents and the children had gouge marks in them that had apparently been made by the upswing of the ax. This would imply that the killer had used a fairly decent amount of force when striking his victims, which would also suggest that the striking of their skulls, as well as the contact with the ceiling, would have made a fairly loud noise. Strangely though, no one in the family seems to have been awakened during the murders. All of them were slain in their beds, apparently asleep at the time. There is no indication how the killer could have managed this during an obvious "spree" murder but somehow he did.

In each case, he covered the faces of his victims with their bed sheets after he killed them. Modern criminal psychologists would suggest that the killer either knew the victims or that he had a great amount of guilt for what he had done. Some have suggested that this could not have been a stranger, or traveling serial killer, because he covered their faces but this is short-sighted thinking. It's very possible that the murderer may simply have possessed a condition that caused him to immediately regret the murders, even though he was incapable of stopping himself from committing them.

Whatever his state of mind might have been, the killer did not immediately leave the house when he was finished with his work. The first thing that he did was to draw the curtains on all of the windows in the house. Two of the windows did not have curtains, so he covered them with clothing that he found in the Moores' closets. This was likely to ensure that he could light lamps in the house and not be seen from outside. If lights were seen burning in the house in the pre-dawn hours, it could have raised suspicion, or attracted attention, from the neighbors. A pan of bloody water was later found in the kitchen, where the killer had attempted to wash up. It was sitting next to a plate of food that he had prepared but had not eaten. The killer spent quite some time in the house, likely calming down after the murders. But why prepare the food if he did not plan to eat it? It's possible that he may have realized the lateness of the hour, as the sun was starting to lighten the sky, and left with the food untouched. The killer also locked all of the doors of the house, something not usually done in this little town at the time, ensuring that the bodies would not be discovered until he had plenty of time to escape.

This was the list of information that the investigators compiled but with no fingerprints to match and without technology to look for hair and blood samples, footprints or trace evidence, there was little to go on. The only piece of evidence recovered was a piece of a keychain that was found on the floor in the downstairs bedroom. It did not appear to belong to anyone in the house and the police deduced that it must have been left behind by the killer.

But was it? We may never know for the killer has undoubtedly taken his gruesome secrets with him to the grave --- but this does not keep us from delving deeper into this mystery. Could the answers to the murders lie with the identities of the victims? Or does this even deepen the mystery?

THE VILLISCA VICTIMS

Josiah Moore, known as J.B., was one of Villisca's most prominent businessmen. He married Sarah Montgomery in December 1899 and together, the two of them had four children. Moore was a member of the school board and the Presbyterian church. He was born in Hanover County, Illinois, and came to Iowa with his parents. Growing up in Page County, he was one of 16 children, although four of his siblings died as children. Another, Willie, died at age 20 and his sister, Anna, died in November 1910. For a brief time, Anna's husband, Sam Moyer, was considered a suspect in the murders.

At the time of his murder, J.B. had been a resident of Villisca for 13 years and had been employed by Frank Jones at his farm supply and hardware store for nine of those years. A few years before, he had left his position with Jones, another of the town's most prominent residents, and opened his own implement store. Thanks to this kind manner and generosity, Moore's business became an immediate success. After a short time, his hard work managed to take away the John Deere franchise in the area away from Jones. It was an action that some believed gave Jones a motive for the murders. Could his animosity towards his former employee have boiled over into murder?

Sarah Montgomery Moore seemed to have even fewer enemies than her well-liked husband. She had been born in Knox County, Illinois, in 1873 and had moved to Iowa with her parents and her sister, Mary, in 1894. She was also an active member of the Presbyterian church in Villisca and was beloved by all of the children that she taught in Sunday school. Sarah was also considered to be a generous and kind-hearted person and her murder was a mystery to everyone who knew her. On the night of the murders, she and J.B. were sleeping in the largest bedroom on the second floor, located at the top of the stairs from the lower level. It is unknown as to whether the adults or the children were murdered first but neither of them stirred while the killer was at work.

Even more tragic, and bewildering, than the slaughter of Sarah and J.B. were the murders of the children in the house. Herman and Catherine were the oldest of J.B and Sarah's four children. On the night of the murders, they were sleeping in separate beds in the second upstairs bedroom of the Moore home. The bedroom, located at the front of the house, held three beds. The younger boys, Boyd and Paul, were sleeping in the third bed in this same room. According to testimony given in the coroner's inquest by Dr. J. Clark Cooper, the children were also killed in their sleep. "Not a face was exposed." Dr. Cooper testified. "The windows were all down, the curtains were all down and when I went into the south room, I reached up to run the curtain up, and in so doing I knocked that curtain down, I did not put that back up. It seems there was sort of a three window effect, one big window and one little window on each side. I gave it a quick jerk, and I knocked it off, it was so dark in there, and the other in the back room, I ran that up myself." Other witnesses also stated that the bodies were completely covered with sheets or had pieces of clothing draped over them. Strangely, the mirror in this room was also covered.

The bodies of the Stillinger girls were both found in the downstairs bedroom. Lena and Ina were both members of the Presbyterian church and its Junior Society, which was led by Sarah Moore. They were good friends of Catherine and the other Moore children and were survived by their parents and seven brothers and sisters.

Joséph Stillinger, the father of the two girls, had come to Villisca when he was 14 years old. His father, a Civil War veteran, died young and his mother settled a few miles north of Villisca on land that was given to her as the widow of a soldier. His brother, George, bought another farm nearby. When Joseph married Sarah Hastings, he built a large home across the creek from his mother and brother and did so well with his farm that he eventually bought out his brother's land and incorporated it into what came to be known as Doddy Hollow Farm. Joseph became an expert in horticulture and the farm boasted several fine orchards of fruit and nut trees. He also raised cattle and sheep, operated a seed corn business and was involved in a small coal-shipping venture. He received great acclaim for his orchards and traveled widely to speak to farmers under the sponsorship of Iowa State College. On a number of occasions, he even appeared before the state legislature to discuss a statewide horticulture program. At one point, he was even nominated as a congressman for the district but refused to take the time to campaign. Even so, he was so popular that he only lost to his opponent by two votes.

The murder of the two girls seemed to start a series of tragic events for the Stillinger family in 1912. During the same week that Ina and Lena were murdered, Sarah gave birth to a stillborn child and a few months later, while the family was away, their home burned to the ground, destroying all of their belongings. Sarah Stillinger died in November 1944 and Joseph lived just a few years longer, dying in April 1945. They are both buried in the Villisca Cemetery, next to the graves of their murdered daughters and stillborn child.

As the reader can see, the lives of the Villisca victims offer no more clues to the murders today than they did to the authorities in 1912. According to contemporary accounts, the Moores were well liked, as was Joseph Stillinger. There seems to be no reason why the family would have been killed or why anyone would have been targeting Stillinger by slaying his daughters. The only person in town who seemed to have a grudge against anyone involved was Frank Jones, the owner of the implement store where Moore had previously worked. But were business problems enough to make someone kill a man and his entire family? Or was there more between the two men than was publicly known? Or could the murders have been the work of a random stranger --- making them even more horrific and sinister?

THE VILLISCA SUSPECTS

While no one was ever convicted of the Moore/Stillinger murders, there was never any shortage of suspects in the case. In the days that followed the crime, there were at least four suspects mentioned in every edition of the newspaper. However, leads were quickly exhausted, alibis were established and possibilities began to dwindle. The local police, state investigators, private detectives who were hired and even amateur detectives looking for the reward that had been offered combed the town and the surrounding region, following every clue that was presented. Dozens of theories were pursued by each time the investigation seemed to be getting close to something, it all fell apart again. As time wore on, the possibility of solving the crime began to fade and eventually, the trail went cold.

Today, historians, and those with an interest in the case, have their own ideas of who committed the murders. There are many who believe the killer was a local man, known to the victims, while others believe a deranged preacher, a traveling hobo or serial killer was responsible for the deaths of the Moores and the Stillinger girls.

One of the most popular suspects of the time was Frank F. Jones, the prominent Villisca resident and state Senator. Jones had been born in Bath, New York, and he and his family moved from New York to Southern Michigan in 1862, then on to Illinois the following year. In 1875, they relocated and settled in rural Iowa. Jones started out his working life as a schoolteacher but later became a bookkeeper for Baines and Waterman, a farm implement store, in 1882 and moved to Villisca with his wife, Maude. When the Baines and Waterman partnership dissolved, Jones stayed on and worked for J.S. Baines.

In 1886, Jones purchased what was then known as the "Jackson Corner" on 5th Avenue in Villisca and in 1898 began construction on one of the grandest homes in town. In 1890, he took over the Baines implement business with J.L. Smith. The two men remained partners until 1892, when the Waterman Hardware store came up for sale. Smith traded his farm in Nebraska for ownership of the hardware store and Jones took over as the sole owner of what was soon known as "Jones of Villisca." He later reorganized the business as Jones & Co. in 1984, when he became a partner in the Farmers Bank, and took on new partners, Henry and Horace Farlin and John Garside. In 1898, the Farlin brothers became the sole owners of Jones & Co. but Jones once again became a partner in 1901 when he bought out Horace Farlin The store operated as Jones & Farlin until 1902, when Jones took over again as sole proprietor and renamed the place The Jones Store.

In 1903, Jones entered politics and was elected to the Iowa legislature. Around the same time, he also founded the Villisca National Bank, which took over the Farmers Bank, which put him in control of just about all of the finances in Villisca and the surrounding region. Jones served for a total of three years in the House of Representatives and two years in the Iowa Senate. He and his wife had two children, Albert and Letha, and he also served as a Methodist and Episcopalian Sunday school superintendent for over 30 years.

Senator Frank F. Jones has long been considered to have had some hand in the Moore murders.

J.B. Moore worked for Jones for several years until his opened his own implement company in 1908. According to many residents, Jones was extremely upset that Moore left his employ and managed to take the lucrative John Deere franchise with him. Jones was undoubtedly the most powerful man in town during this era and it's not likely that he

William "Blackie" Mansfield

would have suffered what he considered a "defeat" lightly. But would this have been enough to murder Moore and his family? Some believe that matters were made even worse by the fact that J.B. Moore was rumored to be engaged in an affair with Jones' daughter-in-law, Dona. Although no actual evidence of any affair exists, it was a rumor that was going around at the time of the murders. This may have enraged not only Jones but his son, Albert, as well.

After the Burns Detective Agency from Kansas City got involved in the case, their detective in charge, James Newton Wilkerson, became convinced that Jones was involved in the murders. He openly accused Frank and Albert Jones of hiring a man named William Mansfield to carry out the crime. He believed that J.B. Moore was supposed to be the only target but Mansfield had killed everyone in the house instead. Neither of the Joneses was ever arrested and both of them vehemently denied any connection to the killings. Detective Wilkerson was never able to gather enough evidence to get the authorities to charge the men.

If Frank and Albert Jones were innocent of any involvement in the Moore/Stillinger murders, they also became victims in one of the most horrible crimes in Iowa history. But were they innocent? Detective Wilkerson didn't think so…

The man accused of carrying out the crime for the Joneses was William Mansfield, who came from Blue Island, Illinois. Wilkerson believed that Mansfield, who was also known under the aliases of George Worley and Jack Turnbaugh, was a cocaine "fiend" and a killer who was also responsible for other murders. The detective believed that Mansfield murdered his wife, infant child and his wife's parents in Blue Island on July 5, 1914, two years after the Villisca murders, killed a married couple in Paola, Kansas four days before the Villisca murders and murdered Jennie Peterson and Jennie Miller in Aurora, Colorado.

Wilkerson's investigation revealed that all of these murders were committed in precisely the same manner, which led him to believe that one man was responsible for all of them. In each case, the detective believed that the evidence showed the killer was either a maniac or a man who was crazed by drugs. In all of the murders, the victims were hacked or bludgeoned to death with an ax and the mirrors in the homes were covered. A burning lamp with a chimney off was left at the foot of the bed and a basin where the killer washed up was found in the kitchen. The killer also avoided leaving fingerprints at all of the crime scenes. Wilkerson believed that this was because Mansfield knew his fingerprints were on file at the federal military prison at Leavenworth. He also stated that he could prove that Mansfield was present in each of these places on the night of the murders.

Wilkerson managed to convince a grand jury to open an investigation in 1916 and Mansfield was arrested and brought to Montgomery County from Kansas City. However, the accused managed to produce payroll records that showed that he was in Illinois at the time of the Villisca murders. Without any other evidence, Mansfield was released. He later won a lawsuit against Wilkerson and was awarded $2,225 in damages. Regardless, Wilkerson always believed that Mansfield, along with Frank and Albert Jones, was responsible for the Villisca murders. He maintained that political pressure from

Jones resulted in not only Mansfield's release but also in the subsequent arrest and trial of Reverend George Kelly.

Reverend Kelly, a traveling preacher, became another prime suspect in the Moore/Stillinger murders. Lyn George Jacklin Kelly was born in England in 1878 and came to America with his wife, Laura, around 1904. He desperately wanted to be a minister and soon joined the Presbyterian Church. Kelly was described as a "spidery little man" with protruding ears, a prominent noise, high forehead and a wide mouth with large lips that seemed to turn down at the corners even when he smiled. People recalled the odd expression in his dark eyes and were disconcerted by his mannerisms. He was easily excited and often ranted and spoke so fast that he was often impossible to understand. He was also said to drool excessively and sprayed spit all over those who were close to him when he talked.

Kelly and his wife settled in Macedonia, Iowa, in 1912 after several years of preaching throughout the Midwest. He continued as an itinerant preacher and was present at the Children's Day program at the Villisca Presbyterian church on the night of the murders. His presence there, and his departure from town during the early morning hours on June 10, made him a prime suspect in the killings. Kelly had arrived in Villisca and was to attend the program and then stay overnight at the home of Reverend Ewing, pastor of the church, and his wife.

When Kelly arrived in Villisca, Seymour Enarson, the son of Henry Enarson, met him at the train depot. He was driven from the depot to the home of Louis Enarson, Seymour's uncle, for supper. After that, Kelly was taken to the Henry Enarson home for the evening.

According to Enarson family accounts, Kelly acted very nervous when he arrived at their farm house, which was located six miles north of Villisca. Almost immediately, he began pacing the living room floor and at one point, told Mrs. Enarson and the children to leave the room because they were too noisy. Kelly spent the night in a small downstairs bedroom and Mrs. Enarson was so alarmed by his strange behavior that she wrapped herself in a blanket and spent a sleepless night on the steps leading to the upstairs bedrooms, listening carefully to any sound the preacher might make.

The next morning, which was the day of the murders, Henry and Seymour Enarson took Kelly to the Pilot Grove Church for a picnic. Prior to lunch, Kelly gave a sermon that Seymour later described as "the strangest he had ever heard." Kelly returned to the Enarson home for supper and then Seymour drove him to Reverend Ewing's home. That was the last time that the Enarson's saw him prior to the murders but they always believed that he had

The strange Reverend Lyn G.J. Kelly and his wife, Laura. Kelly would later "confess" to the Villisca murders but his odd behavior and possible mental illness would bring his involvement into question. A common theory is that he might have witnessed the murders but was not actually involved.

something to do with the killings. They always heard that the minister confessed to the crime on the train going back to Macedonia and that he had committed the murders because he had a vision that told him to "slay and slay utterly," a phrase that allegedly came from the Bible. The Enarsons had no reason to believe that this strange man was not guilty of the crimes that he was accused of.

Before his "confession" though, Kelly wrote a number of letters to the authorities about the Moore/Stillinger deaths. In the letters, Kelly appeared to be obsessed with the murders and supposedly wrote things that only the killer would know. His uttering on the train ("slay and slay utterly") was said to have been overheard by witnesses and he spoke to other passengers about the killings --- before they were even reported, some said. True or not, Kelly did send a bloody shirt to the laundry in Council Bluffs but it was never recovered.

In 1914, Kelly was arrested but not for the murders. He was jailed in South Dakota for sending obscene materials through the mail and was sentenced to prison. Instead, he ended up in a mental hospital in Washington D.C. By 1917, suspicions had fallen onto Kelly in Iowa and he was arrested for the Moore/Stillinger murders. Kelly supposedly rambled a nearly incoherent confession and the fact that it was accepted at all had led some to call this a "mockery of law enforcement practices at the time." Kelly withdrew the confession before his trial began. His first trial resulted in a hung jury and he was finally acquitted by the second.

It was said that Kelly returned to England after his release and years later, some of the Enarson children would claim that Kelly wrote to their father and asked him for money to help him return to the United States. The Enarsons ignored the letters but many believe that Kelly managed to return anyway. It's been said that he lived in Kansas City, Connecticut and New York but the remaining years of his life, and final resting place, are a mystery.

Despite what many believed was strong evidence against some of the principals in the case, some of the detectives were unable to ignore other similar murders that occurred in the Midwest around the same time as the Villisca murders. There remains a very strong possibility that a serial killer, before anyone even knew what a "serial killer" was, could have been at work during this time.

Although every hobo, transient and otherwise unaccounted for stranger became a suspect in the Villisca murders at one time or another, there were a few of these travelers who stood out from the others. One of them was a man named Andy Sawyer. Although no real evidence ever linked Sawyer to the crime, his name was often mentioned during the grand jury proceedings.

According to Thomas Dyer of Burlington, Iowa, a bridge foreman and pile driver for the Burlington Railroad, Sawyer approached him and his crew in Creston at 6:00 a.m. on the morning the murders were discovered. Sawyer was clean-shaven and dressed in a brown suit, Dyer recalled in his testimony, but his pants were wet to the knee and his shoes covered in mud. He asked for employment and since Dyer needed another man, he hired him on the spot. Soon after that Dyer and his men started to notice Sawyer's odd behavior. Was he simply an eccentric and possibly mentally ill hobo --- or something more dangerous?

Dyer stated that when they reached Fontenelle, Iowa, Sawyer purchased a newspaper, which he went off by himself to read. The newspaper had a front page account of the Villisca murders and according to Dyer, Sawyer "was much interested in it." The crew also began to note Sawyer's peculiarities – he slept with his clothes on, hardly spoke and stayed by himself most of the time. When he did talk, he mostly rambled on about the Moore / Stillinger murders and whether or not the killer had been apprehended. Sawyer told Dyer that he had been in Villisca on the Sunday morning when the murders were discovered but was afraid that he might be considered a suspect and left town before anyone questioned him. One day, as the crew was traveling through Villisca, Sawyer told Dyer's son, J.R., that he could show him how the man who killed the Moore family escaped from town. And while all of this was disturbing, none of it was as disconcerting as the fact that Sawyer slept with an ax at night!

Dyer finally became suspicious enough of Sawyer that he turned him in to the police on June 18, 1912. Just before doing so, he testified that he had walked up behind Sawyer and saw the man rubbing his head with both hands and muttering to himself. Suddenly, he jumped up and shouted "I'll cut your god damn heads off!" and began swinging his ax and hitting the ground with it.

Sawyer was arrested and brought in for questioning but was apparently dismissed as a suspect in the case when it was discovered that police records had him in Osceola, Iowa, on the night of the murders. He was arrested for vagrancy and the Osceola sheriff recalled putting him on a train out of town at approximately 11:00 p.m. on the night of June 9. Could he have still made it to Villisca to carry out the murders that night? Thomas Dyer, and the nervous men on his crew, believed that he could but their concerns were dismissed and Sawyer vanished into history.

Perhaps the most likely suspect in the "drifter" category was a man named Henry Moore. Although accused of some of the same crimes as William Mansfield, Moore was actually convicted of ax murders only a short time after the events in Villisca. Some believe that he was responsible for a bloody spree of murder that wreaked havoc across the Midwest and included the murders of the Moore family and Stillinger girls in Iowa.

An unbalanced man who was prone to violent rages, Moore was prosecuted in December 1912 for the murder of his mother and maternal grandmother in Columbia, Missouri. He had slaughtered both of his victims with an ax and while this was horrific enough, it was just the final act in a bloody rampage that may have spanned 18 months, five states and more than 20 murders. It is thought that the Villisca murders were what finally put federal authorities on Moore's trail.

The discovery of the killing spree might never have been realized if authorities in Villisca had not requested federal assistance in the solution of their local massacre in June 1912. The police had the savaged bodies of the Moores and the Stillinger girls but had no clues or direction for their investigation. A federal officer, M.W. McClaughry, was assigned to the case and his investigation revealed that the Villisca murders were not unique. Nine months before, in September 1911, a similar massacre had occurred in Colorado Springs, taking the lives of H.C. Wayne, his wife and child, and Mrs. A.J. Burnham and her two children. A month later, in October, another massacre claimed the lives of the Dewson family in Monmouth, Illinois, and then a little more than a week later, the five members of the Showman family of Ellsworth, Kansas were also murdered in their beds. In every case, the killer had broken into their homes late at night and had killed everyone with an ax.

On June 5, 1912 --- just days before the carnage in Villisca --- Rollin Hudson and his wife were murdered in Paola, Kansas. The murders were carried out in the same way as the earlier crimes and those that would occur a short time later in Villisca. Detective James Wilkerson believed that this crime had been carried out by William Mansfield, who he believed had been hired by the Joneses to commit the murders in Villisca. However, McClaughry did not think so. No suspect had ever been identified in any of the cases and rumors of a "romance angle" in the Hudson case produced no leads. McClaughry believed that he was dealing with a transient maniac after the Villisca murders but even so, clues were in short supply.

While McClaughry was a hard-working investigator but it would be coincidence and good luck that would point him in the direction of Henry Moore. McClaughry's father was the warden of the federal penitentiary at Leavenworth and was a man with many contacts within the prison system. When he heard about the case of Henry Moore, who was serving a life sentence in Missouri for the December 1912 murders of his mother and grandmother, he informed his son. After comparing the evidence in all of the cases, capped by interviews with Moore, McClaughry announced, on May 9, 1913, that the books had been closed on 23 Midwestern homicides. Unfortunately, no one took his findings seriously and most were happier to believe that the real killer was Reverend George Kelly, who had "confessed" to the Villisca murders.

As readers already know, there were many problems with the minister's confession. On the same day they were publicized, Kelly told his wife that the confession was "pure fabrication." Granted, he had signed the statement but he said he was not sure why he had done so. He publicly recanted as the trial approached and his ramblings seemed to bolster pleas of mental illness. Kelly was later acquitted after two trials.

During all of the publicity surrounding the trial, the information collected by M.W. McClaughry had been largely forgotten. In spite of this, McClaughry remained convinced of Moore's guilt and always believed that he had solved the Villisca murders.

Officially however, the case remains open to this day.

THE HAUNTING OF THE MOORE HOUSE

In the predawn hours on June 10, 1912, a small frame house in Villisca, Iowa, became the site of one of the grisliest massacres in Midwestern history when the family of J.B. Moore and two overnight guests were slaughtered as they slept. The house earned a place in American crime history that morning and a place in the annals of ghostly legend as well.

The house on Lot 410 in Villisca had originally been built in 1868 by George Loomis. It was purchased by J.B. Moore in 1903 and he and his wife Sarah, along with the children that came along, made their home there until their deaths nine years later. After the massacre, the house remained in the hands of the Moore's estate until 1915, when it was purchased by J.H. Geesman.

Over the course of the next 90 years, the house had seven additional owners, including the Villisca State Savings & Loan, whose name appears on the title from 1963 to 1971. In 1971, the house was sold to Kendrick & Vance, a mortgage company, and only a month later, was sold again to Darwin Kendrick, owner of the company. He remained as the owner of the house, renting it out to tenants, until it was sold to Rick and Vicki Sprague on January 1, 1994. A few months later, a real estate agent approached Darwin and Martha Linn, local farmers, about the possibility of them purchasing the house. At the time, the Linns already owned and operated the Olson-Linn Museum located on Villisca's town square and they felt that purchasing the house at Lot 410 would give them the opportunity to preserve more of the area's history. Because of its deteriorating condition, the Moore house was in danger of being razed. If the Linns had not purchased it, it's likely that it would have been destroyed. They soon set about obtaining the necessary funds to restore the home to its condition at the time of the murders in 1912.

As Darwin and Martha began researching the house, they found that they had a lot of work ahead of them to try and restore the place. Years of renovation followed and some paranormal researchers believe that it was the restorative work that followed that caused the house to become "active." In many cases of hauntings, an event may occur that leaves an "impression" on the atmosphere of a place. Such an event may include a traumatic occurrence like a murder, or several murders, as was the case with the Moore house. Often this haunting will lay dormant for many years before becoming active again. The activity is often generated by remodeling or renovation, disturbing the physical presence of the location. This disturbance can often cause effects to occur that are related to the haunting and can include sounds like voices, footsteps and cries, as well as physical effects like doors opening and closing, widows rattling and even knocking and rapping sounds. Is this merely a "recording" of the past that has been activated again or could there

The Ax Murder House in 2005

be an actual presence that generates the activity? In some locations, like the Villisca Ax Murder House, it may be both.

As the Linns attempted to work on the restoration, they found that 13 previous owners were listed on the deed to the Moore house and that it was often used as rental property. At this date, they have started to compile a list of tenants who lived in the house but progress has been slow and many of the renters stayed for only a short time. They did learn that between 1936 and 1994, the house had undergone extensive changes. The front and back porches were enclosed, plumbing and electricity were added and the outbuildings were either removed or replaced. The structure barely resembled the Moore house of 1912 but that was soon to change.

Using old photographs, the Linns began the renovation work in late 1994. The restoration included the removal of vinyl siding and the repainting of the original wood on the outside, the removal of the enclosures on the front and back porch, the restoration of an outhouse and chicken coop in the backyard and the removal of all of the indoor plumbing and electrical wiring in the house. The pantry in the original house had been converted to a bathroom years before and this room was now restored to its 1912 condition. Then, using testimony and records from the coroner's inquest and grand jury hearings, the Linns placed furniture in approximately the same places it had been at the time of the murders. Unfortunately, the original furniture that had belonged to the Moores vanished many decades ago but antiques replaced what was lost.

The Moore home was added to the National Register of Historic Places in 1998 and remains today as a colorful time capsule of 1912, the ghastly murders that occurred there and the mystery that followed. The walls hide many secrets, from the identity of the murderer to just how he managed to carry out his bloodbath without awakening the occupants of the house. These secrets still bring many visitors to the door. Some come looking for the history of the place but most of them come looking for the ghosts.

Ever since the Moore house was opened to overnight visitors several years ago, ghost enthusiasts, curiosity-seekers and diehard paranormal investigators have come here in droves. Some have stayed here alone, like the Des Moines disk jockey who awoke in the night to the sounds of children's voices when no children were present. Others have come in groups and have gone away with mysterious audio, video and photographic evidence that suggests something supernatural lurks within these walls. Tours have been cut short by falling lamps, moving objects, banging sounds and a child's laughter. Psychics who have come here have claimed to have communicated with the spirits of the dead.

If even a fraction of the stories circulating about this place were true, I reasoned when I first heard about the so-called "Villisca Ax Murder House", then this would have to be one of the most haunted places in America. The history of the place certainly provided a possibility for the story of the haunting to be true --- but was it? I would find that out for myself in May 2005, when I arrived for my first investigation of the house.

I arrived in Villisca just an hour or so before the sun went down. I met up with the rest of the group at Darwin and Martha Linn's museum, located on the town square just steps away from Villisca's bank and its only restaurants. The museum is in what was once one of the town's thriving businesses and features a jumbled assortment of old cars, farm equipment, advertising signs and historical records, displays and artifacts from days gone by. A visitor could spend hours in the museum and still not see everything that has been jammed into the two overflowing floors. I met Darwin and Martha for the first time (I have since cultivated a warm friendship with this wonderful couple) and spent a little while chatting with them before Darwin introduced the group to the bloody history of the Villisca murders through magazine articles and a video that had been produced about the family's last hours in June 1912.

After the introduction, we followed Darwin to the town cemetery, where the Moores and the Stillinger girls are buried. The grave markers of the family had been purchased from the sizable reward fund that had been collected in hopes of capturing their killer. Since the reward was never claimed, surviving family members donated the money to be used for the tombstones in Villisca's small cemetery. After leaving the burial ground, Darwin pointed out the once-grand mansion that had belonged to Frank Jones, one of the leading suspects in the murders, and then he led us back to the square and to one of the local restaurants. We fortified ourselves with a hearty meal --- it would be a long night ahead --- and then we all met at the Moore house, where we would spend the rest of our time in town.

As previously mentioned, walking into the Moore house is like stepping back in time. There is no plumbing or electricity in the house; the only illumination comes from candles and kerosene lamps. There is now a bathroom in the small barn that has been built on the property but at the time of my first visit, there was only an outhouse, which was authentic to 1912. The house is small and we entered through the back door, which let us into the kitchen. The parlor is located at the front of the house, with the bedroom leading off from it where the bodies of the Stillinger girls were found. Just off the kitchen is a small pantry and the staircase that leads to the second floor. At the top of the steps is the bedroom that belonged to J.B. and Sarah Moore and beyond that, at the front of the house, is the children's bedroom, where the blood-soaked bodies of the Moore children were discovered. There is also an unfinished attic room leading off from the Moores' bedroom.

It had been a warm afternoon, fading into evening, when I arrived in Villisca. The heat of the day had generated a line of fierce thunderstorms and soon after arriving at the house, we began to hear rumbles of thunder and see flashes of lightning above the distant, rolling hills. By 11:00 p.m. or so, the rain began to pound on Villisca but it only lasted for a short time. In less than an hour, the storms had moved off, leaving the night warm, still and humid. Our investigations were now set to begin in earnest.

In many cases during ghost hunts, I am relegated to the proverbial "back seat" and spend the evening observing the investigations and research that my invited guests are carrying out. I like to allow them to experience the locations for themselves and while I try to help when necessary, I usually stay out of the details of their experiments. In some cases, though, as it happened in Villisca, I couldn't help but get involved.

Two of the guests that night, Anney Horn and her daughter, Jada, had been to the Moore house on another occasion and Anney told the group about some rather strange happenings that she had experienced in the children's room on the second floor. She was convinced that one of the Moore children, five-year-old Paul, remained behind in this room and would interact with visiting researchers in exchange for candy. She had brought along a pocket full of treats and suggested that the group try and make contact with Paul. Everyone agreed and a couple of the other guests, David and Josie Rodriguez, who were part of an investigation team called PRISM (Paranormal Research and Investigative Studies Midwest) from Omaha, Nebraska, set up an array of video equipment in the bedroom to record any strange events that might occur. It would be the camera that was trained on the closet that would capture the most dramatic evidence of the night.

The closet door in the children's room on the second floor that this author personally saw opening and closing under its own power. Despite a thorough search for a possible explanation, nothing could be found that was causing the door to behave this way.

Within a few minutes, a number of the guests assembled in the room. As mentioned, I usually just like to observe whatever is going on and I chose to stay downstairs rather than make the small bedroom any more crowded than it already was. I was in the parlor as the communication attempts began upstairs but David was monitoring what was going on by way of a video feed that he had set up in the kitchen. After 20 minutes or so had passed, he called to me and invited me to come in and watch. There was something odd going on, David said, and I should come and take a look.

I went into the kitchen and looked over his shoulder at the monitor. The picture and sound were being fed to a laptop computer and I watched as the guests in the bedroom tried to coax the "ghost boy" into performing on cue for them. They were asking him to close a closet door that they had opened up and as far as we could tell, the door was closing just as they asked it to! This happened several times in a row and after watching it for a little while, I decided that I had to see it for myself.

I hurried upstairs and walked into the back room, which was now filled with excited investigators. I squeezed in as they described what had been happening. What they told me matched perfectly with what I had been watching on the monitor in the kitchen. I sat down and watched as Anney began to again try and coax "Paul" into closing the closet door that had been opened for him. To be honest, I was very skeptical about what was occurring. I had come upstairs, not because I was excited to see the antics of the alleged ghost but to find a logical explanation for what was going on. There had to be a reasonable answer for the closet door closing and I was determined to find out what that could be.

Anney called to Paul a few times and promised to leave some candy for him if he would make the closet door close for her. We all watched in silence as the door remained standing open about eight inches. Nothing happened for several minutes and then all of the sudden, for no apparent reason, the door slowly swung closed. It did not slam shut but rather seemed to just gently close, as though someone was pushing it. There was absolutely no one near it at the time.

I'm not sure how I managed to do it but I convinced the ghost hunters to take a break from the investigation and go downstairs for a few minutes. I wanted to check out the room and the closet. I was still dubious about the "ghost boy" and I was sure that there had to be a reason as to why the closet door seemed to be performing on command. I looked at everything ---- I looked for wires, for slopes in the floor, for loose hinges and I even tried opening the door and pushing it closed several times. Could it be a draft? I went through the entire upstairs and closed all of the doors and windows so that I could be sure that there was no air current coming in. Could it have been the distance that the door stood open that allowed it to swing closed? I made a note to try coaxing the door closed from other distances. Was it just a coincidence? If the door was left open long enough would it just close anyway? I tried leaving the door standing open for minutes at a time, much longer that it had been left with the room full of people, but it simply refused to close.

Finally, after 20 minutes or so, I was ready to try again. I invited the guests back into the bedroom and instructed them to try and get the door to close now that I had sealed off the windows from any outside air. Everyone sat down again and Anney went to work, once again calling out to Paul and asking him to close the door. A minute or two passed and the door swung shut again ---- something that I had been unable to duplicate a short time before. There was no way I could say that this was caused by air currents or drafts from the windows. The door was opened back up again and she asked Paul to close it again --- and again.

This happened several more times before we stopped and decided to try something else. If the door was not closing because of an air current, could it close on its own anyway, if we waited long enough? I had tried waiting several minutes, but what if we waited for an hour or so? Would the door eventually just swing closed? And if so, was it because the doorframe was slanted in some way, which would explain why the door was closing, seemingly on its own?

I wanted to see what would happen if we did not ask Paul to close the door. We made an agreement to leave the door standing open and for all of us leave the room. Anyone who wanted to watch it could do so from the monitor downstairs in the kitchen. With that, we all went downstairs or outside to have a midnight snack and to wait around and see what might happen in the bedroom.

We waited for nearly two hours and did not go back into the room during that time. Through most of that time, someone was watching the door from the monitor, or at least checking in periodically to see what was happening. During that entire time, the door never moved. Nothing had changed with it ---- except that no one was asking Paul to close it. It never budged. It just stood there, open about eight inches, apparently just waiting for us to return.

Finally, at about 2:00 a.m., several of us filed back into the room. The door was standing open, just as we had left it, and we sat down with a clear view of it. It had now been standing open for almost two hours and Anney spoke out loud, asking Paul to close the door.

"Paul? Are you there?" she queried. "Would you close the door for us again? If you do, I'll leave some more candy inside of the closet."

Seconds ticked by and then, without anyone moving, speaking or coming close to the door, the wooden panel slowly swung shut and latched with a click. It had never moved --- until someone asked for it to and then suddenly, the door had closed. I would love to provide one but I have no rational explanation for how this could have happened without some sort element of the unexplained being involved.

Is the Moore house in Villisca really haunted? There are many who maintain that it's not. They say that many people lived in the house over the years and none of them ever mentioned ghosts or mysterious activity. It was not until the renovations began that visitors began to say that strange events were occurring within the walls of the "Ax Murder House." Are these events merely the products of overactive imaginations or wishful thinking? That's what some would like you to believe but don't be fooled --- and don't take my word for it either.

I have come to believe that this house is haunted because of my own experiences here. I hope the reader will reserve his own judgment until the time comes when he can spend a night inside this house. It's not a place for the faint of heart but if you are looking for a place where you might be able to experience paranormal phenomena on your own, then search for Villisca, Iowa, on the map and make your own plans to step back in time to this historic ---- and haunted --- place.

13. ONE OF CALIFORNIA'S MOST HAUNTED HOUSES
SPIRITS OF THE LEONIS ADOBE

BY ROB AND ANNE WLODARSKI

"Although Miguel and Espiritu Leonis died nearly a century ago, the current owners of their ranch house insist that they still roam the grounds. Miguel, a Basque settler, spent much of his time shooting trespassers and suing his neighbors over property disputes. He was once called the most hated man in California. The haunting began in 1922 when the occupants, the Agoure family, began to notice strange noises and unexplainable odors throughout the house. Today, there are regular sightings of the cadaverous couple by visitors and caretakers."
Dennis William Hauck

The history of the Leonis adobe is integrally tied to the Native American occupation of the region, and in particular with a village situated a few miles away, called Huwam. This village located in Bell Canyon, contained a shrine site called Castle Peak, and it was here that Miguel Leonis met his future wife, Maria de (Espiritu) Santo Cheboya. The adobe dates to the early 1840s, and was most likely used by a homesteader who raised sheep or cattle, or grew crops. It wasn't until around 1870 that the name Leonis became synonymous with the adobe. For over 50 years the two-story, hacienda-style adobe remained in the Leonis family until Juan Menendez (The son of Espiritu Leonis and her first husband) sold the Leonis Adobe to Martin and Frances Agoure in 1921. From a residence, school, restaurant and finally, a cultural landmark, the adobe continued to fall into disrepair. It was not winning its battle with nature.

On August 6, 1962, the Leonis Adobe became officially designated "Historic Cultural Monument Number 1," the first in a series of cultural properties recognized by the City of Los Angeles Cultural Heritage Board for protection and preservation. However, this honor does little to dissuade investors from eying this prime piece of real estate and shortly after achieving landmark status, the adobe was scheduled to be razed. Decaying and dilapidated, the more than 100-year-old structure was an eyesore and a safety hazard. On the verge of destruction, this historic landmark was saved by the late Catherine S. Beachy of Woodland Hills, among the founders of the non-profit Leonis Adobe Association. Although the venture failed to raise enough money and to save the building from impending demolition and conversion of the site to a strip mall, Beachy ended up purchasing the adobe and the adjoining five acres for $240,000 on March 28, 1963. She added $30,000 to ensure that the building would be restored. Nature had shrouded the old home in weeds and vines, and the wood was rotting, but The Leonis Adobe had been spared

The Leonis Adobe

from destruction at the last minute and so, too, had its bountiful, spirited population.

Volunteers found artifacts from the house scattered around the grounds. An oversized antique mirror was found in a streambed and a staircase railing was discovered mysteriously stuffed up a chimney.

THE HISTORY

There are no spirits without history. Any place on this planet where ghosts are thought to reside has an integral tie to history or the landscape. Spirits do not exist without a strong relationship with the constructs of time and space. The Leonis Adobe, considered one of the most haunted buildings in California, is a perfect example of history not only leaving historic imprints on the building, but providing the basis for a continual, interactive spirited population dating to the time when Native Americans occupied the landscape. With this in mind, the following is a history that gives a context to the spirits of the Leonis Adobe. (Special thanks to the Leonis Adobe Museum and San Fernando Valley Historical Society for the use of the historical photographs in this story.)

1769: Captain Gaspar de Portola led the first overland expedition into Alta California accompanied by his chaplain, a Franciscan friar named Juan Crespi who kept a diary of the expedition. The Portola party discovered the San Fernando Valley, and named it Valle de los Encinos (Valley of the Oaks). Returning from San Francisco, the expedition followed the Camino Real (present-day Ventura Freeway), setting up camp near present-day Calabasas. A historic bell marker commemorating the royal road linking all the Spanish missions, is located in front of the Leonis Adobe.

1783: The earliest mention of the Native American village Escorpion dates to September 17, 1783 from a journal entry at the Santa Barbara Presidio that stated, "it was decided to postpone an attack on Conejo and Escorpion Rancherias, who have stolen cattle." El Escorpion (the scorpion), is the name given to the area by Spanish soldiers. It is situated at the foot of a hill that has a distinctive shape that reminded them of a scorpion. This landmark hill (now referred to as Castle Peak) is recognizable from miles away.

1821: Maria de (Espiritu) Santo Cheboya was born

1824: According to local lore, Calabasas obtained its name because Antonio Jauregui, a Basque farmer from Oxnard, accidentally dumped a load of pumpkins along the road leading to Los Angeles. A few months later, vines sprang up along both sides of the road. This mishap led to christening of the area "Las Calabazas" meaning "the pumpkins" or "the gourds." Michel "Miguel" Leonis was born on October 20, in the village of Cambo-les-Baines, France, in the Basque Province of the Pyrenees Mountains, near the border of Spain.

1834: San Fernando Mission was secularized. Over 120,000 acres within the mission's purview encompassed most of San Fernando Valley. Rancho El Escorpion lands became a horse and cattle ranch.

1839: On July 5, Native American José Odon, a neophyte at Mission San Fernando, received his Decree of Emancipation, giving him permission to leave the mission.

1844: Researchers believe that the construction of the two-story Leonis adobe began.

1846: The construction of the Leonis adobe was presumed completed.

1850: The census listed about 90 individuals living at Rancho E1 Escorpion with all of its inhabitants joined under two households: those of Urbano and Joaquin Romero. Urbano Chari was listed as a 50-year-old Indian and his household included his wife, Juana, and 38 Indians. Co-owner, Joaquin Romero, was listed as a 28-year-old single male, a non-Indian, with 53 Indians in his household.

1858: Miguel Leonis, 34, a native of a Basque province in southern France, arrived in Southern California after leaving his country to escape the law. He worked as a sheep-herder for Joaquin Romero, co-owner of Rancho El Escorpion. Horse thief Dolores Aguirre was killed on Rancho El Escorpion.

1859: Espiritu, the daughter of Urbano Romero and Eusebia, a Native American woman, married a man named Menendez and had a son named Juan. Espiritu and her husband inherited her father's holdings in Rancho El Escorpion. Miguel Leonis, became a resident at Rancho El Escorpion where he raised sheep. The owners allowed Leonis to graze his livestock on their land.

1860: Espiritu's husband died and she was left with part of a ranch and a young son. Joaquin Romero who drank excessively, promoted Miguel Leonis as majordomo over his ranch. During this time, Leonis lived in a small adobe in the northwest corner of

(Left) Miguel Leonis   (Right) Espiritu Menendez

the rancho. Miguel Leonis began courting Espiritu Menendez, which ultimately led to their marriage by contract the Gabrielino way (essentially common-law marriage). Miguel and Espiritu now jointly owned the entire rancho. Miguel refused to allow Espiritu's son, Juan Menendez (also spelled Melendez and Melendrez) to live in their home on Rancho El Escorpion.

1861: Miguel Leonis and Espiritu had a daughter named Marcelina.

1871: On January 23, Odon sold his share of Rancho El Escorpion to Miguel Leonis for one dollar and "other valuable consideration." On March 2, Miguel Leonis attempted to re-adjust the lot lines to his rancho by deeding his ownership of El Escorpion to his wife, Espiritu Chijulia, and resubmitting new deeds with an extended northerly lot line. Espiritu's father Urbano sued Leonis claiming he accidentally sold

Marcelina, the daughter of Miguel and Espiritu

Leonis all his land. The court ruled in favor of Leonis and the new northern lot line is upheld. Miguel Leonis had his eye on an abandoned adobe (the present-day Leonis adobe) around this time. The abandoned adobe in Calabasas, which Leonis coveted, reportedly had walls two feet thick and consisted of two levels. Leonis slowly began restoring the adobe, eventually making it his place of residence. Leonis also began claiming additional land around the adobe.

1872: Leonis reportedly constructed a two-story barn on Rancho El Escorpion land, which, along with the adobe, stood near the southwest corner of present-day Bell Canyon Road and Valley Circle Boulevard. Through his marriage to Espiritu, Leonis now owned all of Rancho El Escorpion

1872: Leonis seized large amounts of land by homesteading. The Homestead Act of 1862 provided that anyone could claim unappropriated public land, provided that they established residency and made improvements to the property. Leonis put up crude buildings; paid an employee to live there;

then filed a claim on the land. Leonis accumulated land and cattle and eventually became known as the "King of Calabasas." Leonis had over 100 Hispanic and Native American employees.

1875: A land dispute occurred between Miguel Leonis and a band of squatters led by an ex-Union soldier named Andrew Banks and other Civil War veterans. Banks, threatened by Leonis, hired prominent attorney Horace Bell to stop Leonis. The conflict ended with the death of Banks and the scattering of his comrades.

1879: Miguel Leonis began enlarging the adobe on Calabasas Road while still living at Rancho El Escorpion. He enclosed the outside front of the house by building a veranda. Leonis installed a clapboard roof and the rear and northeast side porches were walled in at both levels to create additional rooms. Leonis placed wooden paneling on the living room walls and laid wood planks over the original earthen floor.

1880: The U.S. Census listed Joaquin Romero as living with Maria, Marcelina and José Odon. José Odon's fourth child, Espiritu, age 48, living with Miguel Leonis, 54, and their family at the present-day Leonis Adobe.

Miguel and Espiritu's daughter Marcelina died from smallpox at the Rancho El Escorpion adobe. According to some historians, Miguel was on the verge of moving the family to the adobe along Calabasas Road when the tragedy took place. Some say that Leonis was so distraught after the death of his beloved daughter that he tried to commit suicide. He reportedly tied a rope around his neck and tossed the other end over a branch of a large oak tree near the present-day Sagebrush Cantina; however, his horse refused to budge and his suicide attempt failed. He was so upset that he cut off the branch. The stately oak (now gone) earned the name, "Hangman's Tree."

1886: Without heirs, Miguel Leonis (who did not consider Juan Menendez his son) sent for his nephew from France, John Baptista (J.B.) Leonis, to prepare him to run his estate. J.B. Leonis became his uncles' accountant, until finally setting off on his own. J.B. had no desire to run a ranch.

1889: While heading home through the Cahuenga Pass after celebrating a legal victory in Los Angeles, an intoxicated Miguel Leonis reportedly fell under a rear wheel of his wagon and was crushed. As one story goes, on the morning of September 21, the lifeless body of 65-year-old Miguel Leonis was discovered in the pass (Some believe that he was ambushed by one of his numerous enemies, while others claimed that he was a victim of armed robbery). A coroner's inquest conducted just after Leonis' death, reported that on September 17, Miguel Leonis, while en route from Los Angeles to Calabasas with four other men including Espiritu's son Juan Menendez, fell from his seat when the wagon jerked, and landed between the wheels. Before the wagon could be stopped, a rear wheel crushed his abdomen, gravely injuring him. Those with him rushed him to the Six Mile House, a stage stop along the road to the Cahuenga Pass. Leonis suffered four broken ribs and internal injuries and died three days later. On September 23, Miguel Leonis was interred at the old El Campo Santo cemetery at the end of North Broadway in Los Angeles. At the time of his death Leonis' estate was valued at $303,474.40 and included over 10,000 acres of land, 17-1/2 acres of prime real estate in Los Angeles, 3,000 head of cattle, $85,000 in cash, a store, a saloon, and a two-story adobe home in

Calabasas.

1889: Miguel Leonis bequeathed $5,000 to be invested by his friends, the proceeds to care for Espiritu, "because of her ignorance," and $5,000 in cash if she didn't contest the will. If Espiritu contested the will, she would not be entitled to the inheritance. Espiritu's son Juan Menendez and his wife Juana Valenzuela came to live at the adobe with her. Juan built and operated his own blacksmith shop directly across the road from the Leonis Adobe.

1894: Juan and Juana Menendez adopted six-month-old Maria Johnson, who lived in the adobe until she turned sixteen, at which time she married Pedro Orsua from Santa Monica.

1906: Espiritu Leonis died on April 10, at her home in Calabasas. She was buried at the San Fernando Mission cemetery. The San Fernando Mission was established in 1797 and the first burial there was in 1800. Juan Menendez and his family continued living at the Leonis adobe.

Juan and Juana Menendez

1921: Juan Menendez sold the Leonis Adobe to Martin and Frances Agoure.

1922: The Agoures make several modifications to house by adding two bathrooms through an extension along the north side of the house. The living room was enlarged to its present size by removing a wall that stood between the parlor and the original living room. A doorway was also created between the living room and dining room and the upper level was converted into guest

Modifications and expansions were made to the Leonis Adobe in the early 1920s

... Formal Opening June 5, 1938 ...

MONTEREY RANCHO

23537 Ventura Boulevard
Calabasas, California

Telephone
Canoga Park 6544

Menu

DINNER SERVED IN OUR ADOBE DINING ROOM FROM 1 to 8 P. M.

Our home cooked dinner . . . 85c

Grapejuice Cocktail
Tossed Dinner Salad
Fried Colored Chicken, Jointed
or
Broiled Club Steak, Buttered
Potatoes   Sliced Tomatoes   Chicken Gravy
Hot Biscuits   Orange Marmalade
Homemade Pumpkin or Lemon Pie
Ice Cream   Sherbert
        Coffee   Tea   Milk
Dinner Served to Children Under 12 Years — 50c

A La Carte

SOUPS
Cream of Tomato 15c   Chicken Broth 15c
Split Pea 15c   Vegetable 15c
SALADS
Avocado and Tomato 25c   Chicken 45c
Pineapple or Pear and Cottage Cheese 25c
SANDWICHES
"Our Special" Open Faced Cold Fried Chicken 35c
Fried Ham 25c   Cheese 20c   Avocado 25c   Bacon and Tomato 20c
DESSERTS
Ice Cream 10c   Sherbet 10c   Pie 10c
Pie a la Mode or with Cheese 15c
BEVERAGES
Coffee 5c   Tea 10c   Milk or Buttermilk 10c   Coca Cola or 7 Up 5c

For Party Reservations Telephone Canoga Park 6544

OUR FOODS ARE PROTECTED BY AIR CONDITIONED
ICE REFRIGERATION

We Are Not Responsible for Lost Articles   No Service Less Than 10c
3% Sales Tax will be added to all Taxable Items

The menu for the Monterey Rancho Restaurant, which
opened in the Leonis Adobe in 1938

bedrooms. The City of Los Angeles granted the Agoure family access to the city water system by creating a new boundary line between the city and county of Los Angeles. The odd boundary creation only included the Leonis Adobe, which was now part of the City of Los Angeles. The Agoures also owned a restaurant in Calabasas.

1930: To dispel the rumors that have circulated over the years regarding the sudden demise of Miguel Leonis in 1889, his body was exhumed. A thorough examination revealed marks on his upper abdomen consistent with the reported wagon accident; he was not murdered.

1938: On June 5, the Leonis Adobe opened as a restaurant called the Monterey Rancho. A home-cooked dinner cost 85 cents, with coffee and a Coca-Cola cost 5 cents, ice cream was 10 cents and an open-faced cold fried chicken sandwich was 35 cents.

1960: Actor John Carradine, Sr. and his family moved out, after renting the adobe for six years. Vandals began breaking windows and destroying the building.

1962: On August 6, the Leonis Adobe was designated "Historic Cultural Monument Number 1," the first in a series of cultural properties recognized by the City of Los Angeles Cultural Heritage Board for protection and preservation.

1963: Catherine S. Beachy bought the adobe and five adjoining acres.

1965: Renovations began on the Leonis Adobe to return it to its 1870s appearance.

1966: On May 21, the Leonis Adobe opened to the public as a museum.

1975: On May 29, the structure was listed on the National Register of Historic Places.

1978: Death of Pedro Orsua, followed by that of his wife a year later. They are buried in the San José Mission cemetery.

1983: After learning the plight of the Plummer House through the Los Angeles Conservancy, the Leonis Adobe Association stepped in and had the front portion of the heavily damaged building relocated to the Leonis Adobe grounds. The Plummer House was known as the oldest house in Hollywood. The Association repaired, restored and refurbished the house, making it into a visitors' center and gift shop for the Leonis Adobe.

Currently: The Leonis Adobe and five remaining acres of land are now owned and maintained by the Leonis Adobe Association. Today, the adobe is an example of living history and an opportunity for visitors to glimpse the less hectic lifestyle that once existed in the San Fernando Valley. Adults and children love to roam the adobe and surrounding grounds where farm animals graze, and in a sense, return to yesteryear, when there was no freeway, and Miguel Leonis, the King of Calabasas, ruled the local landscape. The Leonis Adobe Museum is located at 23537 Calabasas Rd., Calabasas, CA. It is open to the public Wednesdays through Sundays from 1:00 p.m. to 4:00pm. Donations are requested. Call 818-222-6511 for information regarding group tours and special events or visit www.leonisadobemuseum.org.

THE SPIRITS

The haunted character of the adobe has never been in question; it is unknown, however, just how many spirits occupy the dwelling and surrounding grounds. The International Paranormal Research Organization (IPRO) began researching the building over a five-year period from 2002 to 2007 and conducted numerous investigations in the house during that time. The house was profiled in the British paranormal television series *Most Haunted* in 2005. A group of paranormal investigators spent the night there and said they made contact with the ghosts of Miguel and Espiritu Leonis. Stories from ghost hunters, paranormal investigators, psychics, caretakers, docents and those fortunate enough to be touched by the spirited population of the adobe, suggested that anywhere between six-and-ten spirits occupy the adobe, including Miguel Leonis, Espiritu Leonis, Juan Menendez, Maria Johnson Orsua, an unidentified female housekeeper, a Native American male, a Hispanic male and two girls. This all adds up to a crowded population of unseen houseguests. Following are a few of the ghost stories assembled to date:

"CHICHITA, CHICHITA"

The following information was provided by Ray Phillips, a member of the board of the Leonis Adobe Museum. "This is a transcription of a reel-to-reel tape taken at one-and-seven-eighths speed of Mary Vergara telling a ghost story on September the 14th, 1966. The circumstances are these: Maria Johnson Orsua had been brought to the Leonis Adobe as an infant of about six months old in 1894, and raised by Juan Menendez and his wife as one of their five children. She knew Mrs. Leonis, Espiritu Leonis, very well, and called her, Grandmother. She [Mary] was about 12 years old when Mrs. Leonis

A mysterious mist appeared in a photograph that was taken in the living room of the house

died.

"At the time of this [occurrence], Mr. and Mrs. Orsua were using the master bedroom. Mr. Orsua was in a hospital bed, having recently had an operation for lung cancer. Mrs. Orsua was sleeping in another bed in the same room. Mary Vergara, I believe was her oldest daughter, and had come down from northern California, where she lived, to visit the Orsuas. She was sleeping in the farther room, which we call the Juan Menendez study or siesta room, in a cot. She was awakened around midnight, and found a dark, shadowy figure, standing just to the north of her, by the door. It said to her, "pssst, pssst, Chiquita, Chiquita!"

Mary Vergara had never been called Chiquita, and was annoyed at being awakened. So she took her cot and her bed things and went into another room to spend the night. The next morning, she went in to see how her parents were, and asked Mrs. Orsua, why she had awakened her and called her Chiquita. Mrs. Orsua said that she and her husband [Pedro Orsua] had not been up, and had not awakened her, and that Chiquita was the name they called her when she was a child living at the adobe. The assumption is, that it was [Espiritu's] ghost calling to someone she felt was Mrs. Orsua during her last illness [in 1906], because Mrs. Orsua spent the last several months of [Espiritu's] life, sleeping on a cot, or rather a couch near her [Espiritu's] bed, under the north window in the master bedroom, so that she could hear if Espiritu Leonis called for help in the middle of the night."

Another event involved a young couple who visited the adobe on one a rainy afternoon. There were no other visitors on that day and only a single volunteer was present. The couple toured the house without a guide. Once upstairs, they were drawn to a large bedroom, where they noticed a bearded man asleep in one of the beds. Taken aback at first, they decided that that it must be the caretaker taking a nap. Then they saw the man gasp and convulse. The couple wasted no time running down the stairs to find help. They found the docent and explained that there was a man in trouble upstairs. All three people moved a fast as they could to the spot where the man was convulsing but the room was empty. The only explanation they could come up with was that they had intruded on a death scene involving Miguel Leonis who reportedly was brought to the room after suffering lethal injuries from an accident involving a fall from a wagon. The couple had no way of knowing that Leonis had tragically died that way in 1889, over 100 years earlier.

When the Agoure family lived at the Leonis Adobe, unexplained noises were heard in the house on a frequent basis. The family also reported hearing the sounds of footsteps on the upper floor and on the staircase. Occasionally, the family would be confronted by odd smells that would suddenly emanate throughout the house. During the 1930s, the Gregg family owned the adobe. One moonlit evening a woman who lived there (possibly Mrs. Gregg) was leaning against the railing on the second level verandah. The dilapidated rail cracked and was about to give away when a pair of strong hands pulled the woman back, saving her from serious injury. When she turned to look at who saved her, she was amazed to find nobody there. While alive, Miguel Leonis was touted for his great strength and undoubtedly had strong hands. Other supernatural snippets include:

Heavy footsteps are frequently heard coming from the upstairs hallway, kitchen, master bedroom and veranda.

There are reports of a party going on in the living room and dining area when it is unoccupied. The noise is often so loud that it seems as if a group of people has just gathered. Other times, people report hearing heated conversations. When they check the areas where it seemed the discussion was taking place, the room is always empty.

Doors frequently open and close by themselves in the upstairs hallway area. This happens when there is no wind and no one is ever found to be responsible for the strange slamming sounds.

Loud knocking sounds will often come from the front door. When someone checks to see who might be trying to get in, there is never anyone there.

Occasional sounds of phantom children playing are heard coming from the Orsua room, the upstairs hallway, the stairwell and the living room.

Misty forms have been sighted in the upstairs hallway, on the upstairs verandah, in the master bedroom and in the living room. Most of the apparitions are without a discernible form, so no one is sure if they are male or female, young or old.

One day a group of startled women witnessed an apparition while they were resting at the rear of the adobe. A tall and dark figure of a man materialized before their eyes and proceeded to walk in their direction. They saw the figure instantly disappear into an oak tree. They claimed that it was the spirit of Miguel Leonis, who in life was a tall man. The spooked ladies never forgot their encounter with the unknown.

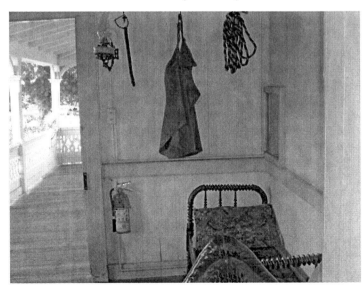

Another group of women were frightened by the sounds of an unseen presence digging somewhere in the backyard. They could hear the shovel penetrate the ground and the dirt being tossed, but they couldn't find an excavation going on anywhere around the building.

A lone guest at the house reported observing a misty, floating image in the upstairs hallway and said that it spoke in a soft, pleasant female voice. The words were unclear but the frightened guest recalled that

The bed where the spirit of Miguel Leonis is often witnessed the sound was very eerie.

Witnesses occasionally report seeing a tall man appear in front of the adobe entryway. This eerie male apparition, resembling Miguel Leonis, materializes for a few seconds, and then quickly vanishes in front of the stunned onlookers.

An apparition frequently sighted at the adobe is the famous Lady in Black. She is usually spotted standing on the front verandah by guests and staff during the time the adobe is open, or by people driving by after the place has been locked up for the night. The woman is always described as wearing a long, black dress and she stares silently at those who dare gaze back. The spectral lady [probably Espiritu Leonis], has also been sighted downstairs, in the back yard by the large oak tree. She has even visited the caretakers who live on site. The mysterious lady seems to be checking up on the place and the people who come to visit, just as Espiritu might have done while she occupied the adobe.

A guest, while strolling through the upstairs hallway after coming in from the veranda, began hearing heavy footsteps in back of her. She turned quickly, but no one was behind her. Attributing it to the old floors creaking, she continued. Passing through the doorway that leads to a main east-west corridor, the footsteps followed closely behind hers. Turning again, she found she was alone in the hallway. Becoming a little spooked, the woman picked up her pace and reached the stairwell. The footsteps echoed in the hallway behind her, matching her movement, step for step. By now, she was afraid to see who might be following her. This time, she felt a chill and the distinct sensation that she was being watched, and that was enough to send her scurrying down the stairs and out the front entrance. She did not feel threatened, but rather unnerved at being followed by one of the spirits she had heard tales about over the years.

A psychic once visited the adobe and was strolling along the upstairs veranda when one of the rocking chairs began moving back and forth for about fifteen seconds before suddenly stopping. The person felt that a female presence had decided to sit down for a few seconds before resuming her daily routine.

Once, while filming at the adobe, another strange incident took place. Just after the director had called, "quiet on the set," and the cameras were about to roll, a loud crashing sound was heard in the background. Although everyone in the room denied making the sound, they all heard it. However, no one could find the source of the sound. Nothing had fallen in the house. After a few minutes, the director set up for another take. Just after he called for quiet once again, the loud banging noise (like someone slamming a door) disrupted the silence. This unnerved the crew because no one was able to determine the source of the disturbance. After some time, the director and crew were able to get the take they wanted.

Two visitors once entered the front doorway of the adobe, when one of them noticed a woman off to the left side of the living room, passing through the kitchen/dining area. Having visited the place before, the visitors were startled, because the figure didn't look like a docent or another guest, but rather like a Native American or Hispanic woman from another era. Without wasting a moment, the visitors ran into the adjacent room, which was empty. Quickly looking around the kitchen, there wasn't a soul to be seen. Just then, a docent came into the house. The visitors eagerly told her what had happened. According to the docent, the description of the figure would have fit one of the housekeeping staff during the time that Miguel and Espiritu Leonis occupied the adobe.

PARANORMAL INVESTIGATION
DECEMBER 1, 2001

One of several paranormal investigations conducted by the International Paranormal Research Organization (IPRO) took place on Saturday, December 1, 2001. The group consisted of: Robert Wlodarski; Anne Wlodarski; Ginnie McGovern; Kevin Patrick; Daniel Smith; Matt Cope; Karen Camus; Richard Senate; John Anthony Miller; Alma Carey; Wayne and Diane Bonner; Dan Larson; Michelle Garforth; Matt Wlodarski; and Leonis Adobe board members: Sheryl Saul, Angela Adams, Don Adams, Michelle Fix, Deanna Saul and Margaret Daly. Equipment included an Aurameter; two Tri-field EMF Meters; two Gauss Meters; three analog recorders: two digital thermometers; one 35mm camera; one VHS and one 8mm camcorders; a Cyber Probe II - static Electrical Field Detector; and four sets of dowsing rods.

The investigative group and guests began arriving around 3:30 p.m. The outside temperature at 3:00 p.m. was around 64 degrees F, and it was a partly cloudy afternoon with rain expected the next day. There would be a full moon that night. Inside, the ambient temperature ranged from 68 degrees upstairs to 64 degrees downstairs. By the time the investigation was over at 10:00 p.m., the temperature outside was roughly 45 degrees. The temperature downstairs was 58 degrees while the temperature upstairs was 61 degrees. The downstairs area contains a dining room, family room, kitchen, caretaker's kitchen (former guest room) and storage room for food (display area). Upstairs, there is a master bedroom, two corridors, a caretaker's bathroom (formerly a bedroom), the caretaker's bedroom (formerly a guest bedroom), and a multipurpose room. There are wrap-around verandas on the east and south-facing, upstairs and downstairs portions of the house.

The psychics and paranormal investigators walked through the adobe, documenting their impressions of any anomalous phenomena. Several pieces of monitoring equipment were used to help document or confirm potential paranormal "hot-spots" and possible anomalies. A cameraman documented the investigation of the building. After about two hours of investigating, the results of the walk-through were gathered from each investigator for later compilation.

In the dining room, a moving energy that registered sudden drops in temperature from 64 degrees to 52 degrees occurred near the entryway to the living room and near the entryway to the kitchen. The EMF and Gauss meters recorded extreme fluctuations that went off the scale numerous times (no external source could be found for these readings). Several individuals with dowsing rods also pinpointed two main areas in the dining room, which conformed with the temperature and EMF readings.

In the kitchen, a very strong energy (most individuals felt a dominant Hispanic, female energy on the east and west sides of the room). The temperature and EMF readings picked up numerous spikes and anomalies

The haunted kitchen

The Stairway to the second floor

there. Several individuals came into the room during the measurements in an attempt to communicate with the seemingly disturbed spirit. Three people with dowsing rods and an Aurameter, pinpointed two primary anomalous areas in the kitchen which conformed with the odd temperature and EMF readings. By communicating in Spanish, several team members tried to assure the woman (who was felt to be a housekeeper for the Leonis or Menendez families) that no one was there to harm her or intrude on her space. The sense of anger and confusion was tempered through a discussion with the entity. The readings in the room confirmed this. After communication was established, the areas where the female spirit seemed to be, did not yield the same, high-spiked readings and temperature fluctuations. There was a simple request by the woman relayed by a psychic, that she (the female spirit) had much work to do, and that she would like us to leave HER kitchen; which we did.

In the living room, the dowsing rods and EMF and Gauss meter readings pinpointed three hotspots: one, near the entry door into the dining room; one near the large mirror on the west side of the entry door to the adobe; and another near the door leading from the original adobe to the back entryway and stairway. These areas were monitored a number of times and they did not change in intensity, always exhibiting, strong, anomalous readings on all the equipment.

At the base of the stairwell on the first floor and on the landing on the second floor, the equipment registered distinct anomalies in temperature and EMF fluctuations, as if a presence were standing in those locations. There was also a chill surrounding those spots.

Near the entryway to the Orsua Room on the first floor (connected to the house but just outside the original adobe), a strong, pulsing energy was felt and picked up with the dowsing equipment. The EMF and Gauss meters showed strong fluctuations, and one investigator remarked that he was being watched.

The upstairs bathroom produced intense EMF and Gauss meter reactions at the doorway and near the bathroom mirror. The dowsing equipment also picked up energy near the bathtub and doorway area. One investigator said he heard the sounds of a girl or girls giggling or laughing. It was later determined that at one time, this bathroom was used as a girls bedroom.

The corridor separating the master bedroom from the current caretaker's room also showed signs of activity as evidenced by strong spikes in the EMF and Gauss meters, dropping temperatures as registered by the digital thermometer, and reactions of the dowsing rods. These readings carried into the master bedroom where numerous paranormal events have been reported over the years, including imprints appearing on a freshly made bed, lights turning on and off and people being touched by unseen hands.

The northeastern room upstairs also exhibited fluctuations on the EMF meter and with the dowsing rods. There was a consensus among investigators that a male presence dominated this area. Frequent cold spots were felt and the energy seemed to move around the room and out the door to the veranda. The EMF meter and dowsing rods picked up fluctuations throughout the veranda after leaving this room and essentially the energy continued along the veranda until reaching the south-facing entryway and corridor which connected to the master bedroom and caretaker's room. It was as if the investigators were following someone unseen as they walked around the building on the upstairs veranda.

The equipment registered fluctuations and anomalous readings around the veranda. Once the investigative team

A séance during the investigation of the house

reached the south-facing doorway, the readings dropped off. When the group entered the doorway, the equipment began registering strongly again, particularly in front of the master bedroom.

There was an overall feeling that the energy that was in the building was friendly but very curious as to what we were doing there. Several people felt as if they were constantly being watched and followed. These feelings were particularly strong in the kitchen and dining room, where one spirit seemed to follow behind two investigators for brief periods before trailing off.

Psychics reported the following:

* Strong dowsing rod movement was recorded in the living room, near the mirror. This area seems to be a strong energy vortex or portal.

* A male presence was sensed around the bed and desk in the northeastern room upstairs.

* Espiritu's presence is very strong in the master bedroom.

* Strong activity from the dowsing rods in the upstairs bathroom. There was an impression that children were present.

* Strong movement from the dowsing equipment and Aurameter on the right side of the dining room.

* In the hallway adjacent to the living room, near the door threshold, a lot of energy and movement is sensed along with noticeable dowser activity.

* A guest who joined the investigator felt cold air on her legs which slowly moved up her back in

the kitchen/dining room entryway. The energy felt happy and seemed to be a male energy.

* Someone heard a child humming and rocking in a chair on the veranda. The following words were heard: "Mama coming home," "Papa coming home," and, "Oh, where is the puppy?"

* A young man was sensed, standing near the front door, looking into the mirror and waiting for a woman wearing lilac. The mirror is perceived as an energy portal for many spirits to enter the house.

* The downstairs kitchen has sharp feeling of sudden pain; fire.

* The cellar has a feeling of resolve and darkness. There was a noxious smell emanating from there, and the investigator felt intoxicated, confused and experienced equilibrium problems.

* On the second-floor balcony in front of the master bedroom window there was a scattering of energy and a static spot. Since numerous people pass this spot, it is a focal point for nervous energy.

* In the second floor hallway, just below the attic access, there is a playful spirit at work. It felt like a game of hide-and-seek was being played. A male child who has happy memories pervades this area.

* The upstairs bathroom had a great deal of movement. The energy felt as if it was from a later period, perhaps post-1920s.

* A woman and two girls were sensed working near the north side of the house facing the oak tree.

* An unhappy female spirit may inhabit the kitchen area. The female is possibly a Native American, with dark hair and one eye that seems out of alignment and a slight scar on her chin. She is wearing a cross or religious medal and has a slightly pock-marked complexion.

* The dining area and kitchen registered intense fluctuations on the Cyber Probe. There were at least three strong areas in the dining room, which seemed to move about, particularly near the door between both rooms.

* Several psychics agreed that the master bedroom is inhabited by two spirits who are short in stature. One is a younger girl and one is a heavy-set person. Several strong reactions were noted on the Cyber probe.

* The first floor Orsua Room is dominated by a strong presence accompanied by an intense cold. The spirit seems to be a male with light-colored hair and a scar on the left side of his face. He wears a white shirt under a brown vest.

* Strong equipment readings were picked up at a trunk in the corridor under Espiritu's picture on the second floor.

* A Native American woman roams the downstairs area. She reportedly has dark hair, a ruddy complexion, and wears a buttoned shawl and brooch.

All participants adjourned to the living room, where the communication circle was to be held. A round table and eight chairs were set up. From around 7:20 p.m. to 10:00 p.m. the circle was convened in front of the large mirror to the left of the entryway. Video and audio cassette taping were conducted by Rob Wlodarski and Matt Cope. Participating at various times throughout the evening, were: Ginnie McGovern, John Anthony Miller, Daniel Smith, Alma Carey, Deanna Saul, Kevin Patrick, Anne Wlodarski, Karen Camus, Richard Senate, Sheryl Saul, Michelle Fix and Robert Wlodarski. The opening meditation/prayer was led by Ginnie McGovern. Items brought to the table were a cassette player, a wind chime, a candle, a child's teddy bear, a feather, and sage. The spirits are asked to use the candle, the table or any other of the items on the table to communicate. If the candle was to be used by the spirits, it was requested that the flame rise high if a "yes," answer and shrink for if the answer was "no". Here are some of the highlights of the séance (a complete transcript can be found in the book *Spirits of the Leonis Adobe* (www.ghostpublishingco.com). In a few cases, words or parts of sentences were difficult to distinguish. The entire session was also videotaped by Sacred Mesa Productions.

Both Albert Einstein and Sir Roger Penrose believed that the universe does not expand in a ball-like fashion, but rather, most likely expands in a cubic manner. Decades later, they were proven correct. Furthermore, they suggested that our concepts of time and its calculation were inherently flawed. Recent advancements in our perception of our universe have resulted in the "thread" or "string" theory, which suggests that there are multiple dimensions interconnected by a common thread of energy. This theory further intimates that we are all simultaneously connected to each other in this, as well as in other dimensions, and that the past, present, and future exist simultaneously. Time and space, therefore, are functions of the physical world, not the metaphysical or cosmic world where these precepts have no bearing on our soul or spirit (energy). Some researchers feel that we all carry a cosmic or meta-DNA code which identifies us through lifetimes and dimensions. This code makes us unique, yet binds us to all living matter or life form energy. This DNA code resonates at a specific frequency, vibration or wavelength, which defines us in relation to all life forms. Like the nature of all physical things, change is a part of the universe. The only constant is our resonant quality, our cosmic DNA; or our vibration, which does not change. Without a body, we still exist and we still give off measurable energy. All life forms produce specific and measurable dimensional frequencies and wavelengths: Humans, animals, rocks, trees, ghosts, angels, extra terrestrials, etc. Some people are more aware or more receptive than others and can tap into these frequencies and dimensions more easily.

Nothing ever dies or is wasted in the universe; it simply morphs, changes, or transforms itself into another form. With each transformation, our energy or life force resonates at a different frequency. Electronic Voice Phenomena (EVP) and Instrumental Transcommunication (ITC) provide ways in which people on the physical plane of existence tap into other dimensions, such as that of spirits or ghosts. They resonate at a different frequency than we do, and therefore different techniques must be used to allow them to communicate with us. Some believe that it is within the range of low frequency sounds that we can connect with other dimensions. We are relying more and more on the expertise of EVP and ITC specialists to help decipher the language of the dead and other-dimensional life forms through equipment designed to discover imbedded responses recorded on tape, or through television, radio or computer imaging.

Karen Camus, in addition to her Electronic Voice Phenomenon (EVP) work, is a certified hypnotherapist and Reverse Speech Interpreter trained by David John Oates, and is also experienced in Technical Remote Viewing. From 1995 to 1997, Camus lived in a house in which she experienced a wide range of dramatic paranormal activity. This led to a renewed interest in and passion for paranormal investigation. Based on her own work with EVP, as well as the work of others in this field, Camus is convinced that EVP is indeed "spirit voices." She agrees with current opinion on the mechanics of EVP, which hypothesize that spirits of people who have passed over can and do use the sound of human voice and other background noise, as well as the energy of the living, to form their own their own audible messages which can be recorded on tape.

Camus provided us with the following information from our December 1, 2001 investigation at the Leonis Adobe. The information contained herein is only the tip of the paranormal ITC/EVP iceberg. We believe that this data adds further credibility to the concept that all life forms operate on different vibrational levels or frequencies and communication between levels or dimensions seems to be difficult for all concerned. However, there may come a time when we can readily tap into the right frequency via short wave radio, television, computer or other electronic devices and communicate with other dimensions for long periods of time and find answers to questions we have been searching for since time began.

According to Camus, at the Leonis Adobe, as in other haunted locations, when we tape audio (via analog or digital technology) we are finding a tremendous amount of embedded speech when the tape is played back. This embedded information seems to come from at least two sources: from people who have passed on, and (less frequently) from the minds of the living people present. Although there is a large amount of embedded speech in the audio, deciphering exactly what is being said is a very difficult and rather tedious process. When the spirit voices (AKA, EVP or ITC) occur at the same time as the speech of living people present, most often at least part of the message being conveyed is muddled by the overlapping human speech. When EVP occurs independently of human voice, most often it's more like a whisper, too low and soft to be able to document with any level of confidence. While sometimes independently occurring EVP is louder, it is often multi-layered itself, with two or more spirits talking at the same time. Therefore, analyzing audio for EVP takes a great deal of time and patience. However, this work is so fascinating and important, that it is well worth the effort. From what I can tell, it seems that spirits need both the energy of living people and ambient sound to be able to produce clearly audible speech on tape. We find that when we leave recorders running in empty rooms at a haunted location, we hear EVP when the tapes are played back, but generally it is just too faint to interpret with any certainty. On the other hand, if we tape record audio during a séance, or leave the tape running when we take a break from the séance and are all standing around talking, the EVP which is captured is stronger and louder. However, as I mentioned above, problems still occur in deciphering this phenomenon, because the spirit voices often overlap the sound of humans or other spirits talking at the same time. Our team, like many others currently doing this work, is constantly learning and experimenting with new and different techniques. Below are some of the clearer EVP messages documented from the Leonis Adobe.

Near the beginning of the séance, people seated at the table asked questions aloud to Espiritu and Miguel Leonis. During these questions, there are overlapping EVP messages in two different female voices. An older female voice says, "I left something here in the room. It's important." The younger female voice says "Mama's talking; she's giving you the wrong answer." The older woman may be Espiritu, and the younger one, her daughter Marcelina. Another possibility, of course, is that the mother and daughter in this EVP are Juana and her adopted daughter, Maria [Maria Johnson, later married Pablo Orsua], because Espiritu's son Juan and his family also lived in the adobe. In any event, it sounds as if the mother was not in a very lucid state at that point, and therefore was not responding to the questions being asked. Instead, she seems to be preoccupied with something she left behind in the adobe. What makes this even more interesting is that additional EVP messages also seem to be talking about items, which were left or hidden on the property. In particular, there is mention of a "watch" and some "dinero." Then, when psychic, Ginnie McGovern, described how she sensed some of the family members upstairs, a younger-sounding female voice exclaims happily "She's saying I am here, Mama." I can't say for sure that this is the same younger female spirit mentioned above, but it certainly sounds like it could be and she appreciated being sensed and acknowledged by the psychic.

Early on in the séance a male voice came through who said his name was "Chuck." This personality came through a few different times. One of the people associated with the adobe and the Leonis family was Charles Bell. Bell was the son of the early pioneer and noted Los Angeles attorney Major Horace Bell. In 1917, while Bell was the Calabasas Justice of the Peace, he was arrested in Los Angeles on a morals charge. After being released from jail, Charles reportedly went to his house, located on the adobe property, and committed suicide by taking poison. Can the "Chuck" coming through be Charles Bell? While we can't be sure, there is another exceptionally clear EVP message, in a male voice, which says "I killed myself." There is also a very strong loud female voice that comes through saying "I am Terry." It's interesting to note that Charles Bell's wife's name was Maria Teresa, so perhaps she went by that name. When the words "I am Terry" are played in reverse, it says "Teresa."

During the séance, when Miguel's fall from the wagon is being discussed, a male voice says "Both his hands were crushed." During that same discussion, again in a male voice, the message "made a mistake" comes through. Perhaps the latter information is relevant to the issue of whether foul play could have played a part in Miguel's death, as it is heard when psychic Alma Carey poses a question related to that matter [A.C. - Juan has something to do with Miguel's accident].

Prior to the séance, when one of the psychics was walking around the adobe, attempting to tune into the spirits in various rooms, the message "Come over here" was heard in a low raspy female voice. At another point in the investigation, while in the kitchen area trying to communicate with a female spirit sensed by the psychics, a question was asked regarding a garment on the mannequin across from the kitchen area. Specifically, the spirit was asked whether she was comfortable having the mannequin positioned there all the time. Since the psychics sensed that the spirit spoke Spanish, the question was asked in Spanish. A response of "No, no me gusto" ("No, I don't like it.") comes through in a female voice. In addition to EVP messages which, based on content and context, seem to be coming from the Leonis family and associates, there are other messages in the audio which are of more uncertain origin. For example, There are references to a "gun on a shelf" and a male voice saying, "I blew my head off." Also, two overlapping messages say "Aunt Dolly" and "I like to party." We have no idea what these last messages relate to, but they could be from the large group of spirits who have no association with the property, but are still anxious to communicate with this dimension. This tends to occur at all of our on-site investigations, and does sometimes complicate matters, as far as identifying the spirit who is speaking.

In order to be able to more easily tell who is coming though, at the beginning of our séances we try to impress upon the spirits that they need to communicate in an orderly manner. We ask the spirits who once inhabited the property to come through first, but promise to allow some time at the end for other spirits to talk. We also ask that they attempt to identify themselves each time they speak, since many different families have lived on the premises. However, considering how desperate some of these beings are to make contact, and how long they have been waiting to do so, it is understandable that sometimes they sometimes get carried away and can't wait their turn to speak!

In closing, there is one further complexity in analyzing the audio from on-site investigations. In addition to hearing messages from people who have passed on, and thoughts of the living people present, we are also hearing messages that appear to be predictions about the future. However, we have not yet been able to ascertain the origin of these predictions, so we cannot assess their reliability at this point.

CONCLUSIONS

This site is extremely active. There seem to be layers of energy imbedded in the adobe. However, most of the energy is not an imprinted or passive energy, but rather active/interactive. Investigators who have visited the adobe over the years have reported numerous strong energy spots or portals throughout the house. There are very few areas in the house that have not exhibited anomalous readings when tested with equipment. The energy often follows people, so in essence, the house is alive with psychic energy that is very possessive. The spirits watch over their domain and seem to take offense to people who do not treat the house with respect. For the spirits, they are still actively performing their tasks from beyond the veil. They get upset when they are distracted, but are also curious when people who are sensitive come to visit. They struggle to contact us, just as we do in trying to find a way to communicate with them.

There are certain areas of the house, which appear to exhibit much stronger readings or provide more vivid impressions for psychics and investigators. The strongest spot in the house seems to be the master bedroom, followed in order of reported energy by the living room, kitchen, dining room, northeastern room, Orsua room, caretaker's bathroom, hallway, stairs, veranda and storage area. The barn, oak tree in the back and upper room in the windmill have also yielded strong impressions/readings. The following spirits seem to be active in the house: Espiritu Leonis; Miguel Leonis; Juana Menendez; Maria Orsua; Marcelina Leonis; Juan Menendez; Pedro Orsua; Charles Bell; and, a few other unidentified phantoms. We will be back to conduct numerous follow-up investigations and attempt to refine our questions and focus our answers based on the results of the Electronic Voice Phenomena.

WHITECHAPEL PRESS

Whitechapel Productions Press is a division of Dark Haven Entertainment and a small press publisher, specializing in books about ghosts and hauntings. Since 1993, the company has been one of America's leading publishers of supernatural books and has produced such best-selling titles as *Haunted Illinois, The Ghost Hunter's Guidebook, Ghosts on Film, Confessions of a Ghost Hunter, The Haunting of America, Sex & the Supernatural* the *Dead Men Do Tell Tales* crime series and many others.

With more than a dozen different authors producing high quality books on all aspects of ghosts, hauntings and the paranormal, Whitechapel Press has made its mark with America's ghost enthusiasts.

You can visit Whitechapel Productions Press online and browse through our selection of ghostly titles, plus get information on ghosts and hauntings, haunted history, spirit photographs, information on ghost hunting and much more. by visiting the internet website at:

WWW.AMERICAN HAUNTINGS. ORG

AMERICAN HAUNTINGS TOURS

Founded in 1994 by author Troy Taylor, the American Hauntings Tour Company (which includes the Illinois Hauntings Tours) is America's oldest and most experienced tour company that takes ghost enthusiasts around the country for excursions and overnight stays at some of America's most haunted places.

In addition to our tours of America's haunted places, we also offer tours of Illinois' most haunted cities, including Chicago, Alton, Decatur, Lebanon and Jacksonville. These award-winning ghost tours run all year around, with seasonal tours only in some cities.

Find out more about tours, and make reservations online, by visiting the internet website at:

WWW.AMERICAN HAUNTINGS. ORG

ABOUT THE EDITORS

TROY TAYLOR

Troy Taylor is an occultist, crime buff, supernatural historian and the author of more than 60 books on ghosts, hauntings, history, crime and the unexplained in America. He is also the founder of the American Ghost Society and the owner of the American Hauntings Tour company.

Taylor shares a birthday with one of his favorite authors, F. Scott Fitzgerald, but instead of living in New York and Paris like Fitzgerald, Taylor grew up in Illinois. Raised on the prairies of the state, he developed an interest in "things that go bump in the night" at an early age and as a young man, began developing ghost tours and writing about hauntings and crime in Chicago and Central Illinois. His writings have now taken him all over the country and into some of the most far-flung corners of the world.

He began his first book in 1989, which delved into the history and hauntings of his hometown of Decatur, Illinois, and in 1994, it spawned the Haunted Decatur Tour -- and eventually led to the founding of his Illinois Hauntings Tours (with current tours in Alton, Chicago, Decatur, Lebanon & Jacksonville) and the American Hauntings Tours, which travel all over the country in search of haunted places.

Along with writing about the unusual and hosting tours, Taylor has also presented on the subjects of ghosts, hauntings and crime for public and private groups. He has also appeared in scores of newspaper and magazine articles about these subjects and in hundreds of radio and television broadcasts about the supernatural. Taylor has appeared in a number of documentary films, several television series and in one feature film about the paranormal.

Troy and his wife, Haven -- when they are not traveling -- currently reside in an undisclosed location.

ROB WLODARSKI

Born in the very haunted Queen of Angels hospital in Los Angeles, California, Wlodarski has BA's in history, anthropology, and an MA in anthropology from California State University, Northridge. As the President of Historical, Environmental, Archaeological, Research, Team (H.E.A.R.T.) and Cellular, Archaeological, Resource, Evaluations (C.A.R.E.) since 1978, Wlodarski has administered over 1400 archaeological and historical projects for federal, state, county, city agencies and private companies, and has authored and co-authored over 20 articles for journals and magazines throughout California and the Southwest. Mr. Wlodarski has served as a consultant for numerous television shows on the History Channel, Food Network, Travel Channel, TLC and many others.

ANNE WLODARSKI

Born in San Antonio, Texas, Ms. Wlodarski is a registered art therapist. She received her MA in behavioral science from the University of Houston, and has published several articles including a chapter in California Art Therapy Trends. She has been an exhibiting artist and is the president and founder of HEARTWORLD Arts Center for Children, a non-profit organization for abused and disadvantaged youth. Ms. Wlodarski served as an education outreach coordinator and gallery assistant for the City of Los Angeles' Artspace Gallery from 1989-1993 and has been featured in the media for her work with children and the arts. She was honored as a "Sunday Woman" by the Daily News, and was a J.C. Penney Golden Rule Award nominee. She is also a member of the Daughters of the Republic of Texas (DRT), and the Southern California Art Therapy Association (SCATA).

Together, they are the founders of G-Host Publishing and the authors of more than 20 books about American ghosts and hauntings.

ABOUT THE CONTRIBUTORS

DALE KACZMAREK
Dale Kaczmarek is the president of the Chicago-based Ghost Research Society and the author of number of books about Chicago ghosts and paranormal research. Born in Chicago, he served in the U.S. military and following his discharge, returned to the Chicago area and became active in ghost research. He has served as the president of the Ghost Research Society in 1982 and the organization now boasts members all over the country. He has devoted countless hours to the study of anomalous spook lights and has one of the largest collections of spirit photographs in the county.
Kaczmarek lectures and conducts ghost tours of the Chicago area. He is also a frequent guest on media shows and has been featured in numerous publication and books. His books and articles can be found on his website at www.ghostresearch.org

ROSEMARY ELLEN GUILEY
Rosemary Ellen Guiley has written 41 books and hundreds of articles on the paranormal. She is the author of The Encyclopedia of Ghosts and Spirits, and Talking to the Dead (2010), co-authored with George Noory, the host of Coast to Coast AM. Her website is www.visionaryliving.com. Information on Frank's Box can be found in her topics library.

RICHARD SENATE
Richard Senate was born in Los Angeles, California. His father was a painter at MGM studios and worked on such classic films as "The Wizard of Oz." Richard's Family moved to Thousand Oaks in 1952 and he has been a resident of Ventura County for most of his life. He went to Ventura High School, Ventura Community College and Long Beach State University where he earned a degree in History. He worked his way though school doing odd jobs. He did a years post graduate work in Anthropology at UC Santa Barbara with plans to do archaeology. While at a field school held by Cal Poly San Luis Obispo, held at Mission San Antonio de Padua, he saw a ghost. This chance encounter changed his whole life. He began to study ghosts and related supernatural topics becoming one of the pioneers in the study of the paranormal. He has continued his work investigation from that time one. He has appeared on such TV shows at the "Search for Haunted Hollywood" (Fox) "Sightings" (UPN), "Haunted Houses" (A&E) "Haunted Hotels and Haunted History" (History Channel) Most recently he appeared on "DeadFamous " (UK). He is the author of 14 published works on ghosts and history including "Hollywood Ghosts", "Ghosts of the Haunted Coast" and "Ghost-stalker's guide to Haunted California". His newest work "The shocking psychic solution to the Lizzie Borden Case," (with

Debbie Senate) is published. He leads tours of haunted sites and holds classes on ghost hunting in his home town of Ventura, California. He also managed two historic museum as well as served the city of Ventura as a historian for 22 years.

He writes a column in the Ojai Valley View newspaper of psychic subjects and contributes to Ghost Village Newsletter. He currently resides in Ventura, California with his wife of 25 years and their 19 year old daughter Megan. Richard continues to research and investigate the unknown seeking answers to the riddles of ghosts and haunted houses. He is currently updating his work "The Ghost Stalker's guide to Haunted California," and he hopes to re-publish this work soon. His novel "The Flight of the Hercules" is about to be published in hardback by Lost Continent Magazine.

RENE KRUSE

Rene' Kruse has lived in small towns in the Mid-West and Texas but has lived in southwestern Pennsylvania for the past 20 years. She holds a PhD from Texas A&M and teaches Applied Engineering and Technology at California University of Pennsylvania when she is not watching over her 4 children and 2 grandchildren.

Rene' has been fascinated in ghosts and all things haunted for as long as she can remember and has been actively investigating haunted sites for over 30 years. Since her first investigation in 1976, she has been involved in nearly 250 investigations in 23 states. She has had the opportunity to meet and work with some of the most respected paranormal investigators from around the country.

MARITZA SKANDUNAS

A genealogist with over 30 years of experience, Maritza has assisted many individuals and organizations in discovering their past. Major projects have included teaming with Richard Milligan and John Miles of the Linn County Historical and Stage historical Societies of Oregon from 1980 to 1990, assisting Evergreen Production Studios, Inc's Larry Reaney for a television production focusing on the pioneers of Oregon, moving script development support with Cindy Clarke on the Harden Family history, and investigation support for paranormal historian and author Rob Wlordarski.

Currently, Maritza is working with the famously haunted San Diego Whaley House Museum, the Historical Department of the Hotel Del Coronado, and spearheading the San Diego Ghost Hunters' investigation agenda. She brings her intuitive gifts and vast research experience to unlock the spirits of history.

KAREN RIDENS

Currently I am retired (hopefully I get it right this time!) and enjoying day to day life with family and friends. In my previous life I worked as Vice President of Client Services for a small specialized management/consulting and assessment processing organization providing comprehensive information processing services to the California K-14 education community. Prior to this position I worked in the capacity of Systems Analyst for Information Management Services of San Diego County Office of Education retiring for the first time after Y2K programming was in place! In this position my responsibilities included, but were not limited to, writing all system documentation, providing the software quality assurance, and comprehensive training/support for in house developed software products.

The gift of always having been intuitive helped immensely in my professional career and has carried me in good stead into the paranormal investigation arena. My specialty in the paranormal world has been the ability to connect with children and mothers. My main form of communication is speaking and feeling the spirits near me (many times clinging or tugging at me for attention), although occasionally they will allow me to see them.

SHARON GAUDETTE HIESERICH

Sharon has had countless paranormal / supernatural experiences in her life, several of them shared-experiences with other family members, including sister and sdGH Founder, Dawn. With her avid interest in history and the realm of the spirits, she finds it fulfilling to work with such a close group who share her perspectives, and with whom she can relate and trust. Sharon comes from a large family, quite a few with "gifts".   She has known Maritza for almost 40 years, as Maritza and her sister Dawn met in high school and have been close friends since then. Maritza, Dawn and Sharon have shared many paranormal experiences together over the years. They sense the same things, and many times have the same dreams on the same nights.

In her professional life, she has worked in health care as a medical language specialist for 30 years.   Working in the field of medicine gave her an insight which has helped sharpen her intuitiveness.   As well, her gifts have helped her with her chosen field of health care. Sharon is married, and has two children - a daughter and a son.

JOHN AND KELLY WEAVER

Kelly L. Weaver grew up in a haunted 19th century Hummelstown, PA home. Following years in advertising, she is today a nationally recognized psychic-medium, regional rep for the American Ghost Society and founder of the Spirit Society of PA. www.spiritsocietyofpa.com   Her first book, *Whispers In the Attic - Living with the Dead* was published in 2004. Kelly is a regular guest on paranormal internet broadcasts and has appeared on MTVs "Fear", Discovery Channel's "A Haunting" and numerous other television programs. She is a popular speaker who lectures regularly on a variety of paranormal and esoteric subjects. Kelly and husband John live in Camp Hill, PA and have been investigating the paranormal as a team since the early 1990s. For more on Kelly, please visit www.kellysmagicalgarden.com   John D. Weaver is a native of Mechanicsburg, PA who works as an Advertising/Art Director. He has been a hockey goaltender for 40 years and is passionate about history, sports cars and road racing. As the co-founder of SSP with Kelly, he specializes in obtaining evidence at haunted locations and has extensively investigated the Gettysburg Battlefield, which he first visited as an 8 year old. John's interest in the strange stems from a UFO sighting in 1967 and today he is a Field Investigator for the Mutual UFO Network (MUFON).

CHAD PATTERSON

Chad Patterson is President and Founder of the California Society for Ghost Research and resides in Fontana, CA. He has investigated claims of paranormal phenomena for the past 19 years. In the summer of 2002, he founded the California Society for Ghost Research (CSGR), after serving as Co-Director of the San Gabriel Valley Paranormal Researchers (SGVPR), and being a member of the Orange County society for Psychic Research (OCSPR). Check out the CSGR website at www.csgr.us. If you have any questions regarding a specific case or need an investigation, please contact Mr. Patterson at sentrylight@att.net.

DUSTY SMITH

Dusty Smith is the founder & president of the Daytona Beach Paranormal Research Group, Inc. She began the group in 1997 and has been helping homeowners, business owners and other clients with her investigators ever since.

The Daytona Beach Paranormal Research Group, Inc. are proud members of The American Ghost Society, TAPS Family Members and recommended by The Light and have worked thousands of cases all over the south east and beyond.

You can learn more about Dusty and her teams work at: http://www.dbprginc.org

PETER JAMES HAVILAND

Peter has been investigating the paranormal for over 20 years in Houston, Texas and the surrounding cities of Texas. He and his team, Lone Star Spirits have been documented in many books, newspapers, and local/national radio and television. Peter has worked on many projects with his fellow colleagues over the years in support of television pilot projects and has provided research on cases for book projects, radio and ongoing television shows for friends and colleagues. Peter is often contacted by fellow investigators to consult on cases that colleagues are working on to help their client or maybe to give a new perspective on the case. It was Troy Taylor that encouraged Peter to write and through the many years of giving Troy grey hair and headaches, he learned the confidence to sally forth and speak publicly. He has been well received by convention audiences, as well as, school speaking events that he has been invited to. Peter is an advanced certified clinical hypnotherapist and obtained his certification from Dr. Ed Martin and Cheryl Martin of The PATH Foundation. Through Dr. Ed Martin and his mentor Loyd Auerbach is where Peter gets his understanding and practice of Parapsychology, how it relates to the human condition and paranormal events. Since 1998 Peter has been an American Ghost Society Member, a regional representative for the state of Texas and has just recently been named its Communications Coordinator. Peter has been in practice since 2002 and has just opened his office this July in Houston.

You can get more information about Peter at www.lonestarspirits.org

ROBERT HUNNICUTT

A ghostly encounter 33 years ago in an Arizona theater was the beginning of Robert Hunnicutt's journey into the world of ghosts and hauntings. Since then, he has investigated cases of phenomena associated with a wide variety of hauntings at private residences, businesses and historical landmarks throughout the state of Georgia, the Southeast and portions of the Mid-west.

Robert is the Founder and Executive Director of the Georgia Ghost Society and the Central Georgia Representative for the American Ghost Society. He has worked with renowned members of the paranormal community that include paranormal investigator Patrick Burns and psychics Reese Christian and Sharon Johns. In 2008, he was selected as one of the Top 10 Paranormal/Ghost Investigators in America by Haunted America Tours.

He has been the featured guest on prominent radio programs that include Coast to Coast AM with George Noory, The "X" Zone Radio Show with Rob McConnell, Paranormal Radio with Captain Jack, Ghostly Talk Radio and Georgia Public Radio.

LaVergne, TN USA
23 September 2009
158847LV00003B/9/P